BETWEEN ANARCHY AND SOCIETY

For my Parents

Between Anarchy and Society

Society

Trusteeship and the Obligations of Power

WILLIAM BAIN

OXFORD
UNIVERSITY PRESS

OXFORD
UNIVERSITY PRESS

Great Clarendon Street, Oxford OX2 6DP

Oxford University Press is a department of the University of Oxford.
It furthers the University's objective of excellence in research, scholarship,
and education by publishing worldwide in

Oxford New York

Auckland Bangkok Buenos Aires Cape Town Chennai
Dar es Salaam Delhi Hong Kong Istanbul Karachi Kolkata
Kuala Lumpur Madrid Melbourne Mexico City Mumbai Nairobi
São Paulo Shanghai Taipei Tokyo Toronto

Oxford is a registered trade mark of Oxford University Press
in the UK and in certain other countries

Published in the United States
by Oxford University Press Inc., New York

© William Bain, 2003

British Library Cataloguing in Publication Data

Data available

Library of Congress Cataloging in Publication Data

Data available

ISBN 0-19-9260265

1 3 5 7 9 10 8 6 4 2

Typeset by Newgen Imaging Systems (P) Ltd., Chennai, India
Printed in Great Britain
on acid-free paper by
Biddles Ltd., Guildford and King's Lynn

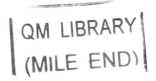

Preface

The origins of this book can be traced to my interest in questions of humanitarian intervention while I was a graduate student at the University of British Columbia. Thinking about those questions eventually led me to ask: what might come after humanitarian intervention? This book, which is based on my doctoral dissertation, considers the idea of trusteeship as one possible answer. Some of my earliest attempts to think about trusteeship in international society were presented in papers at the British International Studies Association Conference in 1999, 2000, and 2001, and at the International Studies Association Conference in 1999 and 2001. I also presented some of the ideas and arguments contained in this book at the Pan-European International Relations Conference in 2001 and to the Failed States and Global Governance Conference in 2000 and 2001, which was organized by Michael Stohl. These papers eventually evolved into essays published in *Canadian Foreign Policy* (1999) and *Global Society* (2001). Also, parts of Chapter 1 appeared in *The Round Table* (2003) and parts of Chapter 6 in *International Relations* (2003). I would like to thank all who were involved in these conferences, as well as the journal editors and reviewers, for their comments and suggestions on these papers.

I would like to thank the University of British Columbia for providing financial support for my doctoral research, and Mrs Alice Li, whose generous endowment of the Li Tze Fong Doctoral Fellowship also assisted me in that regard. I would also like to thank the faculty and staff of the Department of Political Science at UBC, where I began this project. Barbara Arneil, Kal Holsti, Brian Job, Sam La Selva, and Mark Zacher have all made very important contributions to this book. To each of them I offer my heartfelt thanks and gratitude. Thanks also to my fellow doctoral student, Mikulas Fabry, who has enriched my thinking in several ways. Since moving to the University of Glasgow, I have enjoyed the conversation of several of my new colleagues in the Department of Politics. I have been fortunate to discuss ideas explored in this book with Chris Corrin, Jane Duckett, Paul Graham, Michael Lessnoff, Andrew Lockyer, Sarah Oates, Barry O'Toole, and Alasdair Young. Alasdair has been exceptionally patient and supportive as I struggled to revise the manuscript into its final form. I am particularly grateful to Chris Berry, who made several very helpful suggestions that sharpened and focused the claims of this book.

I would be negligent in failing to thank several other people who have in some way or other contributed to this book. My thanks go to Cornelia Navari, Adam Roberts, Sasson Sofer, Peter Lyon, and Georg Sørensen for taking the time to engage me in conversation; and especially to James Mayall for his encouragement and interest in my research. I would also like to thank the reviewers for Oxford University Press, who made several suggestions that improved this book. To Jennifer Jackson Preece I owe an enormous debt of gratitude. Jennifer helped me to conceptualize this project as well as to think through some of the key arguments upon which it rests. My greatest debt, however, is owed to Robert Jackson. It has been my great fortune to be able to converse with Robert over a period of several years about the ideas contained in this book. Indeed, it is hardly possible to read what I have put on paper without noticing his influence on my thinking. I shall be forever grateful for his guidance and friendship.

Finally, I would like to thank my friends and family for their unyielding support. Erin Tettensor has relieved many bouts of despair with her impeccable humour. I am especially thankful to my dear friend Hamish Telford, who has been like an older brother to me in offering sound advice and a sympathetic ear. To my wife and best friend I would like to express my deepest gratitude. Diana has supported me with a seemingly endless well of patience, encouragement, and understanding. For that I am eternally grateful. And, above all else, I would like to thank my parents, who have supported me at every turn and through every difficulty, and at times probably more than they should have. It is to them that I dedicate this book.

W.B.

Glasgow
January 2003

Contents

1

Introduction

While reflecting on the differences that were said to divide the human family, P. H. Kerr posed the question: 'What is the obligation on those who by reason of their own claim to superior civilisation have the responsibility for saving the weak from the ravages of the strong?'[1] He answered this query by suggesting that some people, on account of superior virtue, a sharp sense of personal responsibility, and great achievements in the fields of politics, law, education, commerce, science, and industry, may rightly regard themselves as the leaders of mankind. In contrast, so-called backward peoples, those mired in a state of ignorance, idleness, and poverty, were destined to obey until they were able to take their place alongside more advanced peoples. The superiority that Kerr ascribed to civilization—European civilization to be precise—did not, however, issue licence for the domination and exploitation of the disadvantaged. Alien rule could be justified only so far as it encouraged backward peoples to the ranks of civilized life. Public order, the rule of law, and useful education had to be instituted in places where they were absent; and conditions of human suffering, poverty, and the sort of cruelty that was the hallmark of uncivilized society, had to be eradicated wherever they were found. Civilization was something that had to be shared collectively by a humanity that embraced both the 'zenith of civilisation' and the 'nadir of barbarism'.[2] Indeed, Kerr understood the claim of superior civilization as transcending the particular allegiances of citizenship. Europeans were obliged to assist Africans and Asians, he argued, 'not from any pride of dominion, or because they wish to exploit their resources, but in order to protect them alike from oppression and corruption, by strict laws and strict administration, which shall bind foreigners as well as the native, and then they must gradually develop, by education and example, the capacity in the natives to manage their own affairs'.[3] To act in any other way would be to deny underdeveloped segments of the human family a chance at improvement and progress.

In this understanding of obligation we are able to discern the main contours of the idea of trusteeship in international society. But in order to grasp

---

[1] P. H. Kerr, 'Political Relations between Advanced and Backward Peoples', in *An Introduction to the Study of International Relations* (London: Macmillan, 1916), 149.
[2] Ibid. 142.   [3] Ibid. 149, 166.

the character and limits of this idea, it is useful to consider, if only briefly, trusteeship against a backdrop framed by its opposite: the idea of liberty. John Stuart Mill defended the value of liberty by asserting: 'neither one person, nor any number of persons, is warranted in saying to another human creature of ripe years that he shall not do with his life for his own benefit what he chooses to do with it'.[4] For it is in the activity of choosing, that is, in observing, interpreting, reasoning, and judging one's situation, that human beings develop a plurality of experiences upon which progressive society depends. These choices may strike some people as being strange, uncomfortable, and even repugnant; and, as a result, they may evoke feelings of pity, contempt, or the wish to encourage a different course of action. But the tolerance of such conduct is justified, Mill argued, because freedom to innovate and to experiment is a necessary condition of flourishing individuality and of civilized society. Hence a man's liberty must not be subject to interference so long as the consequences of his actions do not inflict injury on others.[5]

The idea of trusteeship is distinguished from the idea of liberty in so far as it invokes a paternal mode of human conduct—the idea that 'interference with a person's liberty of action [is] justified by reasons referring exclusively to the welfare, good, happiness, needs, interests or the values of the person being coerced'.[6] Thus, an arrangement of trusteeship always entails a loss of liberty; for a ward must be coerced, just as parents coerce their children, towards some good for the sake of his own happiness. And like a child in Aristotle's *polis*, whose faculty of reason is present but underdeveloped, a ward is excluded from participating in the goings-on of public life.[7] Immaturity may obscure some fundamental truth or inexperience may obliterate the moderation, restraint, and discipline required of orderly social intercourse so that someone must choose for him. It is in this context that trusteeship presupposes a relationship in which a natural person or a legal person is responsible for the general well-being of one or more persons who are deemed to be incapable of directing their own affairs.

The purpose of this book is to interrogate the character of trusteeship as an idea of international society. By that I mean: I want to investigate the assumptions, claims, and justifications that render trusteeship intelligible as a recognized and settled mode of human conduct in international life. My task, then, is to understand the idea of trusteeship in terms of its postulates. I want to explicate, elucidate, and clarify these postulates, rather than explain a pattern

---

[4] J. S. Mill, *On Liberty*, ed. E. Rapaport (Indianapolis, IN: Hackett Publishing Company, 1978), 74.   [5] Ibid. 53–60, 73–5.

[6] G. Dworkin, 'Paternalism', in R. A. Wasserstrom (ed.), *Morality and the Law* (Belmont, CA: Wadsworth Publishing Company, 1971), 109.

[7] See Aristotle, *Politics*, trans. T. A. Sinclair (London: Penguin Books, 1992), 95.

of causal relationships, in an attempt to understand a particular type of human relation. It is the contention of this book that the character of trustee-ship is discernible in full relief at the intersection of two dispositions of human conduct: the good of assisting persons in need and the good of respecting human autonomy. Good in the first instance, assisting our fellows who may be in peril, is perhaps most clearly conveyed in the biblical injunc-tion: love your neighbour as yourself. Jesus tells of the nature of this obliga-tion in the parable of the Good Samaritan. For it was the Samaritan who, on encountering a man beaten and half-dead, 'had compassion, and went to him and bound up his wounds, pouring on oil and wine; then he set him on his own beast and brought him to an inn, and took care of him'.[8] In order to sub-scribe fully to this obligation, to act on the compassion that is felt for human beings who are in distress, advocates of trusteeship must accept that for some reason they are unable to make good use of their liberty. And modern-day Samaritans must concede that, on account of this inability, some people should not be entitled to direct their own affairs. Thus, the person who is favour of trusteeship must be prepared to overturn the normative settlement that emerged out of decolonization, a settlement that for better or worse accepts the advice offered by Satan in Milton's *Paradise Lost*: 'Better to reign in hell than serve in Heaven.'[9] But in accepting the worth of this claim—a claim that understands good in terms of being the author of one's own actions—people who defend the sanctity of liberty above all else must be prepared to accept failure when people fall short of the mark. They must be content not to interfere and to set things right, but to recognize tragedy and to express sympathy in the face of human suffering and cruelty. The good expressed by both Jesus and by Satan are ubiquitous dispositions of human conduct; how-ever, there are times when we must draw upon all our wisdom and courage in order to choose between them.

In times of uncertainty, times when it seems as if our institutions, practices, moralities, and modes of knowledge are unable to cope with the realities of everyday life, the conditions of this choice are not as obvious as they might be in times of quiet and satisfaction. At times, when our ideas no longer furnish meaningful answers, when the course we normally travel appears to be blocked, we tend to subject the ways of our lives to cutting scrutiny. We tend to ask questions about prevailing notions of obligation, authority, and justice, as well as the conditions of peace, order, and security, all in the hope that we might say something meaningful about how human beings should live their

---

[8] Luke, *The Old and New Testaments of the Holy Bible*, revised standard version (Philadelphia, PA: Lutheran Church in America, 1971), 10.25–34.
[9] J. Milton, *Paradise Lost and Other Poems* (New York: Mentor Books, 1961), 44.

lives and how they should treat their neighbours. Thus, if we find, for example, that theology no longer provides meaningful answers to these questions then perhaps we might turn to science; and if not science, perhaps to philosophy, history, or aesthetics. In times of crisis human beings tend to agitate for reform, maybe to restore the glory of a past golden age; and if reform is impossible, or appears to be so, they might seek something entirely new, something revolutionary, which sweeps away the old for a new order of things. It is then, times when 'normal' ways of thinking no longer seem normal, that we are apt to ask: might there be a better way? It seems as if we live in such times. For it is a development of considerable significance that the idea of trusteeship, an idea that was relegated to the dustbin of history along with the legitimacy of empire, is increasingly put forward as a way of responding to problems of international disorder and injustice. For instance, Stanley Hoffmann suggested, before the outcome of the American-led war in Afghanistan was clear, that there might be 'a need for a temporary United Nations trusteeship over a post-Taliban Afghanistan, to preserve peace, to rebuild an administration, and to reconcile factions'.[10] And it has been suggested as well that a 'provisional' Palestinian state, a status promised to the Palestinian people on the condition that they opt for a leadership 'not compromised by terror', might take the form of an American or United Nations administered trusteeship. Martin Indyk, who was twice the American ambassador to Israel, recently proposed an international trusteeship that would see an American-led group assume administrative responsibility for Palestinian territories that 'would oversee the building of the new state's democratic institutions, election of its leadership, and Israeli–Palestinian negotiations to define its permanent borders'.[11]

But thinking about trusteeship in contemporary world affairs need not be confined to the realm of speculation. So-called international administrations in Bosnia and Herzegovina, Kosovo, Eastern Slavonia, and East Timor are frequently held out as examples of a new form of trusteeship—the former incorrectly so, as will be argued in Chapter 6—that is untainted by the ignoble experience of empire. These cases are said to offer useful precedents for dealing with states that have collapsed into anarchy: they point the way to how peace might be substituted for war, human rights for persecution, and democracy for despotism. It is in this respect that Paddy Ashdown, who,

---

[10] S. Hoffmann, 'On the War', *The New York Review of Books*, 48/17 (2001).

[11] See G. W. Bush, 'President Calls for New Palestinian Leadership', The White House, Office of the Press Secretary, 24 June 2002; and M. Indyk, 'A U.S.-Led Trusteeship for Palestine', *Washington Post*, 29 June 2002. Thomas Friedman has also called for a NATO-run Palestinian state along the lines of Kosovo and Bosnia and Herzegovina. See T. Friedman, 'A Way Out of the Middle East Impasse', *New York Times*, 24 August 2001.

as High Representative of the international community in Bosnia and Herzegovina, is responsible for superintending the implementation of the Dayton Peace Agreement, contends that international involvement in 'Bosnia will be seen as a new model for international intervention—one designed not to pursue narrow national interests but to prevent conflict, to promote human rights and to rebuild war-torn societies'.[12] Out of these experiments in international administration a spirited debate has emerged, particularly within American foreign policy circles, with proponents of nation-building extolling the virtues of engagement and sceptics deriding extensive involvement in local and regional crises as according too prominent a place to ill-considered 'ethical' or 'humanitarian' considerations. A foreign policy underwritten by hope, the sceptics argue, a virtue Martin Wight once described as having more to do with religion than politics, is no substitute for a foreign policy that is grounded in a sober assessment of discordant interests, some of which are manifestly more important than others.[13] However, the terrorist attacks on New York and Washington on 11 September 2001 have brought home the reality that failed and unjust states cannot be summarily dismissed as being peripheral to the 'hard-headed' calculations of great power interests. The notion of 'local conflict' has been drained of much of its meaning; and, seeing that much of what was once local is now unavoidably global, and often dangerously so, distant islands of anarchy are now ignored only at the risk of great peril. Indeed, in marking the first anniversary of the 11 September attacks, George W. Bush proclaimed in the pages of the *New York Times*: 'More than ever, we know that weak states, like Afghanistan can pose a great danger to the peace of the world.'[14]

It is thus said with a monotonous regularity that the collapse of the World Trade Center's twin towers, which carried nearly three thousand innocent civilians to their deaths, changed the world. Ours is a world in which the smallest of groups, aided by modern technology, exceedingly modest sums of money, and the sanctuary of weak states like Afghanistan, can inflict catastrophic destruction on even the strongest of states. But the Bush administration's published national security strategy, a purportedly forward looking document that has been crafted with an eye towards meeting the challenges of

---

[12] P. Ashdown, 'What I Learned in Bosnia', *New York Times*, 28 October 2002.

[13] See C. Rice, 'Promoting the National Interest', *Foreign Affairs*, 79/1 (2000), 45–62; S. Mallaby, 'The Lesson of MacArthur', *Washington Post*, 23 October 2002; M. O'Hanlon, 'The Price of Stability', *New York Times*, 22 October 2002; and M. Wight, 'Christian Commentary', BBC Home Service Broadcast, Friday 29 October 1948. For a brief overview of Wight's understanding of hope, see Hedley Bull's introduction to M. Wight, *Systems of States*, ed. H. Bull (Leicester: Leicester University Press, 1977), 11–14.

[14] G. W. Bush, 'Securing Freedom's Triumph', *New York Times*, 11 September 2002.

this changed world, casts a curious gaze, not into the future, but into the past. It is a document that is acutely conscious of the preponderance of American power, the responsibilities and obligations that attach to that power, and, crucially, the opportunities it offers for extending throughout the world the benefits of a singular notion of the good life. The enemies of civilization, the most immediate of which are terrorist groups and the (failed) states which harbour them, must be eradicated in cooperation with other like-minded champions of freedom. Only then will it be possible for every man and every woman, irrespective of their nationality, race, or creed, to enjoy the freedom that is 'the birthright of every person—in every civilization'.[15] It is a document that aspires to a union of values and interests in a righteous mission to make the world a better place than it is at present; in other words, it is premised on the conviction that American power can and should be used to make the world right. Indeed, it promises to seize upon the opportunity created by America's unprecedented power in order 'to bring the hope of democracy, development, free markets, and free trade to every corner of the world'—what are for the Bush administration irreducible conditions of human dignity.[16] And in that promise we obtain insight, not into a vastly different world of the twenty-first century, but into the humanitarian and philanthropic inclined imperialism of the nineteenth century.

There is very little about the Bush administration's claims that would be out of place in the age of empire, an age during which trusteeship was the most obvious outward manifestation of a similarly righteous mission to propagate the virtue of civilization and to eradicate its enemies. In 1903 Roger Casement described the Congo Free State as a society stricken by the most appalling instances of hardship and cruelty. Native subjects were forced to labour without remuneration, courts were either unable or unwilling to grant relief of grievances, and official edicts were enforced through fear, mutilation, and murder. He concluded by observing that the native population 'endured such ill-treatment at the hands of the Government officials and the Government soldiers in their own country that life had become intolerable'.[17] These words may well describe life in the Congo today or, in recent years, life in Angola, Bosnia and Herzegovina, Cambodia, East Timor, Kosovo, Liberia, Rwanda, Sierra Leone, Sudan, and, of course, Afghanistan. And just as it is the declared policy of the United States to bring the hope of freedom, democracy, and free markets to these places of despair, so also

---

[15] Government of the United States of America, 'The National Security Strategy of the United States of America', September 2002, vi.   [16] Ibid. pp. iv–vi, 1–5.
   [17] R. Casement, 'Mr. Casement to the Marquess of Landsdowne—(Received December 12), December 11, 1903', *Parliamentary Papers*, Cmd. 1933 lxii (1904), 23–52.

missionaries, soldiers, traders, and colonial administrators set out to bring hope to the Congo and to wherever else that the light of civilization did not shine. As self-proclaimed trustees of civilization they endeavoured to redeem peoples that fell well short of the (self-affirmed) perfection of European civilization. They instituted order where it was absent, put down oppression where it was present, and built schools, canals, irrigation systems, and hospitals, which in the jargon of our world would fall under the rubric of international development assistance. And in doing all of these things they disclaimed, as does the United States today, the pursuit of unilateral advantage. For they too understood themselves as having a special role to play in world affairs, as having a mission to propagate values that were regarded as right and true for all people in all places, which was guided by the belief that imperial power should be used as a force for good.[18]

This common sense of mission suggests that in some ways the problems of the past are also those of the present. The landscape of contemporary world affairs is conspicuous, as it was when empires spanned the globe, for enormous disparities in power, wealth, and development, uncertainty about the right relation of man and citizen, and a diversity that endures in the face of attempts to fashion a universal community of humankind. These were the problems of the East India Company's government in Bengal just as they are the problems of the United Nations administration in Kosovo; and they are the problems that continue to attract scholarly interest in spite of vast differences in time, place, and personality. Thus, Martha Nussbaum takes on the problem of inequality and the status of women by outlining a 'capabilities approach', in an attempt to provide an account of basic principles that deserve the respect of all governments in all nations. Respect for human dignity, she argues, requires that the lives of women should be judged from the standpoint of 'what people are actually able to do and to be—in a way informed by an intuitive idea of a life that is worthy of the dignity of the human being'.[19] Nicholas Wheeler seeks to escape the vexing dilemma of having to choose between man and citizen by taking refuge in the idea of common humanity, so that it is then possible to argue that subscribing to international humanitarian obligations may enjoin the use of force in order to save strangers. And Robert Jackson's notion of a global covenant, the procedural and prudential norms of which seek the unity of the human family through recognition of its manifest diversity, represents an attempt to come to terms with the problem of difference internationally. The global covenant is on this view 'a response

---

[18] A. P. Thornton, *Doctrines of Imperialism* (New York: John Wiley & Sons, 1965), 61.
[19] M. Nussbaum, *Women and Human Development: The Capabilities Approach* (Cambridge: Cambridge University Press, 2000), 5.

to the fact and implied value of political diversity on a global scale'.[20] The idea of trusteeship stands as yet another way of making sense of these problems; for it proposes in terms of its own assumptions, claims, and justifications, an answer to the question: how shall human beings best live their lives? And it is in respect of this question that this book may be read as an extended essay on inequality, obligation, and difference in contemporary world affairs.

The Conversation of Trusteeship

A resurrected practice of trusteeship is also deserving of scholarly attention because it challenges norms that are fundamental to something called 'international society': sovereign equality, territorial integrity, and non-interference. This book is written in the idiom of the international society approach, or what is often (and somewhat misleadingly) called the 'English School', because it has, more than any other tradition of international inquiry, given sustained attention to the normative framework within which international life is conducted. The international society approach is in the broadest of terms concerned with interpreting and understanding international life in the context of history, philosophy, and law.[21] It is, in the words of Herbert Butterfield and Martin Wight, 'more concerned with the historical than the contemporary, with the normative than the scientific, with the philosophical than the methodological, with principles than policy'.[22] Thus, human conduct, and, particularly, the moral significance that it imparts, provides the frame of reference within which interpretation and understanding should take place. This concern with the moral content of international life, the nature of obligation, the demands of justice, and the conditions of right, separates the approach that I have in mind from social science approaches that distinguish very sharply between scholarly inquiry and moral judgement. Questions of morality are internal to the subject—and unavoidably so. There is no class of judgements called 'moral' that are distinct from a class of judgements called

[20] N. Wheeler, *Saving Strangers: Humanitarian Intervention in International Society* (Oxford: Oxford University Press, 2000), 309; and R. Jackson, *The Global Covenant: Human Conduct in a World of States* (Oxford: Oxford University Press, 2000), 13–22.

[21] The following discussion of international society is derived from H. Bull, 'International Theory: The Case for a Classical Approach', *World Politics*, 18 (1966), 361–77; and Jackson, *The Global Covenant*, chs 2–4.

[22] H. Butterfield and M. Wight, 'Preface', in H. Butterfield and M. Wight (eds.), *Diplomatic Investigations: Essays in the Theory of International Politics* (Cambridge, MA: Harvard University Press, 1968), 12.

'political', 'economic', or 'social'.[23] And making sense of these questions involves a great deal more than offering prescriptive judgements that follow the formulation of theory, the testing of hypotheses, and the articulation of generalizations. Nor are they adequately understood in terms of a research programme that outlines yet another sub-field of an academic discipline called 'international relations'. Rather, the approach that informs this book assumes that the engagements, practices, and conventions of international life are distorted, if not wholly incoherent, outside of the norms, values, and rules that are distinctive of the realm of human conduct in which they are found.

Before proceeding any further, it is important to distinguish between explaining human behaviour and interpreting human conduct. Whereas the former is concerned with identifying causes that act on and therefore account for what human beings do, the latter is concerned with conscious and thinking human beings that choose their course of action. Human conduct implies what Michael Oakeshott understands as a 'human being responding to his contingent situation by doing or saying *this* rather than *that* in relation to an imagined and wished for outcome and in relation, also, to some understood conditions [emphasis in original]'.[24] Interpreting human conduct does not involve discovering 'true' motives or 'real' intentions, and it does not involve explaining processes or forces that bring a particular state of affairs into being. The character of human conduct is disclosed, not in an unbroken chain of causes and effects, but in a particular context of activity; a context that conceives conduct 'as actions and utterance, wise or foolish, which have reasons, adequate or inadequate, but not causes'.[25] And it is in these reasons, which are the result of conscious deliberation and choice, as opposed to cosmic forces that act on and determine human behaviour, that we are able to detect the character of trusteeship. These reasons rarely, if ever, find their justification in a single corpus of knowledge; nor do they represent the revealed 'truth' of a sovereign and authoritative voice of knowledge that speaks for all humankind. Reasons, and the justifications they entail, represent an amalgamation of different and often contradictory experiences, values, and desires that, taken together, provide insight into the human condition.

I am not, therefore, in case there should be any misunderstanding about the scope and purpose of this book, interested in the uses and limits of international theory as an explanatory tool. I am not interested in articulating

[23] See B. Parekh, *Contemporary Political Thinkers* (Oxford: Martin Robertson & Company, 1982), 96–123.

[24] M. Oakeshott, *On Human Conduct* (Oxford: Clarendon Press, 1996), 32.

[25] Ibid. 234.

a theory of trusteeship that explains the interests and choices of any particular international actor; and I am not interested in specifying a model that predicts how trusteeship might 'work' if it were 'applied' to any particular failed or collapsed state. Interrogating and discerning the character of an idea does not at any point involve a claim of explanatory or predictive power. That enterprise is better cast as a problem of international political theory. Investigating the idea of trusteeship in this way supposes that international theory and political theory are concerned, each in its own right and in its own context, with the conditions of the good life. It recognizes that the goings-on of international life are conducted in an explicitly normative vocabulary; and without knowledge of this vocabulary, and the ideas that it conveys, it is impossible to convey or to contest beliefs about what is good, what is right, and what is just. In other words, political theory and international theory are, as Jackson argues, distinct branches of the same tree.[26] Thus, this book is also written against a tradition of international thinking, influenced by the writings of Thomas Hobbes, that disavows the significance of morality, particularly where there is no sovereign to enforce the law. Some international theorists have taken the absence of an overarching authority in international life—what is often called a condition of international anarchy—to mean that states 'cannot afford to be moral'.[27] The guiding premise of this book holds that the character of an idea, in this case the idea of trusteeship, cannot be separated from the beliefs from which conceptions of the good life spring and the vocabulary required to express those beliefs. It is in this context that I shall interrogate the character of trusteeship in terms of questions that are classically questions of political theory. Who shall rule and by what authority? What is the right relation of ruler and subject? And, towards what end or ends shall the office of government direct its activities?

With these questions set before us it is possible to enter into, and, indeed, to take part in, the conversation of trusteeship. The notion of conversation proposes a way of accessing an inheritance of human belief and wisdom that, in the context of international life, is registered in a repository of treaties, charters, covenants, declarations, resolutions, minutes, speeches, letters, and other related forms of speech. Conversation, Oakeshott maintains, implies

---

[26] See R. Jackson, 'Martin Wight, International Theory and the Good Life', *Millennium*, 19/2 (1990), 26–67; and R. Jackson, 'Is There a Classical Theory?', in S. Smith, K. Booth, and M. Zalewski (eds.), *International Theory: Positivism and Beyond* (Cambridge: Cambridge University Press, 1996), 204.

[27] T. Hobbes, *Leviathan*, ed. M. Oakeshott (Oxford: Basil Blackwell, 1949), chs 13, 17; and R. Art and K. Waltz, 'Technology, Strategy, and the Uses of Force', in R. Art and K. Waltz (eds.), *The Use of Force: International Politics and Foreign Policy* (New York: University Press of America, 1983), 6.

a meeting-place in which 'the participants are not engaged in an inquiry or a debate; there is no "truth" to be discovered, no proposition to be proved, no conclusion sought'.[28] Understanding human conduct in terms of conversation implies a diversity of voices, none of which is the bearer of truth as such. Voices engaged in conversation are not arranged hierarchically, there is no arbiter to judge the merits of what each voice has to contribute, and they are not directed towards any final destination. Conversation is an end in itself; it is an 'unrehearsed intellectual adventure' that is fundamentally and necessarily inconclusive.[29] The claim that the character of an idea is discernible in the context of conversation should not, however, be taken to mean that I am disinterested in argument—that is, a discursive engagement that represents what Oakeshott understands as the purposive voice of science and its concern with problems and their solutions.[30] What it does mean is that argument is internal to conversation. It would be very difficult indeed to make sense of trusteeship and the character it imparts without paying attention to arguments which propose, for example, that preponderant power should be used to propagate the morality of a particular religion; or, better than the dogma of religion the utilitarian would say, to institute rational law; or, better than religion or law, to communicate knowledge of modern natural science. I want to interrogate the claims of these arguments, not to provide an account of the one that is on balance most convincing, but to assess what they reveal about trusteeship, its context of activity, and type of experience it imparts.

It is no less important to understand that conversation, so far as it concerns the idea of trusteeship, is principally an European affair: African and Asian voices do not become audible in any substantial way until the onset of decolonization. These non-European voices were prevented from taking part in the conversation of trusteeship on account of their presumed ignorance and immaturity. They were no more than objects, because they could be no more than objects, of a conversation that was concerned with the conditions of their 'true' happiness. For in the absence of a fully developed faculty of reason, a condition ascribed to most non-European peoples, they lacked the wherewithal to make any contribution to such an engagement. The idea of trusteeship presupposes the belief that the interests of such people, the moral and material conditions of their happiness, must be represented on their behalf: someone must choose for them. Indeed, Edward Malet, the British

---

[28] M. Oakeshott, 'The Voice of Poetry in the Conversation of Mankind', *Rationalism and Politics and Other Essays*, new and expanded edn. (Indianapolis, IN: Liberty Fund Press, 1991), 489; and M. Oakeshott, 'Political Education', *Rationalism and Politics and Other Essays*, new and expanded edn. (Indianapolis, IN: Liberty Fund Press, 1991), 62–3.
[29] Oakeshott, 'The Voice of Poetry in the Conversation of Mankind', 488–95; and R. Grant, *Oakeshott* (London: The Claridge Press, 1990), 65–6. [30] Ibid. 488–9.

ambassador to the Berlin Conference of 1884–1885 that internationalized
the idea of trusteeship, conveyed this belief by saying: 'I cannot forget that
the natives are not represented amongst us, and that the decisions of the
Conference will, nevertheless, have an extreme importance for them.'[31]
Interrogating the conversation of trusteeship in this manner, and, in particular, focusing on European voices that have dominated it through international history, does not mean that human beings always understand what
they say, that what they say is well founded, or that there is any truth in what
they say. Human beings are surely prone to misinterpret their situation as
well as to deliberately misrepresent it. But all human beings, saints and liars
alike, communicate their claims in a normative vocabulary that conveys
beliefs about what is good, right, and just; and in doing so, as John Plamenatz
argues, 'the conscious hypocrite is a victim as well as an exploiter of his professed beliefs'.[32] My purpose, then, is not to separate the apostle from the
hypocrite or the fool from the sage. Nor is it to offer an apology for the
excesses of empire, the many instances of arrogance, hubris, and greed, that
have transformed the word 'empire' into a synonym for the most vulgar type
of domination, exploitation, and abuse. Rather, I want to discern the character
of an idea, its assumptions, claims, and justifications, that for better or worse
represented the sincere convictions of people who imagined it as their duty to
bring the benefits of civilization to those that did not yet enjoy it.

But international society theorists have paid little attention to the idea of
trusteeship and to what place, if any, it might occupy in their thinking.[33] For
example, Martin Wight is perhaps best known for describing the emergence
of international society out of the arrangements of medieval Christendom.
Hedley Bull's most important work, *The Anarchical Society*, is devoted to the
problem of order in world politics and to how that order has been maintained. Gerrit Gong's study of the standard of civilization, that is, the criteria
according to which independent political communities became members of
this international society, provides an account of how outsiders became
insiders. The collection of essays edited by Bull and Adam Watson, *The
Expansion of International Society*, chronicles the 'revolt against the West'
that transformed European international society into a universal association
of sovereign states. And Jackson's *The Global Covenant*, the most recent major
statement of the international society tradition, outlines the distinctive

---

[31] 'Protocol No. 1—Meeting of November 15, 1884', Protocols and the General Act of the
West African Conference, *Parliamentary Papers*, 1885 LV mf. 91.435, 11.

[32] J. Plamenatz, *On Alien Rule and Self-Government* (London: Longman, 1960), 55.

[33] A notable exception is Robert Jackson's chapter on trusteeship in *The Global Covenant*.

normative dialogue that takes place within this universal association.[34] But international society theorists have not as a group had much to say, at least in a sustained and systematic sense, about relations between insiders and outsiders—that is, between members of international society and non-member political communities. The idea of trusteeship represents but one way of thinking about such relations. A conceptual rendering of this claim takes as its starting point the principal assumption of the international society tradition: the existence of an element of society in international life is not disproved or precluded by the fact of international anarchy. This ordered anarchy, Bull's anarchical society, is often juxtaposed with an anarchy of chaos of the sort popularized by Robert Kaplan's coming anarchy.[35] The idea of trusteeship proposes a way of joining Kaplan's zone of chaos with Bull's zone of order. And in that sense trusteeship may be thought of as an idea that inhabits the space between anarchy and society.

Encountering Difference

This space between anarchy and society was in the first instance opened in consequence of the Age of Discovery—an epoch that both Adam Smith and Karl Marx agreed marked a turning point in human history.[36] When the first European explorers set out for the New World, and when they circumnavigated the Cape of Good Hope to reach the shores of India and the islands of the Pacific, they came into contact with people who were different in every way imaginable. Pizzarro, Cortes, de Gama, and those who followed, encountered people who held radically different beliefs about government, economy, morality, and all that is related to the organization of public life. They understood notions of obligation, responsibility, right, and good in wholly different terms. They had their own standards of courage, beauty, honour, and prudence. And they approached questions of religion, community, marriage, and

[34] See Wight, *Systems of States*; H. Bull, *The Anarchical Society: A Study of Order in World Politics* (New York: Columbia University Press, 1977); G. Gong, *The Standard of 'Civilization' in International Society* (Oxford: Clarendon Press, 1984); H. Bull and A. Watson (eds.), *The Expansion of International Society* (Oxford: Clarendon Press, 1984); and Jackson, *The Global Covenant*.

[35] R. Kaplan, *The Coming Anarchy: Shattering the Dreams of the Post Cold War* (New York: Random House, 2000); and Bull, *The Anarchical Society*, 46–51.

[36] See A. Smith, *The Wealth of Nations*, vol. 2, eds. R. H. Campbell and A. S. Skinner (Indianapolis, IN: Liberty Fund, 1981), bk. IV, vii, pt. C; and K. Marx and F. Engels, 'Manifesto of the Communist Party', *The Marx-Engels Reader*, 2nd edn., ed. R. Tucker (New York: W. W. Norton, 1978), 474–5.

family in ways that repelled or frightened most Europeans. But instead of accepting the legitimacy of these practices, that is, granting them recognition as being fully rational and fully moral in spite of their difference, most Europeans responded to the difference of others with the monist ethics of superior civilization. The European explorer, trader, missionary, soldier, and administrator was not prepared to accept that what may be pleasing to a man in Lisbon, London, or Paris may be anything but desirable to a man in Angola, Bihar, or Senegal. Thus, relations based on reciprocal recognition and mutual consent were impossible so long as some people were convinced of the superiority of their God, their science, and their virtue, and possessed the power to impose them on others.

The idea of trusteeship is thus intelligible in the meeting of difference that accompanied the extension of European rule to the distant reaches of the Americas, Asia, Africa, and Oceania. Most popular accounts of this encounter tend to rehearse a sordid tale of domination and exploitation. Some draw upon Lenin's characterization of empire as the final stage of capitalism, an epoch in which rich financiers and powerful industrialists plundered the world for profit. Others portray the age of empire as a dubious and ill-intentioned (great) game of the sort popularized (perhaps unfairly) by Rudyard Kipling's novel *Kim*. But against these less salubrious accounts of this 'encounter with the West', it is also true that some patrons of empire regarded it as their ordained mission to bestow upon the world's less fortunate peoples the blessings of European civilization. These men, as A. P. Thornton described them, 'saw themselves as the trustees of civilization. They reckoned it their duty to see to it that civilization was disseminated among as many beneficiaries as could be contrived.'[37] An enlightened empire called for the joining of power and responsibility in service of righteous purpose; and, thus, empire obtained its most powerful justification in what it could achieve for others. It is with this justification in mind that the British Resident in Nepal suggested in 1843: 'the British government would be ill-represented (in Nepal or anywhere else) if every valuable opportunity were not used to prompt to that which is good, and to deter from that which is evil.'[38] Of course, the spirit of this sentiment, a high-minded sense of purpose, did not move all who came into contact with the peoples of the non-European world. Most colonies were acquired for commercial purposes, some to secure the strategic lifelines of empire, and others for humanitarian reasons, for example, to combat the

---

[37] Thornton, *Doctrines of Imperialism*, 7; and V. I. Lenin, 'Imperialism, the Highest Stage of Capitalism', *Lenin on Politics and Revolution*, ed. J. E. Connor (Indianapolis, IN: Pegasus, 1968); and R. Kipling, *Kim* (New York: Bantam Books, 1988).

[38] Quoted in Thornton, *Doctrines of Imperialism*, 162–3.

slave trade. But the fact that only a few proved to be of any tangible value did not in any way lessen the obligations that attached to preponderant power.[39] Dominion required justification that was grounded in something more fundamental than the impulse of profit or the imperative of strategy.

It is in debates that arose within the Spanish Empire, particularly those relating to the right by which the Kings of Spain claimed title to the 'newly discovered' territories of the Americas, which something like the idea of trusteeship is offered as a justification of dominion.[40] Francisco de Vitoria alluded to the idea of trusteeship in *De Indis* (1537), when he suggested that a European prince may lawfully exercise authority over the Indians of the New World provided that they were incapable of administering a legitimate government by their own efforts. In putting forth this claim to rule he argued that the Indians could not be arbitrarily dispossessed of their lands and property: they may be barbarians, slow-witted and foolish, but they were nevertheless true masters entitled to the rights of dominion. Thus, he denied claims of universal dominion put forward on behalf of the Holy Roman Emperor and the supreme pontiff of the Latin Christendom; and he rejected the right of discovery, refusal to receive the Christian faith, and the commission of mortal sins as adequate reasons for occupying the territories of the New World.[41] However, he admitted, albeit as no more than a point of argument, that Spanish dominion would be justified if the Indians were all so close to madness that they were incapable of managing their own affairs. The Indians would then, he suggested, be like children over whom it would be entirely lawful and appropriate for European princes to exercise authority, but only so long as 'everything is done *for the benefit and good of the barbarians, and not merely for the profit of the Spaniards* [emphasis in original]'.[42]

Arguments of this sort are also disclosed in the mid-sixteenth century debate between Juan Gines de Sepúlveda and Bartolomé de Las Casas, who was, like Vitoria, a member of the Dominican order and an ardent defender of Indian interests. Of Sepúlveda's justifications of dominion the most interesting is the claim that a condition of barbarism, that is, the ignorance, vice, and cruelty that was thought to be definitive of Indian life, justified Spanish possession of the New World. Dominion was justified by appealing to a

---

[39] J. D. Hargreaves, *Prelude to the Partition of West Africa* (London: Macmillan, 1963), 70; Thornton, *Doctrines of Imperialism*, 42.

[40] For an overview of these debates and their bearing on the history of international society, see M. Donelan, 'Spain and the Indies', in H. Bull and A. Watson (eds.), *Expansion of International Society* (Oxford: Clarendon Press, 1984), 74–85.

[41] F. de Vitoria, 'On the American Indians', *Political Writings*, eds. A. Pagden and J. Lawrance (Cambridge: Cambridge University Press, 1991), 252–77.   [42] Ibid. 290–1.

notion of superior virtue and learning. Thus, the Indians were obliged, as Las Casas summarized Sepulveda's position, to 'obey those who are outstanding in virtue and character in the same way that matter yields to form, body to soul, sense to reason, animals to human beings, women to men, children to adults, and, finally, the imperfect to the more perfect, the worse to the better, the cheaper to the more precious and excellent, to the advantage of both'.[43] In reply, Las Casas argued that while the Indians might be barbarians on account of their ignorance of Christian truth, they were not barbarians properly understood as they were not slavish by nature. They were adept in the mechanical arts, demonstrated great artistic ability, and skilled with the written word; and, in spite of Sepulveda's protestations to the contrary, they were 'very ready' to accept the Christian faith and to redeem their sins. Indeed, Las Casas observed that 'long before [the Indians] had heard the word Spaniard they had properly organized states, wisely ordered by excellent laws, religion, and custom'.[44] The Indians must be treated, then, not as child-like creatures that are immature in reason or as wild beasts that are something less than fully human, but as rational creatures that are capable of receiving 'truth' by their own volition.

Although the sort of paternal reasoning that underpins the idea of trusteeship was not unknown in the sixteenth and seventeenth centuries, the organization of the pre-modern European empires in the Americas did not provide fertile ground in which to establish trusteeship as a justification of empire. The notion that colonies and the peoples residing in them required guidance in 'growing-up' so that they might one day stand on their own was, for the most part, lost on Spanish and Portuguese colonial administrators. The colonies of the Spanish and Portuguese Empires were constituted as European settlements that reflected very closely political and social organization at home. They were reproductions of European society, equal in status to the metropolis in the case of the former and an integral part of the metropolis in the case of the latter, which had been transported across the Atlantic Ocean. And, crucially, since settler colonies were in effect 'extensions of Europe', they generally avoided the problems of native administration that confounded the modern empires in Africa and Asia. In New Spain, for example, native persons enjoyed a status equal to that of settlers; and while it was the duty of the colonial power to assimilate them—though not by force—to European religion and civilization, they did not suffer the liability of an inferior constitutional status.[45] In contrast, modern empires in Africa and Asia differed from experience in the Americas in so far as they disclosed a demonstrable and professed

---

[43] B. de Las Casas, *In Defence of the Indians*, trans. S. Poole (DeKalb, IL: Northern Illinois University Press, 1974), 11–12.   [44] Ibid. 41–9.

[45] D. Fieldhouse, *The Colonial Empires: A Comparative Survey from the Eighteenth Century* (London: Weidenfeld and Nicolson, 1965), 11–33, 99.

humanitarian concern for the condition of native peoples. The idea of trustee-ship that embodied this concern evinced both the best traditions of enlight-ened empire and the worst traditions of empire seduced by theories of racial and neo-Darwinian superiority. Still, this concern represents what David Fieldhouse describes as 'the highest product of European imperialism—the alien ruler who associated himself so closely with his subjects that he was prepared to defend them against his own compatriots if he thought they were acting contrary to the interests of his charges'.[46]

Thus it was not for another 200 years that the idea of trusteeship began to take definite shape in territories administered by the British East India Company. The emergence of trusteeship in late eighteenth century British India coincided with several important developments in the current of European thought that forever altered the terms on which alien rule was justi-fied. The most important of these developments, according to Thornton, was the fact that the architects of empire during the eighteenth century had to confront the legacies of the American and French Revolutions in a way that the Spanish and Portuguese empires in the Americas did not. The rights of man and the idea of social contract disallowed all appeals to divine right, Papal blessing, and the right of conquest as justifications of dominion in Africa and Asia.[47] The justification of empire derived, in implicit acknowledgement of the American Declaration of Independence, from the benefit it conferred on the governed. It is no coincidence, then, that in the latter part of the eighteenth century the East India Company came to recognize, at least as a matter of declared policy, that the well-being of its native subjects must be secured before the pursuit of profit; and in Africa missionaries set out to bring light to the 'dark continent' and abolitionists demanded that slavery and the slave trade be put down by the expeditious exercise of imperial power.[48] What is distinctive about empire of this era is that Europeans believed that they could improve the lives of the world's most destitute and oppressed people through direct intervention. And in that respect, as Plamenatz writes, '[t]hey have also, more than other peoples, been deliberate reformers; they have often tried to change institutions in order to improve them.'[49]

This impulse of reform found its most secure footing in a manner of thinking and speaking about the human condition that is emblematic of the Enlightenment. Immanuel Kant argued in his famous essay on enlighten-ment that true freedom comes with making public use of reason in order to

---

[46] Ibid. 376–8.   [47] Thornton, *Doctrines of Imperialism*, 11.
[48] See P. J. Marshall, 'Introduction', *Problems of Empire, 1757–1813*, ed. P. J. Marshall (London: George Allen and Unwin, 1968), 60; and H. A. C. Cairns, *Prelude to Imperialism: British Reactions to Central African Society 1840–1890* (London: Routledge & Kegan Paul, 1965), 118.   [49] Plamenatz, *On Alien Rule and Self-Government*, 38.

speak for one's self. Attaining enlightenment entailed an escape from a self-incurred condition of immaturity, a condition that necessitated the guidance of another, by having the resolution and courage to 'use your *own* understanding [emphasis in original]'![50] That the human condition was in some way self-incurred opened the way for thinking about social life as a problem of history. For Montesquieu, the influence of religion, law, government, and custom, as well as that of climate, cultivated in a nation a general spirit of national character; and his belief that this character was shaped more by moral than physical causes made it possible to suggest, for example, that '[l]iberty itself has appeared insupportable to those nations who have not been accustomed to enjoy it'.[51] The social rather than natural origins of human inequality led Rousseau to characterize peoples as being relatively 'young' and 'old', and fitted differently in respect of law and constitution; '[f]or nations, as for men,' he writes, 'there is a time of maturity that must be awaited before subjecting them to the laws'.[52] And thinkers of the Scottish Enlightenment furnished a framework within which to think about questions of fitness so that understanding the nature of society and, therefore, the law and constitution that best fitted a particular society, was a matter of examining the past. Thus, Adam Ferguson asserted that in order to 'form a just notion of [European] progress from the cradle, we must have recourse to the nursery'.[53] In this way history joined past and present, it provided a mirror and not merely a window of self-understanding, whereby a European past was intelligible in an (North American) Indian present. This progressive notion of history is perhaps most famously and influentially laid out in Adam Smith's *The Wealth of Nations*. Smith attributed the origin of government to a historical process that began with nomadic society, passed through pastoral and feudal stages, and culminated in commercial society. Only then would it be possible to claim that '[t]he separation of the judicial from the executive power seems originally to have arisen from the increasing business of the society, in consequence of its increasing improvement.'[54]

[50] I. Kant, 'An Answer to the Question: "What is Enlightenment?" ', *Kant's Political Writings*, ed. H. Reiss and trans. H. B. Nisbet (Cambridge: Cambridge University Press, 1970), 54.

[51] Montesquieu, *The Spirit of the Laws*, ed. D. W. Carrithers (Berkeley, CA: University of California Press, 1977), 288–9; and 'An Essay on Causes Affecting Minds and Characters', 443, which is reprinted in the same volume.

[52] J. J. Rousseau, 'Discourse on the Origin of Inequality' and 'On the Social Contract', in *The Basic Political Writings*, ed. and trans. D. Cress (Indianapolis, IN: Hackett Publishing Company, 1987), 37–59, 162–73.

[53] A. Ferguson, *An Essay on the History of Civil Society*, ed. F. Oz-Salzberger (Cambridge: Cambridge University Press, 1995), 80.

[54] A. Smith, *The Wealth of Nations*, ii. 722. For a general discussion on the influence of this 'four stages' theory of history, see R. Meek, *Social Science and the Ignoble Savage* (Cambridge: Cambridge University Press, 1976).

Ideas that were definitive of Enlightenment thinking, particularly the ideas of unity, progress, and perfection, prepared the ground for trusteeship as we have come to know it as a practice of international society. For the world of the Enlightenment was not one of disparate peoples that from time to time came into contact with one another; rather, the many peoples of the world were thought to constitute a single and unified human family in spite of the difference they disclosed. It is in respect of this unity that the distinctive vocabulary of trusteeship is intelligible. Indeed, the only way of making sense of the great differences that separated the European and non-European worlds, and yet sustain this claim of unity, was to make distinctions within the human family and to express those differences in terms of degrees of improvement, development, advancement, or maturity. In a world in which this sort of thinking reigned supreme, neither the conditioning effects of climate nor the absolute will of God provided an adequate account of the reasons why human beings lived as they did. A world whose history was told in terms of stages of development understood the Indians of the New World as a 'young' or 'child-like' people just beginning: they were taking their first steps on the ladder of progress. Thus, not only were all men potential brothers in Christian fellowship as the Spanish scholastics would have it; they were brothers that could be perfected, that is, deliberately improved, in their temporal lives as part of a general progress of things on earth. Societies and the peoples residing in them could be in some sense engineered; and the institution of better government, law, and economy could lift these societies and peoples to a higher stage of development. Therefore, the principal task of philosophy, and that of government, commerce, industry, and religion, as Rousseau explained his purpose in writing *Discourse on the Origin of Inequality*, was to show how 'the strong could resolve to serve the weak'.[55] The idea of trusteeship provides one possible response.

Although the Enlightenment exerted enormous influence throughout all of Europe, the idea of trusteeship in international society remains largely an Anglo-American tradition. That is not to say that other European powers did not confront, as did the British, the problem of governing African and Asian populations that were very different from themselves. Indeed, Thornton argues:

[w]hat the Russians said about their task in Central Asia was repeated by Frenchmen, invoking their *mission civilisatrice* in Africa and in the Far East; by Germans, planning to implant their *Kultur* in a world that so plainly needed it; by Japanese, who wanted to westernize others as they themselves had been westernized; and by the British who, without asserting doctrine, took it for granted that their presence

[55] Rousseau, 'Discourse on the Origin of Inequality', 38.

anywhere ensured more peaceful and prosperous conditions than those that had obtained before.[56]

Each of these powers evolved particular ideas, practices, and institutions about how best to govern their colonial dependencies that in some way resembled, sometimes very closely, the idea of trusteeship as it developed in the British Empire. For instance, G. L. Angoulvant, governor of the Ivory Coast in 1908, justified the purpose of French rule in the paternal language of trusteeship: '[f]or a long time yet our subjects must be led to progress despite themselves, as some children are educated despite their reluctance to work. We must play the role of strong, strict, parents towards the natives, obtaining through authority what persuasion would not gain.'[57] The Portuguese and the Belgians too understood themselves as guardians of underdeveloped (child-like) peoples that required guidance in becoming civilized (adult) peoples. And the fact that they were treated as such was not, for example, lost on Congolese nationalists on the eve of independence: 'We do not enjoy always being treated as children. Understand that we are different from you, and while we are assimilating the values of your civilization, we desire to remain ourselves. We ask of you therefore an effort to understand our legitimate aspirations, and to help us to realize them.'[58]

Each of the European imperial powers disclosed a self-assured certainty about their unique fitness for acting as trustees of civilization. The French endeavoured to civilize the 'lower races' by assimilating them to the excellence of French culture; the Portuguese by introducing the Christian religion; the Belgians by imparting their religion and ideology; and the British by bringing their charges to self-government.[59] And, in consequence of their self-assured superiority, all of the colonial powers disclosed an equally pronounced hostility to the idea of subjecting their colonial undertakings to international scrutiny. But in spite of these similarities, the British, and later the Americans, were disproportionately responsible for introducing and establishing trusteeship in international society. The proprietors of empire did not regard, at least for some time, questions of colonial administration—and thereby questions of trusteeship—as matters of international concern. However, the abolitionist movement, a crusade underwritten disproportionately by the British exchequer and the Royal Navy, gradually resulted in the

---

[56] Thornton, *Doctrines of Imperialism*, 154.

[57] G. L. Angoulvant, 'General Instructions, 26 November 1908', in J. Hargreaves (ed.), *France and West Africa: An Anthology of Historical Documents* (London: Macmillan, 1969), 202.

[58] Quoted in S. Easton, *The Twilight of European Colonialism: A Political Analysis* (London: Methun & Co, 1961), 462. For a general overview of Portuguese and Belgian colonial policy, see chapters 16–17.

[59] See generally Easton, *The Twilight of European Colonialism*.

internationalization of the idea of trusteeship. At the Berlin Conference the British government stressed, more than any other, the solemnity of the obligations of trusteeship undertaken in the Berlin Act. And when things went very badly wrong in the Congo Free State, an ostensibly humanitarian venture founded by Belgium's King Leopold II, Britain stood alone in demanding scrupulous adherence to those obligations. The United States played an equally important, though very different, role in internationalizing the idea of trusteeship. American scepticism of empire transformed trusteeship from a justification of empire, as it was in the British tradition, into an alternative to empire that was expressed concretely in the form of the League of Nations mandates system and the United Nations trusteeship system. Most other European powers remained rather indifferent to these efforts or they attempted to obstruct them, as did the French in opposing the creation of the mandates system. Thus, it is the Anglo-American voice which discloses best the character of trusteeship in international society, that goes furthest in charting the space between anarchy and society.

Virtue, Inequality, and Tutelage

This journey through the conversation of trusteeship reveals a character that is intelligible in a particular relation of virtue, inequality, and tutelage. Thus, in the first instance, the idea of trusteeship assumes that the claim to rule must be subject to a test of fitness, for it accepts the principle, expressed in Plato's *Republic*, that each person is fitted by nature to perform a particular task. 'Different people are inherently suitable for different activities,' Socrates explains to Adeimantus, 'since people are not particularly similar to one another, but have a wide variety of natures'.[60] Particular qualities of right conduct, that is, virtue, are what render some men fit to rule. Those men, Socrates continues, must possess a character that is moulded by the virtues of good memory, self-discipline, courage, morality, and a love of truth. Only men of this character are able to see the true nature of things, for it is they who are equipped with the wherewithal to distinguish true knowledge from mere belief and opinion. And it is to these men that the well-being of the republic should be entrusted. For they are entitled, by virtue of their superior character, to command and all others are bound by duty to obey.[61] In the well-founded republic, all that is good and desirable in life depends on the strict maintenance of class integrity. So where Socrates assures Glaucon that

[60] Plato, *Republic*, trans. R. Waterfield (Oxford: Oxford University Press, 1993), 60.
[61] Ibid. 196–212.

no great harm will follow when a shoemaker imitates a carpenter, he warns that disaster awaits the entire community if the unqualified person attempts to enter the ruling class. Thus, the happy man and the good man is one who is true to his nature, just as 'a community's morality consists in each of its three classes doing its own job'.[62]

This dual conception of competence and station underpins the claim to rule that is expressed by the idea of trusteeship. Dominion is the result of excellence of some sort. Individual veracity, rather than strength, duplicity, or cunning, is the fountain of empire. Thus, the British Empire owed its success, according to William Lecky, to the habits and talents of the men who built it, men who possessed the superior intellectual, industrial, and moral qualities upon which the well-being of all nations depend.[63] Kerr believed that these same qualities rendered some people uniquely suited to rule others: '[t]here are peoples who by reason of their character, their truthfulness and integrity, their political institutions, their sense of public responsibility, their resource-fulness and capacity progressively to improve the conditions under which they live, regard themselves as the leaders of mankind.'[64] Of course, these endowments were not enjoyed equally by all: some people were regarded as lacking the patience, knowledge, skill, and self-discipline required to frame and operate government for themselves. Indeed, endemic warfare, despotic rule, slavery, alien customs, and an absence of science, commerce, and industry were taken as demonstrable evidence that non-European peoples were inca-pable of directing their own affairs. The peoples of Africa and Asia were typ-ically derided as being filled with pride, passion, and appetite. They were ridiculed for their seeming preference of superstition to rationality, magic to science, and violence to law. And they were pitied for an apparent lack of spirit that revealed an inability to effect coherent arrangements of public life and to fulfil its conditions. For these peoples, as John Stuart Mill once put it, 'have not got beyond the period during which it is likely to be for their bene-fit that they should be conquered and held in subjection by foreigners'.[65]

But the presumed superiority of European virtue, practice, and achieve-ment did not in any way countenance the exploitation of the disadvantaged; rather, the excellence of European civilization imposed a heavy burden on the strong to act on behalf of the weak. For just as the best men in Plato's repub-lic are obliged to rule, no matter how burdensome or arduous it may be,

[62] Plato, *Republic*, trans. R. Waterfield (Oxford: Oxford University Press, 1993), 142, 153.

[63] W. Lecky, 'The Empire: Its Value and Its Growth', *Historical and Political Essays* (Freeport, NY: Books for Libraries Press, 1970), 53.

[64] Kerr, 'Political Relations between Advanced and Backward Peoples', 141.

[65] J. S. Mill, 'A Few Words on Non-Intervention', *Essays on Politics and Culture*, ed. G. Himmelfarb (Gloucester, MA: Peter Smith, 1973), 377.

proponents of trusteeship believed that the advanced peoples must assume responsibility for the well-being of backward peoples. This responsibility arises, not out of pride or avarice, but out of obligation; for those who are in possession of clear sight and true knowledge must guide those who are shrouded in darkness. Indeed, Kerr argued that the 'decisive mark of a superior civilisation is the readiness of its members to sacrifice themselves in order that their less fortunate fellows may learn how to share in their blessings'.[66] This claim did not embrace pure altruism while disavowing the pursuit of advantage. Instead it rested on the principle of trusteeship laid down by Edmund Burke: 'all political power which is set over men ... ought to be some way or other exercised ultimately for their benefit'.[67] The idea of trusteeship is unavoidably concerned with the justification of power; it supposes that dominion entails great responsibility, and, to that extent, it stands as an unequivocal repudiation of domination and exploitation. Trusteeship is an idea that sanctions the rule of one man over another, in lands that are not his own, so long as the power of dominion is directed towards the improvement of the incompetent and infirm. It is in this conviction, as the Earl of Cromer argued, that empire derived its most powerful defence: 'the Anglo-Saxon in modern times comes, not to enslave, but to liberate from slavery. The fact that he does so is, indeed, one of his best title-deeds to Imperial dominion.'[68]

The superior virtue that entitles one man to rule another, and therefore establishes a claim to rule, prefigures a relation of ruler and subject that is grounded in the belief that all men are not equal in all things. The nature of this inequality, which is indeed a fundamental assumption of the idea of trusteeship, is illuminated in John Locke's idea that freedom and subjection are not necessarily contradictory conditions. While Locke recognized the '*equal Right* that every Man hath, *to his Natural Freedom*, without being subjected to the Will or Authority of any other Man', he asserted that the exercise of that freedom, as well as the capacity for rational action, is something that comes with the maturity of age [emphasis in original].[69] A man who is free possesses full use of reason; and, therefore, he is capable of knowing and understanding the law. Conversely, the man who is incapable of knowing and understanding the law is consigned to a life under the supervision of others. Thus, Locke argues that '*Madmen, which for the present cannot possibly have*

[66] Kerr, 'Political Relations between Advanced and Backward Peoples', 144.

[67] E. Burke, 'Speech on Mr. Fox's East India Bill, December 1, 1783', *The Works of the Right Honorable Edmund Burke*, vol. 2 (Boston: Little, Brown, and Company, 1899), 439.

[68] Earl of Cromer, 'The Government of Subject Races', *Political and Literary Essays, 1908–1913* (London: Macmillan, 1913), 19.

[69] J. Locke, 'Second Treatise of Government', *Two Treatises of Government*, ed. P. Laslett (Cambridge: Cambridge University Press, 1988), 304.

the use of right Reason to guide themselves, have for their Guide, the Reason that guideth other Men which are Tutors over them, to seek and procure their good for them' [emphasis in original].[70] People who were made wards of some corporation, state, or international organization were similarly deemed as being unable to know true law, and, accordingly, they were regarded as being incapable of directing their individual and collective lives by their own will. Darkness prevented them from seeing the true nature of things and irrationality concealed from sight the conditions of their own happiness. Therefore, the condition of inequality that so prominently shapes the character of trusteeship is the consequence of defect.

In order to grasp the significance of this condition of inequality, it is necessary to consider this notion of defect in the context of what Herbert Butterfield calls the whig interpretation of history. The whig historian does not understand what is to some people precious, meaningful, and sacred, on its own terms and for its own value, for these things are not the stuff of historical narrative. Rather, the activity of writing history consists in investigating, understanding, and judging the past with reference to the standards of the present. History is thus reduced to a ratification of the present. The whig historian 'stands on the summit of the twentieth century, and organises his scheme of history from the point of view of his own day'.[71] For James Mill, Thomas Fowell Buxton, Jan Smuts, and others like them, the present with which they were acquainted represented the highest state of achievement; and it was against this standard of perfection that they judged the non-European peoples with whom they came into contact. History, as they understood it, transformed the values, practices, and institutions of others into models of defect. When considered from this vantage point, it can come as no surprise that Mill felt only contempt for the purportedly fantastic tales portrayed in the epics, poetry, and mythology he believed were responsible for leaving the Hindu mind in a shrunken and feeble state; nor is it possible to dismiss as mere mockery Smuts' suggestion that wine, women, and song are for the African the greatest consolation in life. Both Mill and Smuts comprehended, as is typical of the whig historian, a relative Hindu or African past against the backdrop of an absolute European present. Only then was it possible to adjudicate authoritatively between different religions, philosophies, forms of government, and ways of life.[72] In this way the trustees of civilization adopted a uniform and universal scale of (European) values against which

[70] Ibid. 307–8.
[71] H. Butterfield, *The Whig Interpretation of History* (New York: W. W. Norton & Company, 1965), 13.
[72] J. Mill, *The History of British India*, abrg. W. Thomas (Chicago: University of Chicago Press, 1975), 33; J. C. Smuts, *Africa and Some World Problems* (Oxford: Clarendon Press, 1930), 75; and Butterfield, *The Whig Interpretation of History*, 16, 73.

non-European society could appear only as depraved, destitute, and defective. And it is this notion of defect, something that is confirmed as deviance from European standards of perfection, which sustains and justifies the relations of inequality that are at the centre of the idea of trusteeship.

After establishing the imperfect state in which the peoples of the non-European world existed, their European masters were left with the task of determining the end towards which the tutelage of these peoples should be directed. Only then would they satisfy the stringent justification of political power that Burke had laid down. The self-designated guardians of the 'ignorant' believed that for some reason their wards did not understand their situation; and, in that respect, they were a danger to others and to themselves. Thus, the first, and most important, end of trusteeship consists in promoting the welfare of people who were incapable of choosing for themselves the ends for which they should strive. Indeed, the act of choosing, and thereby attending to the welfare of their charges, remained the sacred duty of the supervising trustee. For Charles Grant the remedy of Indian depravity depended on the communication of European knowledge and, especially, the excellence of Christian morality. The perfection of the Christian religion certainly impressed David Livingstone, but he believed that the salvation of Africa depended also on the introduction of legitimate commerce. Lord Lugard recommended that the African be instructed in the qualities of responsibility, initiative, fair-play, discipline, and justice—qualities that were required of a people who were fit to be self-governing. And the architects of the United Nations trusteeship system believed that the welfare of dependent peoples could not be separated from the furtherance of international peace and security, as well as political, economic, social, and educational advancement, and respect for human rights and fundamental freedoms.[73] The many ends of trusteeship surely came into conflict from time to time. For example, acolytes of utilitarianism understood enlightenment quite differently than the apostles of Christianity. However, these differences notwithstanding, the schemes proffered by Charles Grant and James Mill in British India, David Livingstone and Lord Lugard in sub-Saharan Africa, and Cordell Hull and Oliver Stanley in debates about trusteeship in the United Nations charter, were each in its own right directed towards lifting dependent peoples into the ranks of civilized life.

But the idea of trusteeship demanded something more than the promotion of welfare. Hence the second end of trusteeship consists in protecting dependent

---

[73] See C. Grant, 'Observations on the State of Society Among the Asiatic Subjects of Great Britain', *Parliamentary Papers*, 1812–13 (282) x.31, mf. 14.63–64, 76, 91; Cairns, *Prelude to Imperialism*, 192–8; F. D. Lugard, *The Dual Mandate of Africa*, 4th edn. (London: William Blackwood & Sons, 1929), 215; and 'Charter of the United Nations', in A. Roberts and B. Kingsbury (eds.), *United Nations, Divided World* (Oxford: Clarendon Press, 1993), 520.

peoples from the machinations and rapacity of outsiders. For the history of this encounter is often told as a sordid tale of unscrupulous traders, dealing in firearms, liquor, and slaves, who were driven by the impulse of personal enrichment. Of these less virtuous patrons of empire Kerr writes: '[h]aving no defined responsibility for the welfare of the people with whom they are brought into contact, many of them succumb to the temptation to take full advantage of their own superior energy and knowledge, and of the weakness and vices of the backward peoples, to exploit them for their own profit.'[74] There were also those who were deemed to be less able trustees of civilization. It is in this context that Cromer recalled Livingstone's complaint that 'in five hundred years the only thing the natives of Africa had learnt from the Portuguese was to distil bad spirits with the help of an old gun barrel.'[75] While the ranks of the civilized were most definitely assured of their moral and material superiority, they were not indifferent to the exploitation and suffering of their fellow human beings, no matter how debased their lives might have been. Burke's crusade against the East India Company, though unsuccessful in the end, led to parliamentary supervision of the Company's affairs in order to curb abuse of its native subjects. The horror of Leopold's Congo Free State merely confirmed that the protections afforded by the Berlin Act were hopelessly deficient. And the response to this failure eventually resulted in the creation of elaborate 'international machinery', first as part of the League of Nations and then as part of the United Nations, to ensure the faithful performance of duties pertaining to the protection of dependent peoples. It is this duty of protecting backward peoples from the exploitation of outsiders, in addition to the duty of promoting their welfare, which in part justified the idea of trusteeship.

The principle that the strong should assist the weak—the principle that Kerr and other proponents of trusteeship wished to promote—enjoins the fit, the capable, and the wise to seek the good of all human beings for no other reason than that they are members of the human family. Trusteeship assumes that the fit, that is, the virtuous, shall rule on behalf of the incapable. It assumes that some notion of defect joins ruler and subject in a hierarchical relationship, one based explicitly on a condition of inequality, whereby the enlightened instruct the ignorant in the true nature of things. And it assumes that the end towards which this tutelage is directed is concerned fundamentally with promoting the welfare of dependent peoples and protecting them from exploitation, until such time that they are able to exercise the freedoms and responsibilities of 'mature' human beings.

---

[74] Kerr, 'Political Relations between Advanced and Backward Peoples', 145.
[75] Cromer, 'The Government of Subject Races', 11.

2

The Obligations of Power

The idea of trusteeship in international society finds its origin in late eighteenth century British India. Thus the purpose of this chapter is to examine the emergence of trusteeship as a justification of political power in territories administered by the East India Company. This most famous of the great chartered companies is perhaps best remembered for the trial of Governor General Warren Hastings in 1787 and for the Indian Mutiny in 1857, which brought to an ignominious end the political dominion enjoyed by a company of merchants. But in the 60-year interregnum that separated these events, a period during which questions of politics gradually displaced questions of commerce, the Company embarked on a series of experiments that were aimed at securing the happiness of its native subjects. These experiments resulted in the articulation and affirmation of a mode of conduct, or to put it differently, a standard against which to evaluate the justice of alien rule, that is broadly intelligible in the terms of the idea of trusteeship. In short, then, dominion in British India was justified by the belief that the strong should rule on behalf of the weak; that a condition of inequality joined ruler and subject; and that government should secure the happiness of people that cannot secure it for themselves. It is in this respect that the experience of the East India Company prefigures the emergence of trusteeship as a recognized and accepted practice in international society.

From Merchant to Sovereign in British India

At the height of the impeachment trial of Warren Hastings, Edmund Burke denounced the East India Company as a 'state in the disguise of a merchant'.[1] But the Company got its start, not as a vast economic and political power, but as a modest merchant charged by Elizabeth I with the task of discovering and establishing a lawful trade for the benefit of the commonwealth. After a succession of isolated and commercially risky voyages, the Company obtained

---

[1] E. Burke, 'Speeches in the Impeachment of Warren Hastings, Esquire, Late Governor-General of Bengal, February 15, 1788', *The Works of the Right Honourable Edmund Burke*, vol. 9 (Boston: Little, Brown, and Company, 1899), 350.

from the Mughal emperor in 1613 permission to establish a permanent trading station at Surat. Within a decade the Company expanded its presence to Broach, Ahmadabad, and the imperial capital of Agra; and by 1650 the Company established a presence in Madras and in Calcutta.[2] In these early years, the Company's relations with Mughal India were guided by the policy laid down by Sir Thomas Roe: 'Lett this bee receiued as a rule that if you will Profitt, seeke it at Sea, and in quiett trade; for without controuersy it is an error to affect Garrisons and Land warrs in India.'[3] The Company's directors, being convinced of the incompatibility of war and commerce, proceeded on the belief that the prince of a well-ordered state could provide the necessary conditions for conducting a flourishing and profitable trade. Land-based fortifications were viewed as an unnecessary and potentially provocative expense; and, accordingly, agents posted to India were instructed against using force to secure commercial advantage and against interfering in the domestic affairs of Indian society. Thus, the maintenance of the Company's trading privileges, rather than the internal politics of the Mughal Empire, commanded the greater share of their attention.

But as the Mughal Empire entered into a long period of decline during the latter part of the seventeenth century, the Company's prosperity and its policy of non-interference were ever more uncertain. Rebellious chiefs and ongoing war, along with Emperor Aurangzeb's fanatical devotion to Islam and concomitant intolerance of Hinduism, eroded the stability of the Empire. While local officials were increasingly willing to act independently of the imperial court in Delhi for the trappings of personal power and wealth, the Company's agents complained that these officials secured personal advantage through extortion, interfered with trading privileges and commercial transactions, and could not be relied upon to redress grievances.[4] Nowhere did the ensuing disorder evoke greater alarm than in the Company's enclave on the island of Bombay, which felt compelled to raise a sizeable army to fend off marauding Maratha armies in an attempt to protect its rather precarious position at the periphery of Mughal authority. The slow but steady decay of the Mughal Empire convinced many of the Company's agents that Mughal authorities were incapable of ensuring the conditions of peace, order, and security upon which their commerce depended. Indeed, in the absence of an authority

---

[2] P. Griffiths, *The British Impact on India* (London: Archon Books, 1965), 51–2.

[3] T. Roe, 'Sir Thomas Roe on the Wisdom of Pursuing Peaceful Commerce, 24 November 1616', in S. V. D. Char (ed.), *Readings in the Constitutional History of India 1757–1947* (Delhi: Oxford University Press, 1983), 4; and V. Harlow, *The Founding of the Second British Empire, 1763–1793*, vol. 2 (London: Longman, 1964), 7.

[4] Griffiths, *The British Impact on India*, 56; and Harlow, *The Founding of the Second British Empire*, 7–8.

capable of sustaining conditions favourable to a profitable commerce, the Governor of Bombay, Gerald Aungier, suggested to the Court of Directors in 1677 that 'the times now require you to manage your general commerce with your sword in Your hands'.[5]

The Court of Directors, confronted by persistent disorder and lawlessness, eventually conceded that the Company may have to assume greater responsibility for ensuring the security of its commercial interests in India. In 1687 they signalled a newly found assertiveness when they instructed agents in Madras that the Company 'will maintain and defend against all persons, and govern by our own laws, without any appeal to any prince or potentate whatsoever, except our Sovereign Lord the King'.[6] However, the realities of power would soon demonstrate the practical limitations of conducting relations by force: the seizure of Mughal ships and interference in pilgrim traffic provoked an attack on Bombay and nearly led to the Company's expulsion from India in 1689. Impressed with the still formidable power of the Mughal Empire, the Company sought Aurangzeb's pardon in the hope of re-establishing its licensed trade.[7] But in spite of this humiliating setback, the Company persisted nevertheless in charting a new course for superintending its affairs in India. The weakened state of the Mughal Empire suggested rather ominously that the Company's security and prosperity would at some point in the future depend on its ability to defend, by force if necessary, its principal settlements at Bombay, Calcutta, and Madras. Tellingly, Governor Sir Josiah Child communicated to the Company's servants in 1681 his conviction that 'all war is so contrary to our constitution as well as to our interest that we cannot too often inculcate to you our aversion thereunto'; by 1687 the deterioration of conditions in India convinced Child of the need to 'establish such a politie of civil and military power, and create and secure such a large revenue to maintain both ... as may be the foundation of a large, well-grounded, sure English dominion for all time to come'.[8] The latter of these opinions soon became a matter of necessity: palace intrigue so severely weakened Mughal authority that the Company's trade was increasingly vulnerable to the aggrandizement of local officials who had established their de facto independence from imperial authority.

The charter granted by William III in 1698 formalized this shift in thinking by reserving to the Crown the sovereign right, power, and dominion over British possessions in India while authorising the Company to 'raise, train,

---

[5] Quoted in Harlow, *The Founding of the Second British Empire*, 10.

[6] 'General Letter to Fort St. George, 6 June 1687', in S. V. D. Char (ed.), *Readings in the Constitutional History of India 1757–1947* (Delhi: Oxford University Press, 1983), 4.

[7] Harlow, *The Founding of the Second British Empire*, 10; and Griffiths, *The British Impact on India*, 57.   [8] Quoted in Griffiths, *The British Impact on India*, 56–7.

and muster, such Military Forces as shall or may be necessary for the Defence' of the Company's property.[9] Although the Company obtained the right to raise an army, the Court of Directors did not abandon entirely their general aversion to becoming entangled in the politics and wars of quarrelling Indian princes; and they persisted in reaffirming the primacy of trade and the presumption against fortifications and waging war. 'We cannot avoid remarking', they wrote to Fort William (Bengal) in 1759, 'that you seem so thoroughly possessed with military ideas as to forget your employers are merchants and trade their principal object, and were we to adopt your several plans for Fortifying, half our capital would be buried in stone walls'.[10] The imperatives of defence resulted in a departure from the policy articulated by Roe 75 years earlier; however, the Court of Directors continued to adhere to a course of restraint that proscribed interference beyond what was necessary to safeguard the Company's property and trading privileges. Hence, they insisted that the Company's servants conduct themselves in such a way that the people of India be 'allowed to live in the full enjoyment of the privileges of their respective Casts [sic], provided they do nothing to the prejudice of the English Government'.[11]

Rivalry between competing British and French companies, which by the mid-eighteenth century erupted into open conflict, put this policy to a severe test. Agents of the British company demonstrated an increased willingness to intrude into the domestic affairs of Indian states in a bid to parry the growth of French influence in India. They offered gifts in exchange for enhanced trading privileges; they participated in the intrigues of dynastic succession by supporting, installing, and maintaining their preferred candidates for disputed thrones; and, perhaps most significantly, they demonstrated in engagements with Indian armies the superiority of European arms and military discipline. This degree of confidence and assertiveness aroused such suspicion and fear in the Nawab of Bengal, Siraj-ud-Daulah, that he attacked the Company's factories at Kasimbazar and Calcutta in 1756 in an attempt to reduce the commanding position enjoyed by the British in Bengal. Although the Company's army managed to recapture Calcutta six months later, the Nawab's vacillating support of contending British and French interests

---

[9] 'Charter Granted by William III, 5 September 1698', in S. V. D. Char (ed.), *Readings in the Constitutional History of India 1757–1947* (Delhi: Oxford University Press, 1983), 12.

[10] 'The Court of Directors on the Primacy of Trade, 23 March 1759', in S. V. D. Char (ed.), *Readings in the Constitutional History of India 1757–1947* (Delhi: Oxford University Press, 1983), 6.

[11] 'The Court of Directors on the Policy Towards the Native Inhabitants of Madras, 17 February 1726', in S. V. D. Char (ed.), *Readings in the Constitutional History of India 1757–1947* (Delhi: Oxford University Press, 1983), 16–17.

incited Robert Clive, who had gained the support of influential Hindu merchants and bankers, to depose Siraj-ud-Daulah in favour of Mir Jafar after the Battle of Plassey in 1757. Victory at Plassey not only confirmed the Company's predominant commercial position in Bengal, it signalled the beginning of British political mastery as well. The government of Bengal remained nominally independent of British power and the Company's commerce still relied upon government issued licences, but Mir Jafar, and all subsequent Nawabs, could not offend British sensibilities without fear of being deposed. Indeed, a succession of weak and subservient governments met this very fate; and on each occasion, additional concessions were extracted from newly installed rulers who were little more than executives of the Company's interest.

By 1764, after the ruling Nawab again suffered military defeat at the hand of the Company's army, Bengal had been transformed into a British protectorate. The Company pledged to support newly enthroned Najam-ud-Daulah against all enemies and in return he ceded territory to offset some of the Company's military expenses and agreed to receive a British advisor to assist in managing the affairs of government.[12] But the Company's emergence as a Mughal feudatory was by far and away the most significant development in the growth of British power in India. In August 1765, Emperor Shah Alam granted to the Company exclusive and perpetual possession of the *diwani*—the right to collect and administer revenue—of Bengal, Bihar, and Orissa. Securing the *diwani* irrevocably engaged the Company in the defence and public administration of territories in India, for the grant obliged the Company to remit a fixed annual sum to the emperor and to maintain a large army to protect subject provinces. The magnitude and potential danger of such great responsibility did not escape Clive, who conceded that 'so large a sovereignty may possibly be an object too extensive for a mercantile Company'.[13] However, he eventually came to regard the possession of the *diwani* as the best way of redressing persistent problems of instability, disorder, and war, as well as the increasingly errant conduct of corrupt Company agents. This conclusion rested on the conviction, expressed by the Council at Fort William, that a stable and lasting government in Bengal required the abandonment of all schemes of divided power: 'all must belong to the Company

---

[12] 'Agreement Between the Company and Najam-ud-Daulah, Nawab of Bengal, 20 February 1765', in S. V. D. Char (ed.), *Readings in the Constitutional History of India 1757–1947* (Delhi: Oxford University Press, 1983), 32–4.

[13] 'Shah Alam's Farman Granting the Diwani of "Bengal, Bihar and Orissa" to the Company, 12 August 1765', and 'Robert Clive on the Policy of Acquiring Territorial Possessions, 7 January 1759', in S. V. D. Char (ed.), *Readings in the Constitutional History of India 1757–1947* (Delhi: Oxford University Press, 1983), 31, 34–5.

or to the Nabob'.[14] With the assumption of political power the Company ceased to be merely a commercial enterprise concerned with establishing a lawful trade for the benefit of the commonwealth; and as a necessary consequence it had to confront the problem of governing, an activity it was wholly ill-prepared to perform.

The Claim to Rule

Acquisition of the *diwani* did not result in the establishment of conditions favourable to a healthy trade, nor did it arrest corruption amongst the Company's servants. Rather, government in the custody of the Company's servants aided the cause of despotism and rapacity. Disorders of every kind multiplied as territories rich in natural wealth, territories that Clive described as 'abounding in the most valuable productions of nature and of art',[15] lapsed into a state of privation. Mismanagement and corruption continued unabated, war frequented the Company's relations with neighbouring states, the peasant population laboured under a yoke of exploitation, and famine, which struck in 1769, laid waste to the Bengali countryside and killed millions. To compound matters, the belief that acquisition of the *diwani* would bear great financial advantage proved to be hopelessly misplaced, as the Company advised Parliament in 1772 of its inability to meet financial obligations owed to creditors and shareholders. The complete failure to devise a government that approached a modicum of stability, in addition to persistent allegations of corruption and the burden of an increasingly unmanageable debt, hastened the Crown's first attempt to regulate the Company's affairs.[16] It is in the ensuing debates that we encounter for the first time a particular claim to rule that underpins the idea of trusteeship and which is essential to understanding its central assumptions and justifications.

Parliament's first involvement in the affairs of the East India Company resulted in the passage of the North Regulating Act of 1773. Ironically, opposition to the rather modest reforms prescribed by the North Act did not arise in direct response to charges of corruption and misrule in India, but from

[14] 'The Council at Fort William on the Acquisition of the Diwani, 30 September 1765', in S. V. D. Char (ed.), *Readings in the Constitutional History of India 1757–1947* (Delhi: Oxford University Press, 1983), 36–7.

[15] 'Robert Clive on the policy of acquiring territorial possessions, 7 January 1759', in S. V. D. Char (ed.), *Readings in the Constitutional History of India 1757–1947* (Delhi: Oxford University Press, 1983), 32.

[16] P. J. Marshall, 'Introduction', *Problems of Empire, 1757–1813*, ed. P. J. Marshall (London: George Allen and Unwin, 1968), 32–3.

deeply held beliefs and traditions concerning the constitution of the British polity. Indeed, the North Act raised important questions about the status of chartered rights and the protection they afforded against intrusive legislative and executive authority. It is in this context that the Company defended its claim to rule in India. At the end of the eighteenth century the activities of state were still generally regarded as being properly limited to the conduct of foreign policy, the direction of armed forces, and the disposal of revenue. Conversely, the affairs of a private corporation, and especially matters concerning its property rights, were regarded as inappropriate matters for parliamentary attention.[17] For example, the City of London, the most important chartered corporation in England, viewed any restriction of the Company's chartered rights with grave apprehension: 'the said Bill is a direct and dangerous attack on the liberties of the people, and will, if passed in to a law, prove of the most fatal consequences to the security of property in general, and particularly the franchises of every corporate body in this kingdom.'[18] Edmund Burke also came to the aid of the Company, mainly because he feared that interference in the Company's affairs would lead the country to destruction, for it would entail responsibilities far too great for parliament to contemplate. Thus, he opposed the North Act, saying that it is 'impolitic, is unwise, and entirely repugnant to the letter as well as the spirit of the laws, the liberties, and the constitution of this country'.[19]

While any encroachment on the chartered rights of a private corporation required the utmost caution, the North government believed that allegations of corruption and misgovernment in India were of sufficient magnitude to warrant some form of intervention. The North Act prescribed a set of reforms in the hope of placing the Company's finances and its government in India on a more secure footing. It confirmed the Company's right of dominion in India, but in recognition of this right it also charged the Company's Governor General with the responsibility of making rules and regulations in order to promote and to maintain public order. The Company's servants were forbidden to engage in personal trade, to receive gifts, and to exact tribute in the performance of their duties; and, significantly, the long-standing premise positing the incompatibility of commerce and war obtained positive affirmation. Thus, the North Act declared that in the absence of lawful

[17] Ibid. 22.
[18] 'The Petition of the City of London Against Lord North's Regulating Act, 28 May, 1773', in P. J. Marshall (ed.), *Problems of Empire, 1757–1813* (London: George Allen and Unwin, 1968), 107.
[19] E. Burke, 'Speech on North's East India Resolutions, 5 April 1773', *The Writing and Speeches of Edmund Burke*, vol. 2, ed. P. Langford (Oxford: Oxford University Press, 1981), 391–2.

authorization '[i]t shall not be lawful...to make any orders for commencing hostilities, or declaring or making war, against any Indian princes or powers, or for negotiating or concluding any treaty of peace, or other treaty, with any such Indian princes or powers.'[20] In spite of its modest aspirations, the North government advanced a claim on behalf of the Crown that the public interest and national honour justified parliamentary determination of appropriate standards of conduct to guide the Company's commercial and political activities in India. Indeed, the North Act endorsed the Company's argument that certain rights granted by Parliament sustained its claim to rule, but it also registered the principle that these rights were neither supreme nor absolute, and, in doing so, it established a pattern of relations between Crown and Company that formed the basis of future deliberations on the Company's activities in India.

In the years immediately following the passage of the North Act the Company's administration in India disclosed improvement, but efforts to restore stability through principles of good government fell well short of expectations. Allegations of corruption and abuse continued to tarnish the Company's reputation; and for a second time the Company experienced financial crisis that forced it to seek relief from Parliament. But it was the Company's role in a series of controversial wars that fired the passions of its most determined critics, which by then counted Edmund Burke among them. Burke argued during the North Act debates that the disorders associated with the Company's government in India were few in number and, therefore, did not warrant parliamentary interference. Exactly ten years later he argued that 'in its present state, the government of the East India Company is absolutely incorrigible'.[21] A parliamentary committee which investigated these allegations issued a devastating indictment, charging the Company with waging war in contravention of the public faith and reproaching its servants for condemning and defying orders stipulated in an act of Parliament with little discernible reservation. The committee concluded rather gloomily that the North Act had done little to curtail abuses of power in India and that the only plausible remedy entailed subordinating the Company in the strictest obedience to parliamentary supervision. But in an even more startling conclusion, the committee determined that the amelioration of

---

[20] 'North's Regulating Act, 1773 (Clauses relating to the organisation of the Company)', in P. J. Marshall (ed.), *Problems of Empire, 1757–1813* (London: George Allen and Unwin, 1968), 111–14, 153.

[21] E. Burke, 'Speech on Mr. Fox's East India Bill, December 1, 1783', *The Works of the Right Honourable Edmund Burke*, vol. 2 (Boston: Little, Brown, and Company, 1899), 509; 'Speech on East India Regulating Bill, 10 June 1773', *The Writing and Speeches of Edmund Burke*, vol. 2, ed. P. Langford (Oxford: Oxford University Press, 1981), 395; and Marshall, 'Introduction', 36.

misrule in India required that '[t]he prosperity of the native must be previously secured, before any profit from them whatsoever is attempted'.[22] These conclusions implied a rather different principle against which to judge the Company's claim to rule: dominion depended not only on the possession of chartered rights granted by Parliament, but, as well, on the extent to which the welfare and prosperity of its native subjects coincided with the Company's rule.

The underlying justification of this principle was most eloquently articulated in Burke's celebrated speech in support of Charles Fox's motion to abolish the Company's dominion in India. Burke understood the Company's abuse of commercial and political power as constituting a gross offence against the natural rights of men. Rights of this sort, he argued, are not the products of human activity: natural rights exist prior to the creation of positive rights and their fundamental character and inviolability are not debased by an absence of formal recognition in positive instruments of law. Thus, positive rights impose no obligation when they are repugnant to the authority of natural rights; for 'self-derived rights, or grants for the mere private benefit of the holders, ... are all in the strictest sense *a trust*: and it is the very essence of every trust to be rendered *accountable*, and even totally to *cease*, when it substantially varies from the purposes for which alone it could have a lawful existence [emphasis in original]'.[23] But commercial and political privileges, Burke declared, are not rights of men; and the failure to discharge the duties assumed in possession of these rights violated the trust upon which the Company's claim to rule depended. It was for this reason alone that Burke countenanced executive and legislative interference in the Company's affairs, even when it transgressed rights that were intended to restrain such instances of interference. Indeed, he did not deny the Company's right of commercial monopoly; nor did he dispute the Company's authority to administer the revenue of its Indian territories, to command an army of sixty-thousand men, or to rule over the lives of thirty million Indian subjects.[24] However, egregious abuse of commercial and political rights, and the magnitude and extent of misrule in India, left him with little doubt that the Company had forfeited its claim to rule.

It is the notion of trust that underpins Burke's conviction that the affairs of British India must be placed under parliamentary authority and supervision. He believed that the trust that joined ruler and subject in India had been irreparably broken; for he could discern no benefit of sufficient importance

---

[22] E. Burke, 'Ninth Report of the Select Committee of the House of Commons on the Affairs of India, June 25, 1783', *The Works of the Right Honourable Edmund Burke*, vol. 8 (Boston: Little, Brown, and Company, 1899), 39, 41, 191.   [23] Ibid. 439.

[24] Ibid. 439, 522.

to justify the maintenance of the Company's dominion. He protested that the
Company reduced to ruin every prince with whom it came into contact and
that millions of Indians experienced neglect at the hands of the Company's
administration. Treaty obligations were ignored, rights of war and peace were
abused, and young boys, intoxicated by the excesses of power, governed without sympathy for native interests. And he complained bitterly that the
Company's masters had done nothing to compensate for the injustice of an
ignominious rule. Indeed, he feared that '[w]ere we driven out of India this
day, nothing would remain to tell that it had been possessed, during the
inglorious period of our dominion, by anything better than the orangoutang
or the tiger'.[25] Burke's passionate discourse attracted the sympathy of others
that regarded the Company's conduct in India as being repugnant to the honour of the British nation as well as to the law of nations. Perhaps the most
important of these sympathizers was Adam Smith, who attributed the
Company's misconduct to a fundamental contradiction between the interests
of merchant and sovereign: '[a]s sovereigns, their interest is exactly the same
with that of the country which they govern. As merchants their interest is
directly opposite to that interest.'[26] For Smith, a government conducted by
merchants was apt to prefer the meagre profit of the monopolist to the great
revenue of the sovereign; and for this reason he suggested that 'a company of
merchants are, it seems, incapable of considering themselves as sovereigns,
even after they have become such. Trade, or buying in order to sell again, they
still consider as their principal business, and by a strange absurdity regard the
character of the sovereign as but an appendix to that of the merchant, as
something which ought to be made subservient to it.'[27]

   Although Burke did not succeed in seeing the revocation of the Company's
chartered rights, he did register the principle against which all subsequent
governments in India would be judged: 'all political power which is set over
men, and that all privilege claimed or exercised in exclusion of them, being
wholly artificial, and for so much a derogation from the natural equality of
mankind at large, ought to be some way or other exercised ultimately for
their benefit.'[28] Success in this respect resulted in the passage of the India
Act of 1784, which left the Company's commercial rights unmolested but
stipulated principles of good government that were intended to 'secure the

[25] E. Burke, 'Ninth Report of the Select Committee of the House of Commons on the Affairs of India, June 25, 1783', *The Works of the Right Honourable Edmund Burke*, vol. 8 (Boston: Little, Brown, and Company, 1899), 447–64.
[26] A. Smith, *The Wealth of Nations*, vol. 2, eds. R. H. Campbell and A. S. Skinner (Indianapolis, IN: Liberty Fund, 1981), 638.   [27] Ibid. 637.
[28] Burke, 'Speech on Mr. Fox's East India Bill', 439.

happiness of the natives'.[29] The India Act reiterated the principles of good government contained in the North Act without significant deviation. But the India Act went further in establishing the principle of parliamentary supervision in order to curb abuses perpetrated by the Company's servants and to ensure the welfare of its native subjects. Indeed, William Pitt, the Prime Minister who presided over the passage of the India Act, argued that the success of the East India Company 'must chiefly depend on the establishment of the happiness of the inhabitants, and their being secured in a state of peace and tranquillity'.[30] That Burke and his allies shaped both the terms of debate and the character of reform is beyond the pale of doubt. They registered the principles that ruler and subject were joined by a sacred trust and that the native subjects of India ought to be the ultimate beneficiaries of government. Thus, the happiness and security of the native inhabitants of British India could no longer be dismissed as an adjunct or incidental interest to the business of commerce. Recognition of the Company's claim to rule now depended on the performance of duties pertaining to the general well-being of people on behalf of whom the government of India was obliged to act as a faithful trustee.

The Relation of Ruler and Subject

The elevation of the native subject to the foremost concern of government encouraged a manner of thinking that not only affirmed the idea of trusteeship, but presupposed a relation of ruler and subject based on a condition of inequality. If the Company was to be responsible for the happiness and security of British India's native inhabitants, then the conditions of their individual and collective lives took on a practical importance that transcended the scholarly curiosity of the Orientalist historians of the late eighteenth century. The most famous of these scholars, Sir William Jones, held Indian society in high esteem, even if he believed that its population could not be truly happy in the absence of the freedom that comes with rational knowledge. He regarded Indian poetry, drama, architecture, theology, and philosophy as providing evidence of superior achievement and he noted that Indian scientists were adept in the field of astronomy and possessed rudimentary knowledge

[29] W. Pitt, 'William Pitt on his First East India Bill', in S. V. D. Char (ed.), *Readings in the Constitutional History of India 1757–1947* (Delhi: Oxford University Press, 1983), 52–3.
[30] Quoted in Marshall, 'Introduction', 60; and see generally 'Pitt's India Act, 1784', in P. J. Marshall (ed.), *Problems of Empire, 1757–1813* (London: George Allen and Unwin, 1968), 131–6, 167–70.

of the basic laws of physics.[31] Burke similarly regarded India as home to a polished civilization founded on its own particular laws, institutions, and traditions. In one of his many declamations against the excesses of merchant rule he declared that the people of India do not 'consist of an abject and barbarous populace;... but a people for ages civilized and cultivated, cultivated by all the arts of polished life, whilst we were yet in the woods'.[32] Indeed, he compared the constitution of Indian society favourably to that of Britain and viewed it as being roughly equal to the German Empire. And for Burke, the high degree of moral perfection exhibited by Indian society commanded respect as a civilization in its own right, for 'in Asia as well as in Europe the same law of nations prevails'; and Asia, he insisted, 'is as enlightened in that respect as well as Europe'.[33] But the respect that Burke accorded Indian civilization soon gave way to a contemptuous denunciation of Indian difference that established the ostensible inferiority of Indian society, culture, religion, and character.

Favourable assessments of the state of Indian society came to be viewed with considerable scepticism as the universal and progressive values of the Enlightenment took hold; and the tangible results of reform in India lent credibility to the pretension of European superiority and to the claims of the Enlightenment project. This shift in attitude is evident in the programme of reform undertaken by Lord Cornwallis, who was dispatched to India after passage of the India Act in a bid to repair the Company's stained reputation. Before long the oft-maligned government of India was regarded as the custodian of a well-ordered and prosperous territory, as reports of precipitous decline and decay were soon replaced by accounts of rising standards of living and renewed wealth.[34] The apparent success of the Cornwallis reforms pacified the Company's most strident critics and seemingly confirmed the superiority of British ideas, practices, and institutions. The most consequential of these reforms, the introduction of property rights, aimed at creating a progressive landholding class and securing for the government a permanent source of revenue. To establish the permanence of these arrangements Cornwallis endeavoured to promote the rule of law, for 'security of property must be established by a system upheld by its inherent principles, and not by

[31] W. Jones, 'On the Origin and Families of Nations', in P. J. Kitson (ed.), *Slavery, Abolition and Emancipation: Writings in the British Romantic Period*, vol. 8 (London: Pickering & Chatto, 1999), 140; W. Jones, 'The Orientalist Viewpoint', in W. T. de Bary (ed.), *Sources of Indian Tradition* (New York: Columbia University Press, 1958), 590–2; and G. D. Bearce, *British Attitudes Towards India, 1784–1858* (Oxford: Oxford University Press, 1961), 20–6.
[32] Burke, 'Speech on Mr. Fox's East India Bill', 444.
[33] E. Burke, 'Speeches in the Impeachment of Warren Hastings', 382, 447–8, 485; and Burke, 'Speech on Mr. Fox's East India Bill', 444.   [34] Marshall, 'Introduction', 66.

the men who are to have the occasional conduct of it'.[35] But it is imperative to note that in pursuing a rather ambitious agenda of reform Cornwallis did not aspire to restore Indian society to some faded memory of greatness. The character and objectives of reform proceeded from the belief that Indian ways of life were obstacles to achieving stability, prosperity, and good government. Indeed, it was in the years immediately following the passage of the India Act that it was possible to detect both an implied and deliberate change in the British estimation of Indian society. George Bearce argues that the Company's success in bringing order and prosperity to British India fostered a sentiment that ascribed superiority to the character of the British people and ascribed inferiority to an Indian character that was typically described in terms of weakness, timidity, and moral depravity.[36] And, consequently, Indian society ceased to be an object of admiration and study, but instead became an object of denigration and pity.

One of the most influential statements propounding the inferiority of Indian society is found in an essay penned by Charles Grant, a man who, according to Ainslee Thomas Embree, did more to shape the character and assumptions of the Company's government in India than any other of his generation.[37] In a sweeping and total indictment, Grant described Bengal as being inhabited by people who were without qualification in want of the virtues required in a society abounding in comfort, wealth, prosperity, and security. Selfishness operated without restraint or regard for authority. Deception, fraud, and forgery were pervasive habits of Bengali life and acts of gross dishonesty passed without reproach, leaving no mark of dishonour or disgrace on persons who perpetrated them. Despotism framed a society in which persons entrusted with the responsibilities of power knew nothing of moderate and pacific rule. And a principle no more enlightened than fear, which set every man against every man, joined the Bengali to his ruler. Indeed, Grant insisted that in every respect the people of Bengal 'exhibit human nature in a very degraded humiliating state, and are at once, objects of disesteem and of commiseration'.[38] Thus, in one broad stroke, the difference of Bengali society that commanded a measure of respect from the likes of Jones and Burke provided for Grant evidence of a society founded upon irredeemable error.

---

[35] 'Cornwallis and his Council on Reforms in Judicial Administration, 6 March 1793', in S. V. D. Char (ed.), *Readings in the Constitutional History of India 1757–1947* (Delhi: Oxford University Press, 1983), 124; and Bearce, *British Attitudes Towards India*, 45–6.

[36] Bearce, *British Attitudes Towards India*, 40–2.

[37] See A. T. Embree, *Charles Grant and British Rule in India* (London: George Allen & Unwin, 1962).

[38] C. Grant, 'Observations on the State of Society Among the Asiatic Subjects of Great Britain', *Parliamentary Papers*, 1812–1813 (282) x.31, mf. 14. 63–4, 25–44.

The totality of this error compounded the effects of a defective national character that Grant described as mired in ignorance and the excesses of unfettered avarice and appetite. The faults of Bengali society were both ubiquitous and complete, so much so that he asserted: '[i]n Bengal, a man of real veracity and integrity is a great phenomenon; *one conscientious of the whole of his conduct*, it is to be feared, is an unknown character [emphasis in original].'[39] Grant offered no account of life in Bengal or of its people that did not involve the categorical condemnation of what he regarded as a baneful and, indeed, pernicious system of law and religion. He understood law and religion in Bengal as expressing a single unified system of authority, a system whose authenticity was confirmed by a (false) claim of divine origin. But in truth, he countered, the Hindu religion upholds a system of oppression: it prescribes a caste system—a system that is resistant to every scheme of liberal and enlightened change—that consigns the lowest orders of society to a life of perpetual ignorance, superstition, and servitude. And he betrayed no hesitation or doubt in concluding that the injurious effects of the caste system, which are in the main responsible for the depressed state of Bengali society, are the work of a 'crafty and imperious priesthood' and are the necessary consequence of a religion '[e]rected upon the darkest ignorance, and the boldest falsehood'.[40]

The wholly unfavourable estimation of Bengali society that runs throughout Grant's thought obtains validation of sorts in James Mill's famous history of India, a monumental treatise widely regarded during the early nineteenth century to be the most important and authoritative history of its kind. Mill's reading of history suggested that India had not progressed since contact with the Greeks; and the barbarous state of its population suggested further that 'having reached its present stage, Hindu society does not appear that it has made, or that it is capable of making, much further progress'.[41] He rejected as pretentious nonsense the view that the people of India once enjoyed a period of opulence and grandeur; for he could find no evidence, supported by reason or by history, of a great calamity sufficient to reduce them to a state of abject ignorance and barbarism. Rather, Mill attributed the poverty of Indian civilization to the effects of despotic government and defective law, both of which enjoyed the sanction of a fraudulent system of priestcraft that sustained an equally fraudulent religion from which it was impossible to extract a 'coherent system of belief'.[42] He deprecated the native government of

---

[39] Ibid. 26.   [40] Ibid. 45, 73.
[41] J. Mill, *The History of British India*, abrg. W. Thomas (Chicago: University of Chicago Press, 1975), 35, 55, 180.   [42] Ibid. 138, 190–2.

Bengal as being constituted by the unrestrained will of a single person and he doubted that much thought had been given to forms of government that did not combine the offices of sovereign, judge, and legislator. Indeed, he argued that Hindus deprived themselves of well-ordered society by subscribing to a body of law that was both incomplete and inexact. Hindu law created a multitude of rights that Mill believed should not exist and, having little regard for uniformity, it left matters of precedent shrouded in uncertainty. And like other 'rude' societies, these arrangements of public life were all imposed by a divinely ordained caste system, a system 'built upon the most enormous and tormenting superstition that ever harassed and degraded any portion of mankind'.[43]

The conditions of Indian society confirmed for Mill the shrunken and feeble state of the Hindu mind, a mind easily succoured by the fantastic tales portrayed in Hindu epics, poetry, and mythology, but thoroughly unaware of the 'sober limits of truth and history'.[44] Thus, he found the Sanskrit language, like Hindu law, deficient because of its imprecision. Whereas the standard of perfection consisted in having one name to describe all that requires a name, Sanskrit specified many words to describe the same thing. With respect to scientific achievement he found no evidence to suggest that the Hindu mind imagined the universe as a connected and perfect system governed by general laws knowable to all; and what little mathematics and astronomy it did understand was misdirected towards astrology—'the most irrational of all imaginable pursuits'.[45] In matters of social intercourse Mill likened Indians to uncultivated children: '[a]mong children, and among rude people, little accustomed to take their decisions upon full and mature consideration, nothing is more common than to repent of their bargains, and wish to revoke them.'[46] Mill was so impressed with European standards of achievement that he was certain that anyone who exerted the slightest effort, and was not shackled by sentimentality, hubris, and superstition, could 'form no other conclusion, but that every thing (unless astronomy be an exception) bears clear, concurring, and undeniable testimony to the ignorance of the Hindus, and the low state of civilization in which they remain'.[47]

Burke's defence of a highly organized and polished Indian civilization must have appeared as a rather strange and unintelligible fiction to Grant and Mill; for their histories of Indian society were dedicated solely to the illumination of error and defect. History written and understood in these terms accompanied what C. H. Alexandrowicz describes as the abandonment of a natural law tradition that disallowed the notion of geographic morality—the

---

[43] Ibid. 60–72, 108–11, 226.   [44] Ibid. 33.   [45] Ibid. 158, 224.
[46] Ibid. 76.   [47] Ibid. 213.

idea that differences in civilization endowed like actions with different moral qualities. In place of a tradition that embraced all nations within an universal system of law, European powers substituted a system of positive international law, which repudiated the principle of universality and thereby destroyed the general framework within which people of different civilizations, religions, races, traditions, and values might live out their lives in a spirit of coexistence.[48] Currents of thought that induced a startling and relatively sudden transformation in thinking about history and law also resulted in an equally changed understanding of the proper relation of ruler and subject. The superior virtue of the European and the corresponding defect of the Indian established a pattern of relations grounded in a condition of inequality. It is this conception of defect, understood as false religion, despotic government, feeble character, irrational law, or faulty knowledge, which Europeans invoked as justification for treating the people of India as wards, who were incapable of directing their own affairs. Thus, Indians, on account of their presumed inferiority, were thought to be worthy subjects of a benevolent government responsible for securing them in a state of peace and seeing to their improvement.

Lord Wellesley, the Governor General who added more territory to the Company's holdings than any other, took refuge in this type of thinking when he justified the absence of Indian participation in government: 'at the same time that we excluded our native subjects from all participation in the legislative authority, abundant security was afforded to them, that the exercise of that authority would always be directed to their happiness and benefit.'[49] Justifying the organization of society on these terms, namely, the joining of ruler and subject in terms of inequality, raised a question of supreme importance: for what reason should Indians who, for no reason other than the accident of birth live outside the Company's dominion, be excluded from the benefits of British rule? Lord Minto answered this question by proposing a policy of expansion and annexation that he believed would deliver the people of India from oppression and would confer upon them the benefits of liberal, enlightened, and moderate British rule. And, in form, Lord Hastings (no relation to Warren Hastings) claimed that the Company's wars in Nepal and in the Mahratta states helped stimulate public works and educational progress.[50] Thus, out of the presumption of inequality arose the idea that the

---

[48] C. H. Alexandrowicz, *An Introduction to the History of the Law of Nations in the East Indies* (Oxford: Clarendon Press, 1967), 237; and Burke, 'Speeches in the Impeachment of Warren Hastings', 382.

[49] 'Wellesley and his Council on the Constitution of the Government of India, 9 July 1800', in S. V. D. Char (ed.), *Readings in the Constitutional History of India 1757–1947* (Delhi: Oxford University Press, 1983), 155.   [50] Bearce, *British Attitudes Towards India*, 50–1.

possession of knowledge, wealth, power, and virtue imposed an obligation to attend to the social, moral, and material improvement of the weak and disadvantaged. Indeed, the Court of Directors resolved that the duty of raising India from its self-incurred state of stagnation arose from the 'total inability of the people to perform it with their own scanty means'.[51] And in this respect the Company's dominion would be justified by the extent to which it secured the improvement, if not emancipation, of India's population.

The Purpose of the Office of Government

With the imperfect state of Indian society established, its European masters were left with the task of determining the ends towards which the power of dominion should be directed. All agreed that political power ought to be exercised in such a way that it contributed to the security and happiness of the native people of India, but the ways in which their security and happiness might be realized remained a great deal less settled. Indeed, a plethora of disparate and sometimes conflicting voices argued that the well-being of India's native population depended on the introduction of a particular notion of religion, law, education, or some other form of improvement.

Advocates of religious improvement were moved by the fervent belief that the propagation of the Christian religion would remedy the moral depression that shrouded the people of India in a state of darkness. The assumptions that underpinned this view are again brought into sharp relief in the thought of Charles Grant, who understood the poverty of life in India as the consequence of something more fundamental than the Company's misrule. Like most evangelical Christians he believed that the people of India endured a life of misery on account of ignorance; and the remedy of this ignorance depended on the communication of Christian truth so that they might understand the nature of their errors. For Grant, the benefits of this enterprise were beyond scrutiny:

the pre-eminent excellence of the morality which the Gospel teaches, and the superior efficacy of this divine system, taken in all its parts, in meliorating the condition of human society, cannot be denied by those who are unwilling to admit its higher claims; and on this ground only, the dissemination of it must be beneficial to mankind.[52]

---

[51] 'The Court of Directors on the Duty of the Government to Undertake Works of Public Utility, 15 January 1812', in S. V. D. Char (ed.), *Readings in the Constitutional History of India 1757–1947* (Delhi: Oxford University Press, 1983), 136.

[52] Grant, 'Observations on the State of Society', 91.

That such a remedy awaited only an agent to disseminate its truths served to strengthen his resolve that the office of government should assume responsibility for what William Wilberforce described as the 'temporal and eternal happiness of millions; literally million on millions yet unborn'.[53] Inconvenience could not justify leaving the people of Bengal mired in darkness, nor could the consequences of failure be allowed to impede work destined to improve the lives of millions. Grant argued that dominion imposed an obligation far in excess of protecting the people of India from oppression. The office of government should be entrusted, he argued, to look into evil and disorders that afflict Indian society and 'to enact and enforce wholesome laws for their internal regulation, and in a word, with the affection of a wise and good superior, sedulously to watch over their civil and social happiness'.[54]

Although utilitarian thinkers dismissed religion as the veneration of superstition, their prescription for the improvement of India's teeming masses was in its principal assumptions remarkably similar to the Christian theory of improvement. Both utilitarians and evangelical Christians viewed the Indian character as being sufficiently malleable that the institution of 'true' law, albeit law of different origin, would effect its improvement. Whereas Charles Grant believed that improvement would follow the propagation of God's law, James Mill believed that improvement would follow the implementation of law rationally conceived, precisely articulated, and executed with economy and mechanistic efficiency. Indeed, Mill's theory of improvement amounted to little more than a secular Gospel of utilitarianism; for acolytes of utilitarianism, as Eric Stokes points out, merely 'abolished God and substituted human for Divine Justice'.[55] Thus, from the time of his appointment to the India Office in 1819, Mill brought the full force of utilitarian thought to bear on the policies of the government of India, in part to controvert the scholarly authority of William Jones and others who expressed admiration for Indian society. More importantly, though, he remained fixed on the substantive problem of governing the Company's vast territories. 'To ascertain the state of the Hindus in the scale of civilization,' he wrote, 'is not only an object of curiosity in the history of human nature; but to the people of Britain, charged as they are with the government of that great portion of the human species, it is an object of the highest practical importance'.[56]

In this respect, Mill harboured few doubts about the sources of Indian depravity: poverty was the result of bad government and bad law in India just

[53] Quoted in Marshall, 'Introduction', 72–3.
[54] Grant, 'Observations on the State of Society', 24–5.
[55] E. Stokes, *The English Utilitarians and India* (Oxford: Clarendon Press, 1959), 55.
[56] Mill, *The History of British India*, 180, 225.

as it was everywhere else. And true to utilitarian orthodoxy, he proposed to rectify the sources of bad government and bad law—the evil alliance of political despotism and priestly superstition—by unleashing a revolution aimed at radically reordering the system of law in British India. The defects of India's existing system of law, as Mill would have it, had to replaced with a more accurate and rational system. Law must had to be clear, effective, and economical so that presiding judges were able to declare its obligations without delay. Thus, he testified before the House of Commons in 1832 that 'there ought to be but one legislative organ for our whole Indian empire' and that 'there should be no limit to the power of legislation in India in the hands of the organ I speak of, except that the exercise of this power should be under the strict control of the British Parliament'.[57] In other words, Mill believed that the people of India required a human legislator, a will superior to each of their individual wills, to direct them away from harm and to guide them along the path of improvement. Only then would it be possible to erect a vibrant society built upon the veracity of individual effort, in place of one blinded by the narrowing outlook of priest and tyrant.[58] A government invested with supreme authority, he assumed, would also happily avoid what he identified as the fundamental error of the whig theory of dividing the power of government. Government must proceed uniformly: the legislator must determine the course on which to travel and the executive and judiciary must do no more than see to the faithful implementation of the legislator's commands. Thus, Mill shared with Bentham the view that '[t]o attempt to control government in the interests of the community by dividing its powers, and setting them as a mutual check against one another, was to frustrate its purpose'.[59]

The prescriptions offered by Mill, as well as those by Grant, are noteworthy in so far as they imply a revolutionary reformation of Indian society: improvement was something to be achieved in one momentous step. It is this approach to improvement that prevailed through much of the great decade of reform, from 1828–1838, in which the most ambitious attempts at effecting moral and material improvement of India were mounted. For example, Lord William Bentinck, the Governor General most closely associated with these reforms, determined that the people of India needed a wise and knowledgeable overseer, one sufficiently powerful to devise efficient laws in order to erode practices that obstructed or were incompatible with native

---

[57] J. Mill, 'James Mill on India's Need for a Properly Constituted Legislature, 21 February 1832', in S. V. D. Char (ed.), *Readings in the Constitutional History of India 1757–1947* (Delhi: Oxford University Press, 1983), 186–7; and Mill, *The History of British India*, 557.
[58] Stokes, *The English Utilitarians and India*, 69.   [59] Ibid. 72.

happiness.[60] Perhaps no issue better illustrates what he had in mind than the abolition of *sati*—the practice of a widow immolating herself on her husband's funeral pyre. Bentinck disclosed a thorough appreciation of the hazards to British authority that might follow interference in Hindu religious custom, but he maintained that conscience dictated that government should endeavour to separate the Hindu mind from this most odious practice, that is, to separate religious belief from murder. Only then would it be possible for Hindus to accept acknowledged truth, with calmness and clarity, that there can be no inconsistency in the divine law revealed to all men and to all races.[61] Missionaries denounced *sati* as an abominable ritual that should not in any circumstance be tolerated: '[t]he sacred principles of justice are not to be abrogated, because private individuals are mistaken in their notion of the worship which is acceptable to the Deity.'[62] Bentinck seems to have agreed. His government issued a circular in 1828 declaring that the continued toleration by Christians of *sati* incurred before God responsibility for the victims of an impious and inhuman ritual. The subsequent prohibition of *sati* in 1829 marked an important qualification of the long-standing presumption against interference in religious affairs: 'to the full extent of what it is possible to reconcile with reason and with natural justice [the native population] will be undisturbed in the observance of their established usages.'[63]

While Bentinck claimed early in his career that few reforms would benefit India more than wise laws and the impartial dispensation of justice, he eventually came to view education as the greatest of all possible engines of improvement. Indeed, he believed that education had to precede all other attempts at reform: '[g]eneral education is my panacea for the regeneration of India. The ground must be prepared and the jungle cleared away, before the human mind can receive with any prospect of *real* benefit, the seeds of improvement [emphasis in original].'[64] He perceived no advantage in

[60] W. C. Bentinck, 'Bentinck's Minute on Revenue and Judicial Administration', *The Correspondence of Lord William Cavendish Bentinck, Governor-General of India, 1828–1835*, ed. C. H. Philips (Oxford: Oxford University Press, 1977), 111; and J. Rosselli, *Lord William Bentinck: The Making of a Liberal Imperialist 1774–1839* (London: Chatto & Windus, 1974), 135.

[61] W. C. Bentinck, 'Bentinck's Minute on *Sati*', *The Correspondence of Lord William Cavendish Bentinck*, ed. C. H. Philips (Oxford: Oxford University Press, 1977), 344.

[62] 'Petition of the Missionaries to Bentinck', *The Correspondence of Lord William Cavendish Bentinck*, ed. C. H. Philips (Oxford: Oxford University Press, 1977), 192.

[63] W. C. Bentinck, 'Bentinck's Minute on *Sati*', 470; and '*Sati*: Regulation XVII, A.D. 1829 of the Bengal Code', *The Correspondence of Lord William Cavendish Bentinck*, ed. C. H. Philips (Oxford: Oxford University Press, 1977), 360.

[64] W. C. Bentinck, 'Bentinck on Reform in India', *The Correspondence of Lord William Cavendish Bentinck*, ed. C. H. Philips (Oxford: Oxford University Press, 1977), 1287.

maintaining ignorance: the natives must possess the wherewithal to recognize and represent their grievances and to seek redress in case of dissatisfaction. Moreover, he contended that '[i]f their own habits, morals or ways of thinking are inconsistent with their own happiness and improvement, let them have the means provided by our greater intelligence, of discovering their errors'.[65] Thus, Bentinck approved of every plan devised to communicate the accumulated knowledge and wisdom of European civilization, especially the introduction of European school-masters and colonial settlers who would impart formal knowledge and carry with them the imagination, skill, and capital necessary to raise India in the standard of civilization. Providing a proper education entailed the provision of all sorts of useful knowledge, including the gradual implementation of English instruction. However, Bentinck regarded imprudent interference in native education, particularly the sudden substitution of English in place of all local dialects, as 'an intolerable act of arbitrary power, and quite impossible'.[66]

The rather modest degree of restraint exhibited in Bentinck's approach to education is wholly absent in the thought of Thomas Babington Macaulay, the head of the Indian Law Commission, who advocated the wholesale Anglicization of education in India. Bentinck surely looked on European knowledge as the greatest of intellectual achievements, but he did not share Macaulay's utter contempt for Indian learning. Macaulay believed, even more fervently than did Anglicized Indians like Rammohan Roy, that champions of vernacular instruction were mistaken in their belief that native dialects contained any information of literary or scientific value. Indeed, he wrote in his notorious 'Minute on Education in India' that a 'single shelf of a good European library was worth the whole native literature of India and Arabia'.[67] Useful knowledge could be communicated in no other language than English. Thus, Macaulay engaged the debate on education in India as if it presented no vexing dilemma: it concerned nothing more than identifying the best language worth knowing. In this respect it is worth quoting Macaulay's defence of English instruction at length:

[t]he question now before us is simply whether, when it is in our power to teach this language, we shall teach languages in which, by universal confession, there are no

---

[65] Ibid. 1286.

[66] Ibid.; and W. C. Bentinck, 'Bentinck on the Education of Indians', *The Correspondence of Lord William Cavendish Bentinck*, ed. C. H. Philips (Oxford: Oxford University Press, 1977), 1288, 1395–8.

[67] T. B. Macaulay, 'T. B. Macaulay's Minute on Education', *The Correspondence of Lord William Cavendish Bentinck, Governor-General of India, 1828–1835*, ed. C. H. Philips (Oxford: Oxford University Press, 1977), 1405; and R. Roy, 'Letter on Education', in W. T. de Bary (ed.), *Sources of Indian Tradition* (New York: Columbia University Press, 1958), 592–5.

books on any subject which deserve to be compared to our own, whether, when we can teach European science, we shall teach systems which, by universal confession, wherever they differ from those of Europe differ for the worse, and whether, when we can patronize sound philosophy and true history, we shall countenance, at the public expense, medical doctrines which would disgrace an English farrier, astronomy which would move laughter in girls at an English boarding school, history abounding with kings thirty feet high and reigns thirty thousand years long, and geography made of seas of treacle and seas of butter.[68]

Macaulay hoped that the substitution of English for eastern languages would strike a decisive blow against a system of knowledge that disseminated nothing but error. With this objective in mind he recommended the abolition of Sanskrit and Arabic institutions of higher learning and he advised against printing any new books in either of those languages. Only then would it be possible to create a 'class who may be interpreters between us and the millions whom we govern—a class of persons Indian in blood and colour, but English in tastes, in opinions, in morals, and in intellect'.[69]

But not all shared the supreme confidence exhibited by Macaulay and others that believed the reform of India could be accomplished in one revolutionary step. In the thought of John Malcolm, Thomas Munro, and Mountstuart Elphinstone we encounter a more cautious and deliberate approach to securing the population of India in a state of peace and tranquillity. Malcolm was thoroughly sceptical, if not contemptuous, of the haste with which less experienced politicians wished to effect improvement in India 'I do not think they know so well as we old ones,' he said of younger politicians, 'what a valuable gentleman Time is; how much better work is done, when it does itself, than when done by the best of us'.[70] For Malcolm, schemes of improvement must be suited to the peculiarities of Indian society; they must be implemented gradually and, most important of all, sustained by the efforts of Indians rather than their European masters. Munro similarly disparaged what he regarded as the reckless and ill-considered aspiration of remaking the people of India as brown Englishmen. He lamented that '[t]he ruling vice of our government is innovation . . . it is time that we should learn that neither the face of the country, its property, nor its society, are things that can be suddenly improved by any contrivance of ours, though they may be greatly injured by what we mean for their good.'[71] Both Malcolm and Munro were convinced that the reform of Indian society must proceed incrementally, and in light of experience, rather than in accordance with the orthodoxy of abstract theory. Elphinstone

---

[68] Macaulay, 'T. B. Macaulay's Minute on Education', 1406–7.   [69] Ibid. 1412.
[70] J. Malcolm, *The Life and Correspondence of Major-General Sir John Malcolm*, vol. 2, ed. J. W. Kaye (London: Smith, Elder, and Co., 1856), 365–6.
[71] Quoted in Stokes, *The English Utilitarians and India*, 19.

expressed the substance of this conviction in arguing that any sensible programme of reform must carefully preserve what is of value and purge what is
not: 'it becomes of the first consequence to cherish whatever there is good in
the existing system, and to attempt no innovation that can injure the principles now in force, since it is so uncertain whether we can introduce better in
their room.'[72]

The modesty that infuses this conviction implies an approach to improvement that is professedly liberal, but one that is also conservative in tone.
Munro was foremost among those who objected to the exclusion of the native
population from all but the lowest levels of government; for a nation is
enslaved, its spirit extinguished, when it is unable to frame its own laws, raise
its own revenue, and oversee the administration of its affairs. Less patient
advocates of reform, he demurred, 'do not seem to have perceived the great
springs on which it depends; they propose no confidence in the natives, to give
them no authority, and to exclude them from office as much as possible; but
they are ardent in their zeal for enlightening them by the general diffusion of
knowledge'.[73] However, it would be a mistake to interpret the value ascribed to
aspects of Indian society as reflecting an attitude of indifference with respect
to its defects. Munro believed that India lacked principles of good government
and he thought its system of higher education stifled creative thinking; likewise, Elphinstone described education in India as 'medieval' in curriculum
and the Hindu religion as an impediment to the development of law and
morality.[74] Thus, they set out, like the impassioned prophets of Christianity,
utilitarianism, and Anglicization, to remedy these defects, albeit gradually and
in sympathy with the traditions, habits, and practices of Indian society. They
endeavoured to reform Indian society by introducing liberal ideas in order to
prepare it to join the family of nations; and, in doing so, they deliberately
introduced into Indian political and social life alien ideas that would
inevitably undermine and perhaps destroy aspects of Indian society.

For all of the very obvious differences that distinguished the participants
in this debate, they all remained true to the principle that political power
ought to be exercised so that it benefits those persons who are subject to it.
Some disclosed the modesty of Burke, others the intemperance of Macaulay;

---

[72] M. Elphinstone, 'Mountstuart Elphinstone on the Wisdom of Maintaining Indigenous
Forms of Judicial Administration, 1818–19', in S. V. D. Char (ed.), *Readings in the
Constitutional History of India, 1757–1947* (Delhi: Oxford University Press, 1983), 178.

[73] T. Munro, 'Thomas Munro on the Supreme Folly of Excluding Indian Subjects from
Higher Offices, 31 December 1824' and 'Thomas Munro on the Adverse Effects of Foreign
Rule and His Suggestions for Reform, 31 December 1824', in S. V. D. Char (ed.), *Readings in the
Constitutional History of India* (Delhi: Oxford University Press, 1983), 140, 174.

[74] Bearce, *British Attitudes Towards India*, 124–5, 130, 142.

and, to be sure, they often disagreed on the best way in which to proceed. However, they all shared in common the belief that the people of India were unable to direct their own affairs on account of some manifestation of defect; and, consequently, they understood it as the duty of the office of government to take steps towards rectifying this unhappy state of affairs. Thus, each in his own turn proposed a remedy, based on religion, law, education, or something else, in the interest of drawing the people of India into closer contact with British authority and in the hope of eventually lifting them into the ranks of civilized life.

Providing Protection, Directing Improvement

It would be an exaggeration to say that the East India Company governed British India according to a policy of trusteeship as such. The idea of trusteeship exerted rather uneven influence on the policies adopted by the government of India. It is also true that these policies did not amount to an overarching policy of trusteeship that was systematically articulated and implemented. Periods in which the Company's servants consciously pursued the moral and material well-being of India's native population were often followed by periods of imperial expansion that disclosed little care for the obligations of trusteeship. Moreover, the pressures of financial retrenchment often forced the curtailment of the most ambitious attempts to improve the state of society in India. But unevenness in implementation did not in itself negate the normative significance of an idea that more than any other justified the legitimacy of the East India Company's rule in India. Questions about the right of dominion, from the Company's rise to political power in the mid-eighteenth century to its abolition in the mid-nineteenth century, were grounded in beliefs about the obligations of power. And the idea of trust, and that of trusteeship, expressed one such belief, and probably the most important when considered from an historical standpoint. Burke issued the most important statement of the relation of obligation and power proposed by trusteeship when he declared before Parliament that political power should be exercised for the benefit of those persons who are subject to it. This test of political power set aside the right of conquest, economic interest, and national pride as sufficient justifications for British rule in India. Indeed, William Pitt had Burke's justification of political power in mind when he said that the success of the Company must depend on the inhabitants of India being secured in a condition of peace and tranquillity.

But Burke's view was essentially conservative in its outlook. He was no advocate of comprehensive social improvement, and, in that respect, he was no reformer in the spirit of Grant, Mill, or Macaulay. Burke disapproved of revolutionary change in India just as he disapproved of revolutionary change in France. For Burke, the people of India required protection rather than improvement; and their need for protection stemmed, not from a self-incurred condition of ignorance that made them a danger to themselves and to others, but from the rapacity, corruption, and misrule of the Europeans that lorded over them. However, others interpreted Burke's test of political power to mean that dominion had to be justified by a higher calling. They endeavoured to bring India within, and, indeed, to make its people see, a universal order of things, be it an order revealed by divine revelation as evangelical Christians would have it or an order discovered by reason and confirmed by science as students of the Enlightenment would have it. And in pursuit of this end they believed that the drive for improvement must be harnessed to the engine of political power. For the most ambitious reformers ascribed to the office of government primary responsibility for securing the welfare and happiness of its native subjects. Thus, providing protection was not enough to sustain the Company's claim of dominion. Government must also undertake a proactive programme of providing positive entitlements to which all human beings may lay claim. It is this justification of political power that underpinned the emancipatory ideas of Grant, Mill, and Macaulay. To these men Rousseau's notion of the great legislator, an especially wise and gifted 'engineer' capable of guiding individuals from a physical to a moral existence, must have imparted special meaning.[75] Through proper instruction in religion, law, and education, government—the guiding engineer of India—would be able to deliver the people of India from the bonds of false religion, irrational law, and dubious knowledge.

In that respect, the great experiments undertaken in India disclose a particular mode of conduct that is broadly intelligible in terms of the idea of trusteeship. They justified the possession of political power in the belief that the strong should rule on behalf of the weak; that a condition of inequality joined ruler and subject; and that government should secure the happiness of people that cannot secure it for themselves. The Crown did not abandon this justification of political power after Parliament abolished the Company's dominion in the wake of the Indian Mutiny of 1857. Queen Victoria affirmed the principle enunciated by Burke when she proclaimed that 'it is our earnest desire to stimulate the peaceful industry of India, to promote works of public utility and improvement, and to administer its government for the benefit of

---

[75] J. J. Rousseau, 'On the Social Contract', *The Basic Political Writings*, ed. and trans. D. Cress (Indianapolis, IN: Hackett Publishing Company, 1987), 162–5.

all our subjects resident therein'.[76] The idea of trusteeship implied in this pledge would not only come to define the character of British rule in India, it would also profoundly influence the internationalization of trusteeship, first as part of the Berlin Act, and then in the League of Nations covenant and the United Nations charter. And it is in this respect that the experience of the East India Company prefigures the emergence of trusteeship as a recognized and accepted practice in international society.

---

[76] 'Queen Victoria's Proclamation, 1 November 1858', in C. H. Philips (ed.), *The Evolution of India and Pakistan, 1858–1947* (London: Oxford University Press, 1962), 11.

3

The Internationalization of Trusteeship

The partition and colonization of Africa is one of the most noteworthy, and perhaps misunderstood, events of nineteenth century international history. The so-called 'scramble for Africa' is most commonly identified with the machinations of power politics, the search for imperial glory, and the pursuit of private and national wealth. That European powers pursued all of these things in Africa, and committed misdeeds in doing so, is not in doubt. Greed and vanity, as well as feelings of cultural superiority and racial antipathy, are all part of the story of European mastery in Africa. But it would be an exaggeration of some magnitude to say that Africa's encounter with European international society discloses nothing more than a simple and brutal story of domination and exploitation. For the history of imperialism in Africa also provides ample evidence of a novel claim—that the conditions of life for at least a portion of Africa's population constituted a legitimate subject of international scrutiny. In other words, members of European international society internationalized the idea of trusteeship by establishing in international law obligations that explicitly repudiated relations based on domination and exploitation; and, in doing so, they accorded international legitimacy to the principle that the strong should rule on behalf of the weak. The purpose of this chapter is to examine the internationalization of trusteeship as it arose in the context of British colonial administration in Africa, the Berlin and Brussels Conferences, and the experience of the Congo Free State. It is out of these experiences and events that the idea of trusteeship emerges as a recognized and accepted practice of international society.

Attitudes Towards Africa

British attitudes towards Africa at the turn of the nineteenth century were shaped to a considerable degree by an earnest desire to atone for Britain's role in purchasing and transporting slaves to work in the sugar and indigo plantations of the New World. William Pitt expressed the substance of this sentiment before the House of Commons in 1792: 'how shall we hope to obtain, if it be possible, forgiveness from Heaven for the enormous evils we have committed, if we refuse to make use of those means which the mercy of Providence has still reserved for us for wiping away the shame and guilt with which we are now covered?'[1] This sense of shame and guilt provided the seed for a great national crusade to eradicate slavery, not only within the British Empire, but also throughout the entire world. Stations were established along the West African coast for sole purpose of combating the slave trade; and in 1807, the same year that the slave trade was formally abolished within the Empire, the Crown assumed direct responsibility for Sierra Leone—a colony founded by British philanthropists for the purpose of settling freed slaves.[2] The British government also endeavoured to hasten the end of slavery and the slave trade by impressing upon Africa's native rulers the advantages of a free and unencumbered trade, or legitimate and peaceful commerce as it was commonly called in nineteenth century parlance. Agents were dispatched to tell native rulers of the advantages of lawful trade, and to convince them that innocent commerce would be most productive of industry, virtue, and well-ordered society. Native rulers that failed to heed this advice with sufficient vigour often found themselves faced with the persuasive powers of the Royal Navy. Thus, the crusade to eradicate slavery in all its manifestations joined the art of persuasion and armed intimidation, blockade, and bombardment in righteous service of humanity. Indeed, Lord Palmerston wrote in 1851 that 'the Friendship of Gt. B[ritain] is to be obtained by the Chiefs of Africa only on the condition that they abandon Slave Trade and expel the Slave Traders, and that those Chiefs who may refuse to do these things, will surely incur the Displeasure of the British Govt.'[3]

But atoning for past sins imposed on the most ardent abolitionists a responsibility far greater than that of prohibiting slavery within the British Empire and putting down the traffic in human beings on the high seas. For example, Thomas Fowell Buxton insisted that '[o]ne part of our national debt to Africa has already been acknowledged by the emancipation of our colonial slaves. There remains yet, however, a larger debt uncancelled—that of restitution to Africa itself'.[4] The burden of this responsibility weighed most heavily on Christian missionaries who set out, armed with the promise of salvation, to deliver Africa from the oppressive burden of slavery and to inculcate in its people the perfection of their own (higher) morality. While most of these missionaries toiled in obscurity, braving inter-tribal war, infectious

---

[1] Quoted in R. Coupland, *Wilberforce* (Oxford: Clarendon Press, 1923), 169.

[2] L. H. Gann and P. Duignan, *Burden of Empire: An Appraisal of Western Colonialism in Africa South of the Sahara* (New York: Praeger, 1967), 167.

[3] 'Lord Russell: Instructions to Her Majesty's Niger Commissioners, 30 January 1841' and 'Lord Palmerston: Minute, Lagos, 18 February 1851', in C. W. Newbury (ed.), *British Policy Toward West Africa: Select Documents 1786–1874* (Oxford: Clarendon Press, 1965), 155, 349.

[4] T. F. Buxton, *The African Slave Trade and Its Remedy* (London: Frank Cass & Co. Ltd., 1967), 512.

disease, and enormous personal hardship, the travels of David Livingstone awakened the British public fully to the evil of slavery and to the 'debased' state of society in Africa.[5] In Livingstone's theory of social change, we encounter not only the beliefs and assumptions of the missionary purpose in Africa, but major currents of mid-nineteenth century Victorian thought as well. He betrayed no doubt of his fundamental conviction that the salvation of Africa depended fundamentally on the dissemination of Christian truth. But when he wrote to the London Missionary Society that '[w]e must I conceive go forward, and go forward far too, in order to get at the heathenism of this country',[6] he had in mind something more than just spiritual salvation. The remedy of 'evil' in Africa, he argued, enjoined not only the communication of the Gospel, but the introduction and application of all that was good about British religious and economic life. Free trade, in conjunction with the Christian message of fraternity and universal brotherhood, would pacify isolated and warring tribes, create bonds of interdependence, and join them together in a condition of mutual amity, peace, and prosperity. And together these great engines of civilization—Christianity and commerce—would destroy the odious traffic in human beings and ameliorate the barbarism of tribal life.[7]

Livingstone is perhaps best remembered for engaging the imagination of a nation by skilfully combining Christian respect for individual personality with Adam Smith's idea of economic individualism. However, against missionary wishes for greater spiritual and political involvement in Africa, adherents of the so-called Manchester School marshalled principles of Smith's political economy to argue in favour of liquidating Britain's burdensome imperial commitments. Colonies, as John Bright would have it, did not pay: 'I am inclined to think that, with the exception of Australia, there is not a single dependency of the Crown which, if we come to reckon what it has cost in war and protection, would not be found to be a positive loss to the people of this country.'[8] More importantly, though, Bright and Richard Cobden

---

[5] R. Coupland, *The British Anti-Slavery Movement* (London: Thornton Butterworth, 1933), 225.

[6] D. Livingstone, 'Missionary Correspondence (1841–42)', in A. Burton (ed.), *Politics and Empire in Victorian Britain* (Basingstoke: Palgrave, 2001), 177.

[7] See D. Livingstone, 'Cambridge Lecture No. 1 (1858)', in B. Harlow and M. Carter (eds.), *Imperialism and Orientalism: A Documentary Sourcebook* (Oxford: Blackwell, 1999), 276; A. P. Thornton, *The Imperial Idea and Its Enemies: A Study in British Power* (London: Macmillan, 1959), 14–15; and H. A. C. Cairns, *Prelude to Imperialism: British Reaction to Central African Society, 1840–1890* (London: Routledge & Kegan Paul, 1965), 139, 192–8.

[8] J. Bright, 'Principles of Foreign Policy, Birmingham, October 29, 1858', in E. R. Jones (ed.), *Selected Speeches on British Foreign Policy, 1738–1914* (London: Oxford University Press, 1914), 340.

rarely tired of extolling the virtues of private enterprise and restricted government because they believed that markets were productive not only of
material wealth, but of great social energy and individual improvement.
Markets, they argued, cultivate a sense of responsibility, discipline, industry,
and all that was required of the virtuous citizen; and, consequently, moral
refinement and material prosperity would naturally arise in human beings
that were free to think, speak, worship, and work without interference from
the heavy hand of the state.[9] This unbridled commitment to the benefits of
market economy transformed the maintenance of empire into an impediment to moral and material progress. The folly of retaining political control
over vast territories in Africa and Asia imposed an unnecessary financial and
military burden that ran counter, and imprudently so, to the laws of economy. Life within empire necessarily entailed a pattern of relations that devi-
ated from the natural equality of all men and consequently imposed an
unnatural state of dependence that could not be sustained, as the results of
the American Revolution amply demonstrated. Indeed, Britain's colonies,
Cobden argued, 'serve but as gorgeous and ponderous appendages to swell
our ostensible grandeur, but, in reality, to complicate and magnify our
government expenditure, without improving our balance of trade'.[10]

Out of these ideas grew the general belief that the colonies should be cut
loose and that the Crown should avoid assuming new political, financial, and
military responsibilities beyond the jurisdiction of 'Little England'.[11] The
mid-nineteenth century British official was less concerned with ruling distant
lands than with expanding the nation's commerce: free commerce, rather
than the controlling interests of the flag, would see to the prosperity of
Britain and Africa alike. Thus, colonial questions were settled with an eye to
retrenchment; and colonies themselves were generally regarded as temporary
possessions that were to be self-supporting and self-governing at the earliest
opportunity. That the colonies would gradually seek greater autonomy and,
eventually, demand independence was regarded as significant only so far as it
signalled the natural maturation of empire. It is in this context that British
officials remained decidedly indifferent to African affairs; for Africa afforded
little in the way of interest or value—apart from an abiding interest in suppressing the slave trade—that joined it to Britain in common cause. British
trade with Africa compared rather poorly with the commercial ties that

---

[9] R. Robinson and J. Gallagher, *Africa and the Victorians: The Official Mind of Imperialism*
(London: Macmillan, 1965), 1–3.

[10] R. Cobden, 'England, Ireland, America, 1835', in G. Bennett (ed.), *The Concept of Empire:
Burke to Attlee, 1774–1947* (London: Adam and Charles Black, 1953), 165.

[11] C. A. Bodelsen, *Studies in Mid-Victorian Imperialism* (London: Gydendalske Boghandel,
1924), 33–5.

linked Britain to India and to the Americas; and official opinion believed that the constant threat of war, an inhospitable climate, and the financial responsibilities of empire outweighed any advantage that could be had in Africa. James Stephen expressed the fundamental premise of this view, which dominated Colonial Office thinking right up to the eve of partition, with unmistakable clarity: '[i]f we could acquire the Dominion of the whole of that Continent it would be but a worthless possession.'[12] Even Benjamin Disraeli, a man acutely attuned to the prestige afforded by empire, tended to regard colonies in Africa as millstones rather than sources of imperial power. And, in view of avoiding the acquisition of additional millstones, Parliament resolved in 1865 that the assumption of new responsibilities in Africa would be 'inexpedient' and that the administration of all colonial governments, excepting only Sierra Leone, should be transferred to the natives.[13]

The sudden abandonment of this policy of retrenchment has long been the subject of speculation. For instance, John Hobson argued in his celebrated volume, *Imperialism*, that political, racial, and cultural accounts of European expansion in Africa were far less important than economic interests that wished to dispose 'of their surplus wealth by seeking foreign markets and for-eign investments to take off the goods and capital they cannot sell or use at home'.[14] And, of course, no account would be complete without mentioning the British drive for imperial security or French, German, and Italian efforts to secure places in the sun. Still, Alan Cairns insists that cruelty and suffering, more than commercial or strategic interests, provoked the reaction against British indifference towards involvement in Africa. Sir Andrew Cohen sim-ilarly argues that '[t]he abolition of slavery and, in revulsion from the slave trade, the sense of mission toward the people of Africa were the first motives in time in the British penetration of both West and East Africa'.[15] Indeed, to the distant European, life in much of Africa was a sordid tale of anarchy, war, and shocking brutality. The character and effects of inter-tribal warfare and certain native customs struck the British public as being utterly repugnant. For the ordinary person could not possibly reconcile witchcraft, mutilation, trial by ordeal, human sacrifice, and especially the torture and murder of women and children, with any known standard of justice or reason. Thus, to the British mind, savage custom, paganism, and slave raiding so profoundly

---

[12] Robinson and Gallagher, *Africa and the Victorians*, 14–17; Lord Hailey, *The Future of Colonial Peoples* (Oxford: Oxford University Press, 1943), 10; and J. D. Hargreaves, *Prelude to the Partition of West Africa* (London: Macmillan, 1963), 70.

[13] Coupland, *The British Anti-Slavery Movement*, 240.

[14] J. A. Hobson, *Imperialism* (London: George Allen & Unwin, 1938), 85.

[15] Cairns, *Prelude to Imperialism*, 125; and A. Cohen, *British Policy in Changing Africa* (Evanston, IL: Northwestern University Press, 1959), 13.

disrupted the course of ordinary life that humanity and common decency dictated intervention.

This concern for human suffering and pervasive insecurity was at least partially responsible for inducing the British government to abandon its policy of retrenchment. Missionaries were, predictably, the most enthusiastic advocates of intervention, for they believed, as did Lord Wellesley in India at the turn of the century, that the people of Africa would benefit most from the ameliorating effects of British rule. Pervasive lawlessness and disorder left no less a lasting impression on European traders once it became apparent that Cobden's recipe for security—that 'civilized' men should treat 'savages' like men so that no quarrel might arise between them—was simply beyond the realm of possibility.[16] Before long they too began to demand the protection afforded by the flag in contravention of the orthodoxy of Manchester sensibilities. The Crown responded by declaring protectorates over territories— many of which held little strategic or obvious commercial value—that were believed to be incapable of maintaining law and order, dispensing justice, and protecting persons and property. In these places, as John Stuart Mill once said of savage life, there was an absence of commerce, agriculture, and manufactures; and interests were satisfied by asserting strength and cunning rather than by resorting to settled social arrangements—the collective strength of society. Buxton and others who laboured to make amends for the past vowed to remedy this unhappy state of affairs by teaching the African to abandon his affection for cruelty and love of warfare, and to impress upon him that the happiest people are those who conscientiously keep God's commandments.[17] It can come as no surprise, then, that these same people believed that securing the 'savage' African in the *pax Britannica* held out the best opportunity of fastening him to a mild and progressive government and bestowing upon him the advantages of civilization.

The Dual Mandate

If the call of humanity compelled British intervention in order to establish tolerable conditions of peace, order, and security, to conduct a peaceful commerce and to disseminate God's law, then British colonial administrators were also compelled to devise methods by which to rule their new charges.

---

[16] R. Cobden, 'Speech at Manchester, 10 January 1849', in G. Bennett (ed.), *The Concept of Empire: Burke to Attlee, 1774–1947* (London: Adam and Charles Black, 1953), 168.

[17] J. S. Mill, 'Civilization', *Essays on Politics and Culture*, in G. Himmelfarb (ed.) (Gloucester, MA: Peter Smith, 1973), 46; and Buxton, *The African Slave Trade and Its Remedy*, 250–60, 305.

The most important and influential understanding of these methods is expressed in Lord Lugard's notion of the 'dual mandate', which imposed a very simple yet extraordinarily powerful principle of colonial administration: the exploitation of Africa's natural wealth should reciprocally benefit the industrial classes of Europe and the native population of Africa.[18] The underlying claims of the dual mandate are most clearly intelligible in the practice of indirect rule, a method of colonial administration which, at its heart, supposed that vast differences in native custom, tradition, and level of improvement necessarily entailed the rejection of universally applicable rules and administrative forms. Indeed, Lugard submitted that the 'slavish adherence to any particular type, however successful it may have proved elsewhere, may, if unadapted to the local environment, be as ill-suited and as foreign to its conceptions as direct British rule would be'.[19] Prosperity, welfare, and improvement depended on the recognition of at least a degree of tolerable difference. The dispensation of justice, the framing of law, the delivery of health and educational services, attitudes towards race relations, and agricultural, religious, and labour policies must all be fitted to the particular circumstances and sensibilities of particular communities. And native Africans must have a stake in their government; they must be sufficiently free to direct their own affairs through their own leaders and their own institutions, albeit under the supervision of British officials. Thus, for Lugard, indirect rule aimed at constituting native leaders as integral parts of government—leaders endowed with clearly defined duties that were assigned in accordance with a community's capacity for self-government. But, in an obvious affirmation of the justification of political power laid down by Edmund Burke nearly a century earlier, the rights and powers exercised by these native leaders were justified solely by service rendered to the community and to the state.[20]

Lugard's affection for native practices and institutions did not, however, extend so far as to accord them recognition as fully legitimate ways of organizing and conducting human relations. He believed that while custom and tradition varied in proportion to a society's level of improvement, the ends of political life did not. Thus, the district officer must be well acquainted with local customs and social organization; and he must adapt principles of administration to native life so that they are productive of ends common to all. But the danger of imprudent interference in native practices, or introducing the ways of civilization too rapidly, did not escape the attention of colonial administrators in Africa.[21] The Indian Mutiny of 1857 provided an

---

[18] F. D. Lugard, *The Dual Mandate of Africa*, 4th edn. (London: William Blackwood & Sons, 1929), 617.   [19] Ibid. 104, 211.
[20] Ibid. 94, 193–4, 203.   [21] Ibid. 194–8.

ever-present reminder of the dangers presented by overly ambitious schemes of assimilation and Anglicization. Lugard believed that education would help bring the natives into sympathy with British authority; however, he also recognized that the implementation of a thoroughly Anglicized curriculum risked great danger and perhaps disaster. And in that respect the gradualist approach preferred by John Malcolm won out in Africa over the revolutionary approach favoured by T. B. Macaulay. Lugard was also attuned to the fact that the destruction of native authority and institutions, before the reins of government could be turned over to native peoples, would leave an improbably small cadre of British administrators to govern vast stretches of territory. Thus, he counselled that administrative officers must 'make it apparent alike to the educated native, the conservative Moslem, and the primitive pagan, each to his own degree, that the policy of the Government is not antagonistic but progressive–sympathetic to his aspirations and the guardian of his natural rights'.[22]

That expediency shaped the policies of British colonial administrators is universally admitted; however, the character of indirect rule is not fully intelligible without taking account of a quality that, at least formally, under-pinned the dual mandate and British dominion in Africa generally. The reciprocal relationship expressed by the dual mandate is best understood in the context of a professed duty that obliged the 'advanced' to assist the 'back-ward' in becoming what they were not—civilized peoples—rather than as a manifestation of greed, avarice, and ambition. Few people would hold that British rule in Africa was without defect, but it would be a gross exaggeration to say that British officials devised the methods of indirect rule for the sole purpose of conquest, domination, and exploitation. The methods of indirect rule were for Lugard intended to instil in the natives a sense of responsibility, initiative, fair play, discipline, and justice—qualities that were required of a people fit for self-government. Indeed, he defended the principle of supervised self-government by saying:

[t]o abandon the policy of ruling [the natives] through their own chiefs, and to substitute the direct rule of the British officer, is to forego the high ideal of leading the backward races, by their own efforts, in their own way, to raise themselves to a higher plane of social organisation, and tends to perpetuate and stereotype existing conditions.[23]

But not all accepted the value that Lugard ascribed to the practice of indirect rule. Herbert Tugwell, a member of the Church Missionary Society and one of Lugard's contemporaries in Nigeria, argued that indirect rule robbed the

[22] Lugard, *The Dual Mandate of Africa*, 194; also see R. L. Buell, *The Native Problem in Africa*, vol. 1 (New York: Macmillan Company, 1928), 684.
[23] Lugard, *The Dual Mandate of Africa*, 215.

native of desire for progress of any sort. Indirect rule, he claimed, amounted to little more than 'direct rule by indirect means'.[24] Criticism of this sort did not, however, question the professed end of indirect rule, nor did it allege that indirect rule was directed towards an end less worthy than ensuring the happiness and well-being of Africa's native inhabitants. Rather than criticizing the professed ends of British rule in Africa, Tugwell and others of similar opinion merely probed the means by which the trusteeship of its people might be best achieved.

In spite of repeated professions of solicitude for the well-being of Africa's native inhabitants, accounts of economic exploitation provided a seductive explanation for Britain's purpose in establishing and maintaining its empire in tropical Africa. When confronted with this theory of imperial expansion, Lugard did not disclaim all pretence of self-interest:

Let it be admitted at the outset that European brains, capital, and energy have not been, and never will be, expended in developing the resources of Africa from motives of pure philanthropy; that Europe is in Africa for the mutual benefit of her own industrial classes, and of the native races in their progress to a higher plane; that the benefit can be made reciprocal, and that it is the aim and desire of civilised administration to fulfil this dual mandate.[25]

This claim of reciprocal benefit is grounded in the belief that all human beings possess a right to a fair share of the earth's natural wealth. Scripture confirms this right as a gift from God: 'The heavens are the Lord's heavens, but the earth he has given to the sons of men'.[26] And in the Western political tradition John Locke makes this gift from God the basis of property, the protection of which requires the constitution of political society.[27]

Lugard similarly justifies the dual mandate by appealing to the universal right of mankind—the Kantian idea of *jus cosmopoliticum*. On this view, the wealth of the earth is by natural right the common inheritance of all men; and the fact that groups of human beings hold a juridically determined proprietary right to a portion of the earth's surface in no way restrains the exercise of this right. All men, as citizens of the world, are endowed with the right to settle in distant territories so long as they do not injure others in the use of the soil. For this reason, Kant asserts that 'the possession of the soil upon which an inhabitant of the earth may live can only be regarded as possession of a part of a limited whole and, consequently, as a part to which every one has

---

[24] Quoted in Lugard, *The Dual Mandate of Africa*, 223.   [25] Ibid. 617.

[26] Psalm 115, *The Old and New Testaments of the Holy Bible*, revised standard version (Philadelphia, PA: Lutheran Church in America, 1971), 16.

[27] J. Locke, 'Second Treatise of Government', in P. Laslett (ed.) *Two Treatises of Government*, (Cambridge: Cambridge University Press, 1988), 26, 88.

originally a right'.[28] Thus, rather than clothing naked ambition in the garb of humanitarian platitude, Lugard argues that Europeans have a right to a fair share of Africa's natural wealth, an endowment wasted by the natives on account of their inability to comprehend its value or proper use. Indeed, he asks: '[w]ho can deny the right of the hungry people of Europe to utilise the wasted bounties of nature, or that the task of developing these resources was ... a "trust for civilisation" and for the benefit of mankind?'.[29]

The claims and the obligations of the dual mandate inform the understanding of trusteeship that prevailed throughout most of British Africa, including territories that were not administered according to the principles of indirect rule. Experience in India certainly influenced the interpretation and implementation of trusteeship in Africa; however, the practice of trusteeship in Africa marks a clear break with the Anglicist experiments of the East India Company. The Indian Mutiny and the ascendance of race thinking ruled out any attempt at creating a class of Africans who were in every respect English except in blood and colour. In Africa, as in India, rights of dominion were justified by the benefit they conferred on native subjects; but in method, trusteeship in Africa more closely approximated the gradualist approach championed by Mountstuart Elphinstone, John Malcolm, and Thomas Munro. And like trusteeship in India, the condition of native subjects in Africa remained a concern of paramount importance.

This central and, indeed, indispensable tenet of trusteeship eventually obtained a formal recognition within the British Empire, in part certainly because the events of the First World War subjected colonial administration to considerable scrutiny. Thus, in the famous Kenya White Paper of 1923, the Crown declared that as a matter of official British policy:

His Majesty's Government regard themselves as exercising a trust on behalf of the African population, and they are unable to delegate or share this trust, the object of which may be defined as the protection and advancement of the native races. It is not necessary to attempt to elaborate this position; the lines of development are as yet in certain directions undetermined, and many difficult problems arise which require time for their solution. But there can be no room for doubt that it is the mission of Great Britain to work continuously for the training and education of the Africans towards a higher intellectual, moral, and economic level than that which they had reached when the Crown assumed the responsibility for the administration of this territory.[30]

---

[28] I. Kant, 'The Science of Right', in R. M. Hutchins (ed.) and W. Hastie (trans.) *Great Books of the Western World* (Chicago: Encyclopaedia Britannica, 1952), 456.

[29] Lugard, *The Dual Mandate of Africa*, 615.

[30] 'Indians in Kenya, July 1923', *Parliamentary Papers*, Cmd. 1922 xviii (1923), 10.

This declaration of trusteeship does not specify a practice of a peculiar sort; nor does it propose a particular administrative type or specify a particular political form. Rather, trusteeship in this context refers to a standard of rule, as opposed to a substantive empirical condition, which accommodates a multitude of principles and methods with which to raise the natives of Africa in the standard of civilization. And the ultimate test of these principles and methods was such that 'the interests of the African natives must be paramount, and that if, and when, those interests and the interests of the immigrant races should conflict, the former should prevail'.[31]

The Berlin Conference

The principal claims of the dual mandate are fully intelligible in the proceedings of the Berlin Conference of 1884–1885 that effectively internationalized the idea of trusteeship. Although the Conference is notoriously associated with the partition of Africa, in a literal sense, the continent's population did not find itself suddenly divided by arbitrarily drawn boundaries as a result of agreements reached at Berlin. Rather, Prince Bismarck opened the Berlin Conference in a discourse that is more suggestive of trusteeship than territorial aggrandizement:

[i]n convoking the Conference, the Imperial Government was guided by the conviction that all the Governments invited share the wish to bring the native of Africa within the pale of civilization by opening up the interior of that continent to commerce, by giving its inhabitants the means of instructing themselves, by encouraging missions and enterprises calculated to spread useful knowledge, and by preparing the way for the suppression of slavery, and especially of the over-sea Traffic in blacks.[32]

But these words should not be misinterpreted to mean that Bismarck, or the Berlin Conference generally, stood for a single-minded devotion to the cause of philanthropy. Instead, the deliberations at Berlin disclose the same mode of argument that underpins Lugard's dual mandate: the interests of Europe and those of Africa would be served best by the interrelated and reciprocal benefit of free commerce, tutelage, and security from war.

It is neither possible to make sense of the European encounter with Africa, nor of the Berlin Conference in particular, without making some reference to the all-important issue of slavery. By the close of the eighteenth century,

---

[31] Ibid. 10; and Lord Hailey, *An African Survey: A Study of Problems Arising in Africa South of the Sahara*, rev. edn. (London: Oxford University Press, 1957), 246.

[32] 'Protocol No. 1—Meeting of November 15, 1884', Protocols and the General Act of the West African Conference, *Parliamentary Papers*, 1885 LV mf. 91.435, 9.

abolitionists, especially those in Britain, brought the full weight of religious and secular opinion to bear against the practice of slavery. Abolitionists equated slavery with an offence against humanity; it was a cruel, barbarous, and incurable injustice that amounted to an irreparable offence against the sanctity of human personality. Necessity in no way lessened the burden imposed on all civilized members of the family of nations to destroy such evil. Slavery, as William Wilberforce repeatedly explained, constituted an abomination whose perpetuation was not essential to the welfare of slave-holding interests in the Americas.[33] Widespread acceptance of Adam Smith's theories of economy also dealt a blow to the argument of necessity. Smith argued to great effect that the liberal reward of labour encouraged industry, wealth, a growing population, and supplied all the necessities and conveniences of life. Thus, 'the work done by freedmen', he asserted, 'comes cheaper in the end than that performed by slaves'.[34] But in spite of the signal importance that abolitionists and liberal economists attached to the complete eradication of slavery, the issue of slavery enjoyed a rather reserved place in the Berlin Act. Article IX of the Act simply states: 'each of the powers binds itself to employ all the means at its disposal for putting an end to [the slave trade] and for punishing those who engage in it.'[35]

In order to grasp the full significance of Article IX it must be placed in the context of Article VI, which obliged signatory powers to 'watch over the preservation of the native tribes, and to care for the improvement of the conditions of their moral and material well-being, and to help in suppressing slavery, and especially the Slave Trade'.[36] Article VI presupposed the assumption that, more than anything else, slavery and the slave trade had paralysed the development of Africa's people and natural wealth. Thus, all hopes of economic and political progress, and the very future of Africa itself, depended upon the destruction of the 'vulgar' and 'illegitimate' commerce in human beings. Indeed, a report submitted to the Conference equated the slave trade with the denial of every law and of social order itself: '[m]an-hunting constitutes a crime of high treason against humanity.'[37] But the obligations imposed by Article VI consisted in something more than the duty of destroying slavery in all of its manifestations. Article VI also assumed the inability of Africa's native population to direct their own affairs; and on account of some

---

[33] Coupland, *Wilberforce*, 162.

[34] A. Smith, *The Wealth of Nations*, Vol. 1, eds. R. H. Campbell and A. S. Skinner (Indianapolis, IN: Liberty Fund, 1981), 98–9.

[35] General Act of the Conference of Berlin, *Parliamentary Papers*, 1886 LXVII, mf. 92.353, 15.   [36] Ibid. 14.

[37] 'Annex 1 to Protocol No. 4', Protocols and the General Act of the West African Conference, *Parliamentary Papers*, 1885 LV mf. 91.436, 80.

manner of incompetence, they were regarded as being unable to understand their true interests or to defend them even if they were made known to them. Signatory powers to the Berlin Act were, therefore, obliged to act on behalf of the natives, to assume guardianship over their rights, security, and property, and to confer upon them the advantages of civilization. And towards this end, they pledged to protect without distinction all religious, scientific, and charitable institutions which aimed at imparting to the natives the benefits of civilization; for '[t]he necessity of insuring the preservation of the natives, the duty of assisting them to attain a more elevated political and social state, the obligation of instructing them and of initiating them in the advantages of civilization, are unanimously recognized'.[38]

Although the star of free trade had dimmed somewhat towards the end of the nineteenth century, the deliberations at Berlin reveal a firmly held belief that advancing the state of society in Africa would be best served by complete and perfect freedom in commerce. The British representative to the Conference, Sir Edward Malet, conveyed this opinion when he declared before his colleagues: '[t]he principle which will command the sympathy and support of Her Majesty's Government will be that of the advancement of legitimate commerce, with security for the equality of treatment of all nations, and for the well-being of the native races.'[39] The claims of the dual mandate are at once recognizable in this statement of British policy: free trade must not advance national economic interests at the expense of the well-being of Africa's native population. Thus, the Conference made no attempt, as is consistent with the demands of the dual mandate, to separate questions of commerce from questions of philanthropy. Free and unencumbered trade furnished meaningful answers to questions belonging to both categories. Indeed, the declaration on free commerce adopted by the Conference obliged signatories to 'assist and aid the labours of the missions and all institutions having for their object the instruction of the natives, and making them understand and appreciate the advantages of civilization'.[40] It is in view of this end, as well as the national advantage that might be obtained through unrestricted commerce, that adherents to the Berlin Act accepted the principle of the Open Door. They resolved that no nation should enjoy the privilege of monopoly, in the belief that perfect freedom in commerce would advance the economic interests of Europe and at the same time advance the 'cause of humanity, of civilisation, of science, and religious feeling'.[41]

[38] Ibid. 80.   [39] 'Protocol No. 1—Meeting of November 15, 1884', 11.
[40] 'Annex to Protocol No. 1', Protocols and the General Act of the West African Conference, *Parliamentary Papers*, 1885 LV mf. 91.436, 13.
[41] 'Annex to Protocol No. 5', Protocols and the General Act of the West African Conference, *Parliamentary Papers*, 1885 LV mf. 91.436, 151.

To ensure that the advantages of unrestricted commerce would be enjoyed to the fullest extent possible, the Conference felt it necessary to adopt uniform rules for the recognition of future occupations and to establish a system of neutrality in tropical Africa. Only these steps, the parties agreed, would spare the continent of Africa from the intrigues, rivalries, and passions that all too easily lead to war. Thus, a report commissioned to study the prevention of war in tropical Africa concluded:

> after having surrounded freedom of commerce and navigation in the centre of Africa with guarantees, and after having shown your solicitude for the moral and material welfare of the populations which inhabit it, you are about to introduce rules into positive international law which are destined to remove all causes of disagreement and strife from international relations.[42]

The underlying justification of this decision, like the justification of free commerce, is intelligible in the reciprocal relation proposed by the dual mandate. John Kasson, the representative of the United States, argued that it was not enough to safeguard European interests and property from the threat of war; to do so would be to transform Africa into little more than an estate meant to serve the productive forces of Europe and America. Rather, as trustees of civilization, Europeans were obliged to introduce science, literature, the arts, and other forms of useful knowledge; they must encourage the formation of productive labour; and they must assist the natives of Africa in adapting their lives to the customs and usages of civilization. The success of this enterprise, he reminded fellow delegates, was fundamentally dependent on a condition of peace that must be enjoyed by trustee and ward alike; for 'war quickly lets loose every barbarous passion and destroys the progress of many years of civilisation'.[43] Thus, parties to the Berlin Act agreed in Article X to respect the neutrality of territories placed under the system of free trade 'in order to give a new guarantee of security to trade and industry, and to encourage, by the maintenance of peace, the development of civilisation'.[44]

Many of the principles that were adopted at Berlin, especially those related to Articles VI and IX, received more elaborate treatment at the Brussels Conference of 1890. The Brussels Conference was convened for the ostensible purpose of strengthening existing obligations pertaining to the suppression of the slave trade. But the decisions taken there amounted to nothing short of a revolution in Europe's dealings with Africa. Signatories to the Brussels Act

---

[42] 'Annex 1 to Protocol No. 8', Protocols and the General Act of the West African Conference, *Parliamentary Papers*, 1885 LV mf. 91.437, 217.

[43] 'Annex 13 to Protocol No. 5', Protocols and the General Act of the West African Conference, *Parliamentary Papers*, 1885 LV mf. 91.437, 163–4.

[44] General Act of the Conference of Berlin, 15.

declared their 'firm intention of putting an end to the crimes and devastations engendered by the Traffic in African Slaves, protecting effectively the aboriginal populations of Africa, and insuring for that vast continent the benefits of peace and civilization'.[45] To that end they committed themselves to constructing roads and railways, restricting the importation and sale of firearms, powder, and ammunition, regulating the sale of liquor, and, perhaps most ominously, establishing fortified posts in the African interior. They further agreed that the most effective way of combating the slave trade involved the '[p]rogressive organization of the administrative, judicial, religious, and military services in the African territories placed under the sovereignty or protectorate of civilized nations'.[46] It is hardly possible to overstate the implications of this undertaking; for it collapsed the distinction between the juridical status of a colony and that of a protectorate, the latter being a dependency that ceded control of its foreign relations but retained control over its domestic affairs.[47] For Lugard the implications were at once profound and far-reaching: '[t]he moment at which the civilised Powers of the world have asserted the unequivocal right and obligation of the more advanced races to assume responsibility for the backward races seems an appropriate one to brush aside these archaic and anomalous distinctions, and to abandon the farce of "acquiring" jurisdiction by treaties not understood by their signatories and foreign to their modes of thought'.[48] The obligation to undertake the domestic organization of African societies entailed nothing less than the extension of European dominion over the entire African continent.

In order to appreciate the underlying justification of the Berlin Act, as well as that of the Brussels Act, it is necessary to suspend judgement, at least momentarily, of consequences that by all accounts proved to be detrimental to native interests and welfare. It is no doubt true that delegates to the Berlin Conference worked to increase the wealth of their own countries; and, in doing so, they concealed their efforts to obtain greater access to the natural wealth of Africa for their traders and investors. However, they also went to great lengths to establish principles of conduct that were meant to protect Africa's native inhabitants from the ravages of slavery and war, and to promote their advancement in the standard of civilization. And in the attempt to reconcile these ends, and to ensure that decisions taken by the Conference could withstand the scrutiny of doubt, representatives were mindful of the danger that things might go wrong. Indeed, Malet spoke for several fellow

---

[45] General Act of the Brussels Conference, 1889–90; with Annexed Declaration, *Parliamentary Papers*, 1890 LI mf. 96.405, 21.　　　　　　　　　　　　　　[46] Ibid. 20.

[47] See M. Wight, *British Colonial Constitutions, 1947* (Oxford: Clarendon Press, 1952), 7.

[48] Lugard, *The Dual Mandate of Africa*, 38.

delegates at Berlin when he implored that they all remain fully conscious of the proper relation between the pursuit of national wealth and the work of civilization: '[w]hile the opening of the Congo markets is to be desired, the welfare of the natives should not be neglected; to them it would be no benefit, but the reverse, if freedom of commerce, unchecked by reasonable control, should degenerate into licence.'[49] The Berlin and Brussels Acts rest on the belief that the nexus of commerce, civilization, and peace would destroy the institution of slavery that kept Africa in a retarded state of development, and would impart knowledge of science, Christian morality, and the virtues necessary to bring the light of civilization to the 'dark heart of Africa'. Hence the great achievement of the Africa conferences—and perhaps their only lasting achievement—lies in the fact that they internationalized the idea of trusteeship. They established in international law the principle that the condition of Africa's native inhabitants constituted a legitimate subject of international concern.

Trusteeship and the Congo Free State

Whereas the deliberations of the Berlin Conference provide insight into the type of argument that underpinned the internationalization of trusteeship, the character of political rule that followed in the aftermath of internationalization provides insight into its consequences. These consequences are most readily intelligible in the experience of what is surely the most ambitious humanitarian enterprise of nineteenth century, even more so than the crusade to put down slavery and the slave trade. This enterprise owes its existence to King Leopold II of Belgium who, in 1876, founded the International Association of the Congo, a society 'whose exclusive mission is to introduce civilisation and trade into the centre of Africa'.[50] Members of the Conference agreed without controversy that the Association embodied the principles that were the subject of their work. Mr Busch of Germany expressed his satisfaction by saying: 'we all pray that the most complete success may crown an enterprise which may so practically assist the views which directed the Conference.'[51] To this sentiment the Italian delegate, Count de Launay, added: '[t]he whole world cannot fail to exhibit its sympathy and encouragement on behalf of this civilizing and humane work which does honour to the nineteenth century, from which the general interests of humanity profit, and

---

[49] 'Protocol No. 1—Meeting of November 15, 1884', 11.
[50] 'Protocol No. 9—Meeting of February 23, 1885', Protocols and the General Act of the West African Conference, *Parliamentary Papers*, 1885 LV mf. 91.438, 254.   [51] Ibid. 254.

will always continue to derive further advantage.'[52] And so the Congo Free State was born.

In spite of the optimism that greeted Leopold's humanitarian aspirations, the newly constituted Congo Free State proved to be grossly ill-prepared to undertake its self-proclaimed mission of spreading civilization in the heart of Africa. Most accounts of this failure stress Leopold's overriding interest in profit rather than philanthropy.[53] That such assessments bear an element of truth is certainly correct. But in all fairness, the problems of creating a functioning civil society, not to mention the difficulties in imparting the advantages of civilization, were so daunting that today it is hardly conceivable that a private association would attempt such an undertaking. Since Belgium lacked established commercial links with Africa, as well as experience in administering a distant territory, Leopold relied upon volunteers from throughout Europe, including large numbers from Italy, Switzerland, and the Scandinavian countries. Some were drawn by humanitarian sentiment, others by the desire for loot. And their general view of the native African as being naturally idle, and, therefore, wholly ignorant of the principles of Adam Smith's 'economic man', slid quite easily into the coercive atrocities for which the Congo Free State is now best remembered. But the most daunting problem of all stemmed from the fact that 'Leopold faced the task of conquering and holding vast areas with his personal funds and a tiny budget that was more adequate for ruling a county than a country.'[54] Many of the tribes in the Congo had scarcely heard of the Association; and the fact that large tracts of territory to which Leopold laid claim remained under the control of Arab slave-traders only magnified these problems. And in a rather perverse way, the Berlin Act only exaggerated the difficulties in establishing an effective administration, as the government was financially crippled by a free trade system that severely curtailed its ability to raise revenue. Thus, the task of establishing a competent and recognized authority in the Congo, and the duty to eradicate the slave trade, engaged Leopold in a series of ongoing wars that he could ill-afford to fight.[55]

But the most troubling failure of the Congo Free State, one that dishonours its humanitarian justification, involves the reckless and malevolent treatment of the native population. Leopold quickly transformed the Congo into a private commercial estate that was supported by a system of compulsory labour. The

[52] Ibid. 255.

[53] See, for example, A. Hochschild, *King Leopold's Ghost: A Story of Greed, Terror, and Heroism in Colonial Africa* (London: Macmillan, 1998).

[54] L. H. Gann and P. Duignan, *The Rulers of the Belgian Africa, 1884–1914* (Princeton, NJ: Princeton University Press, 1979), 56–61, 217.

[55] A. B. Keith, *The Belgian Congo and the Berlin Act* (Oxford: Clarendon Press, 1919), 69.

totality of this transformation hastened Sir Constantine Phipps to report: 'the State has monopolized the entire fruits of the soil, and has interfered with the whole evolution of native existence.'[56] And to exploit the bounties of the estate the government elevated the provision of labour into a public duty. Able-bodied males were compelled to work on behalf of the state, for a period not to exceed 40 h per month, through the imposition of excessive taxation and through the use of arbitrary force. Sir Roger Casement reported that throughout the country native subjects were inadequately remunerated for their labour, they were forced to supply food to government posts, and they were afforded no protection of their property. District officers enforced compliance with this system of coercion through illegally imposed fines and summary imprisonment.[57] However, the most grievous instances of abuse were perpetrated by armed sentinels that concessionary companies employed to supervise the gathering of rubber. These 'forest guards' extracted industry, demanded obedience, and inflicted punishment with floggings, imprisonment, mutilation, and murder. Moreover, families were held hostage, village chiefs were imprisoned to induce greater productivity, and labourers were retained against their will even after they had completed their term of service. Victims of such abuse possessed no means of redressing their complaints because the courts were reluctant to punish agents of the state, even when they involved serious criminal matters. The pernicious effects of this system of taxation and forced labour led Casement to conclude that the deplorable conditions in which the natives lived 'were to be attributed above all else to the continued effort made during many years to compel the natives to work india-rubber'.[58]

Missionaries performed an invaluable role of criticizing and drawing attention to a state plunged in the depths of rapacity, corruption, and misrule. More effective, though, were efforts undertaken by the Congo Reform Association, which took the lead in exposing the horrors of Leopold's 'humanitarian' venture to the conscience of the world. Indeed, E. D. Morel, the founder of the Congo Reform Association, complained that '[f]rom the ashes of an international conference, summoned in the name of Almighty

---

[56] 'Sir C. Phipps to the Marquess of Landsdowne, November 7, 1905', Correspondence Respecting the Report of the Commission of Inquiry into the Administration of the Independent State of the Congo, June 1906, *Parliamentary Papers*, Cmd. 3002 lxxix (1906), 1.

[57] R. Casement, 'Mr. Casement to the Marquess of Landsdowne, December 12, 1903', *Parliamentary Papers*, Cmd. 1933 lxii (1904), 25–41.

[58] Ibid. 42–52; J. Whitehead, 'The Rev. J. Whitehead to Governor-General of the Congo State, July 28, 1903', *Parliamentary Papers*, Cmd. 1933 lxii (1904), 65; and J. Whitehead, 'The Rev. J. Whitehead to Governor-General of the Congo State, September 7, 1903', *Parliamentary Papers*, Cmd. 1933 lxii (1904), 68–9.

God, has sprung a traffic in African misery more devilish than the old, more destructive, more permanently ruinous in its cumulative effect.'[59] The Association petitioned the British government, recalling that '[e]ver since Sir E. Malet defined at Berlin in 1884 the part Her Majesty's Government took at the conference held to settle the affairs of the Congo, as being that of trustees for the absent native population, the Government of this country have played the leading part in a wholly unselfish effort to obtain for those unrepresented African peoples the rights the British people believed at the time had been not only morally but materially secured to them.'[60] The British government eventually internationalized the matter by transmitting to the signatories of the Berlin Act a diplomatic note that called attention to allegations of abuse in the Congo. The Congo Free State parried these complaints, saying that its administration was not unlike the administration of British and other European possessions. It also repudiated the right of the Hague Tribunal to adjudicate disputes, as stipulated in Article XII of the Berlin Act, relating to the internal administration of the State. Still, Leopold undertook a programme of reform that stripped concessionary companies of their rights to collect taxes and to employ sentinels, and which granted to the natives extended land rights. But (well-founded) scepticism of the government's ability and willingness to reform itself persisted, and in time the preponderance of British opinion reached the consensus that the situation called for a more radical remedy.[61]

Belgium's annexation of the Congo State in 1908, which Britain belatedly recognized five years later, finally put to rest the great philanthropic experiment that Leopold initiated. However, it is in the debates that transpired in the intervening years that we are able to discern in full relief the idea of trusteeship that was internationalized at Berlin. Opponents of Leopold's African government generally believed that redressing mistreatment of the natives required nothing less than a change in administration; and yet they also understood that administrative change would not yield the desired effects unless the principles of administration were changed as well. The British government hoped to induce reforms that would, once and for all, destroy a system of taxation and forced labour that kept the natives in a state of poverty and which denied them a fair share in the natural wealth of the land. Thus, the British government declared that 'the Belgian Government are under

[59] E. D. Morel, *Red Rubber* (London: T. Fisher Unwin, 1906), 180; and Whitehead, 'July 28, 1903', 65. For a general history, see W. R. Louis and J. Stengers, *E. D. Morel's History of the Congo Reform Movement* (Oxford: Clarendon Press, 1968).

[60] 'Congo Reform Association, Memorial, June 7, 1912', Correspondence Respecting the Affairs of the Congo, February 1913, *Parliamentary Papers*, Cmd. 6606 lix (1912–13), 23.

[61] Keith, *The Belgian Congo and the Berlin Act*, 131–5.

treaty obligations in regard to their treatment of the natives of the Congo, and that ... His Majesty's Government will not recognise the annexation until they are satisfied that these obligations are in a fair way to be fulfilled.'[62] Of these obligations, the government indicated that the most urgent consisted in granting the natives relief from the system of taxation that supported the rubber monopolies. Indeed, the government decided that '[t]he first and foremost subject of complaint under Article VI of the Berlin Act are the abuses resulting from the system of labour.'[63]

It is an event of signal importance that the British government pressed its claims by appealing to the Berlin Act and to the declarations that bestowed an international legal personality upon the International Association of the Congo. The British side recalled the Association's declaration, made at Berlin, that it had been founded 'for the purpose of promoting the civilization and commerce of Africa, and for other humane and benevolent purposes'; and, in turn, the British government proclaimed its 'sympathy with, and approval of, the humane and benevolent purposes of the Association, and hereby recognize the flag of the Association ... as the flag of a friendly Government'.[64] Britain claimed, on the basis of this exchange, a right of interference in order to ensure the faithful implementation of the purpose for which Her Majesty's government recognized the Congo Free State. Therefore, just two days after the Belgian Parliament approved the annexation of the Congo Free State, the British government proposed a comprehensive programme of reform. These proposed reforms included relief from excessive taxation, land reform to encourage the transition from a subsistence to a commercial economy, and permitting traders of all nationalities to establish direct relations with the native population.[65] The British government also expressed apprehension about the exclusive rights possessed by concessionary companies because, as Sir Edward Grey put it, they 'fail[ed] to meet the requirements of Article VI of the Berlin Act, under which the Signatory Powers pledge themselves to

---

[62] 'Foreign Office to Mr. Lamont, May 29, 1912', Correspondence Respecting the Affairs of the Congo, February 1913, *Parliamentary Papers*, Cmd. 6606 lix (1912–13), 22.

[63] 'Memorandum Respecting Taxation and Currency in the Congo Free State', Correspondence Respecting the Taxation of Natives, and Other Questions, in the Congo State, June 1908, *Parliamentary Papers*, Cmd. 4135 lxxi (1908), 4.

[64] 'Annex 1 to Protocol No. 9', Protocols and the General Act of the West African Conference, *Parliamentary Papers*, 1885 LV mf. 91.438, 264; and Memorandum, Respecting the Taxation of Natives, and Other Questions, in the Congo State, November 1908, *Parliamentary Papers*, Cmd. 4178 (1908), 3.

[65] See 'Memorandum, Respecting the Taxation of Natives, and Other Questions, in the Congo State', 3; and Sir Edward Grey to Sir A. Hardinge, March 27, 1908, Correspondence Respecting the Taxation of Natives, and Other Questions, in the Congo State, June 1908, *Parliamentary Papers*, Cmd. 4135 lxxi (1908), 2.

provide for the improvement of the natives' moral and material well-being'.[66] It was believed that, implemented together, these reforms would re-establish the system of free trade established by the Berlin Act, remedy injustices arising from excessive taxation and compulsory labour, and destroy the power of the concessionary companies and the privilege of their rubber monopolies. Indeed, Grey confidently predicted that '[t]he joint effect of these three reforms would go far to ameliorate the condition of the natives in the Congo'.[67]

It should come as no surprise that the Belgians received British criticism as an unwanted and unwarranted intrusion. In 1906, British overtures were rebuffed on the grounds that no foreign power had the right to interfere in matters pertaining to the internal administration of the Congo Free State. Moreover, authorities in the Congo expressly denied that the Berlin Act provided any right or pretext of interference. Mr de Cuvelier stated emphatically the obligations enumerated in Article VI 'were a declaration of general principles and intentions as regarded the treatment of the native populations rather than a binding obligation which the remaining Signatories, or any one of them, had a right to enforce'.[68] The juridical status of the Congo State is of some consequence when considering the veracity of this response. The Congo Free State is sometimes (and mistakenly) regarded as an international philanthropic enterprise. In reality, though, it was an independent state (though not a member of the European society of states) whose independent status was confirmed in a series of separate international agreements between the International Association of the Congo and various European powers. And the British government maintained that the Association assumed, in its exchange of declarations with Britain and other European powers, the obligations of the Berlin Act and 'thus both legally and morally became subject to the full rigour of the provisions of the Act'.[69]

The British government pursued its claims against the Congo State while conceding that Article VI did not imply a right that permitted foreign powers to dictate the character of specific reforms. However, the British government insisted nevertheless that 'no system can be allowed to operate so as to interfere with Treaty obligations to the prejudice of the moral and material well-being of the natives'.[70] The Belgian government eventually abandoned its defence

---

[66] 'Sir Edward Grey to Sir A. Hardinge, March 27, 1908', 3.   [67] Ibid. 4.

[68] 'Sir A. Hardinge to Sir Edward Grey, May 11, 1906', Correspondence Respecting the Report of the Commission of Inquiry into the Administration of the Independent State of the Congo, June 1906, *Parliamentary Papers*, Cmd. 3002 lxxix (1906), 19.

[69] 'Annex 1 to Protocol No. 9', Protocols and the General Act of the West African Conference, 65.

[70] 'Memorandum Respecting Taxation and Currency in the Congo Free State', 5.

premised on the claim of non-interference and it offered assurances that a proposed (new) colonial law would safeguard the rights and interests of the natives. Under this law, natives would no longer be forced to labour, either directly or indirectly; religious, charitable, and scientific institutions would enjoy equal protection; and the system of free trade would be re-established in all of the territories comprising the Congo basin. The Belgian government also recognized obligations of international law pertaining to the welfare of the natives and it proclaimed that its rule in the Congo would be directed at achieving 'an immediate amelioration in the moral and material conditions of existence of the inhabitants of the Congo, and the extension, as rapidly as possible, of a system of economic freedom to the different regions of the vast country'.[71]

Britain's subsequent recognition of the annexation of the Congo Free State marked a major milestone in the development of the theory and practice of trusteeship in international society. There can be no question that the International Association of the Congo failed absolutely in fulfilling its self-proclaimed humanitarian mission. At nearly every opportunity the government of the Congo Free State vacated its obligation to watch over the natives as unselfish trustees of civilization. It is also true that most of the signatory powers to the Berlin Act responded rather indifferently to mounting evidence of misrule in the Congo. Only the United States, Italy, and Turkey responded favourably to a British note that documented flagrant violations of the obligation set out in Article VI of the Berlin Act.[72] But, for all this, the events that transpired between the creation of the Congo Free State and its annexation did not discredit trusteeship or render it merely platitudinous fiction. The British government's repeated references to the obligations imposed by Article VI reaffirmed, and, indeed, vindicated, the legitimacy of the idea of trusteeship. That Belgium eventually accepted the legitimacy of the British position, and, consequently, that it affirmed that 'improving the lot of the natives is not less a matter of solicitude in Belgium than it is in England', gave practical effect to the authority of trusteeship. In that respect the settlement of the Congo question signalled the emergence of trusteeship as an accepted practice of international society.

The Ladder of Civilization

Colonial administration in nineteenth century Africa and the subsequent internationalization of trusteeship marked the triumph of a particular conception of how humanity should be ordered. In Africa, a preference for deliberation,

---

[71] 'Memorandum Communicated by the Belgian Minister, April 25, 1908', Correspondence Respecting the Taxation of Natives, and Other Questions, in the Congo State, June 1908, *Parliamentary Papers*, Cmd. 4135 lxxi (1908), 37–9.

[72] Keith, *The Belgian Congo and the Berlin Act*, 131.

patience, and incrementalism displaced the belief that prevailed throughout much of the East India Company's dominion in India, namely that the improvement of native peoples would come about rapidly and would result in institutional forms and practices that closely resembled those in Europe. An incrementalist approach to imparting the advantages of civilization made it possible to think of societies and peoples as occupying different rungs on a progressive ladder of civilization. It was then possible to make graded distinctions, as did Lugard, between primitive tribes and advanced communities. Primitive tribes were said to languish in a patriarchal stage of development in which superstition and a crude social organization prevailed. In contrast, more advanced communities were said to have moved further along the road of progress on account of some form of enlightenment, such as the adoption of an alien monotheistic religion. Indeed, Lugard viewed Muslim rule as a creative force to the extent that it brought primitive Africa into contact with foreign culture and written language, and destroyed the most heinous of African habits and customs. However, he expressed doubt that the Islamic religion could carry African society beyond a stage of barbarism; for he understood Islam as merely a rung on a ladder that progressed onwards to Christianity and European civilization.[73]

The idea that societies were differently placed along a ladder of civilization is also amply reflected in nineteenth century political theory and international law. For example, John Stuart Mill suggested that the institutions of government must be fitted to the character of the people destined to operate them. Thus, civilized peoples were most suited for a popular constitution, which required the surrender of a portion of personal freedom in order to secure public benefit, because they were able to act as interdependent parts of a complex whole. But representative institutions were inappropriate in 'savage societies' in which each person acts for himself without regard for the interests of the whole. Thus, Mill concluded that savages must learn to obey before taking the first steps towards the ideal of popular government; and until they have done so, so that they are able to act with due regard for the interests of the community, they were fit only for despotic government.[74] James Lorimer similarly reconciled the conventional differences that divide humanity by combining what he called national and cosmopolitan international law. Lorimer proposed that humanity consisted in three concentric spheres: civilized, barbarous, and savage. In that respect he argued:

whether arising from peculiarities of race or from various stages of development in the same race, belong, *of right*, at the hands of civilized nations, three stages of

---

[73] Lugard, *The Dual Mandate of Africa*, 75–8.
[74] J. S. Mill, *Considerations on Representative Government* (Amherst, MA: Prometheus Books, 1991), 34–40, 47–50; and Mill, 'Civilization', 48–50.

recognition—plenary political recognition, partial political recognition, and natural or mere human recognition. Intensively, the first of these forms of recognition embraces the two latter; extensively, the third embraces the two former [emphasis in original].[75]

In this scheme of things, the Christian nations of Europe were entitled to formal political recognition on account of their ability to perform the obligations of a civilized society—domestically and internationally. Barbarians were regarded as not having achieved political age; they were old children, but children nevertheless that could not be expected to reciprocate the duties of civilized society. And, finally, savages were viewed as the undeveloped residue of humanity that was entitled to nothing more than guardianship and guidance 'in becoming that of which they are capable'.[76]

This progressive ordering of human relations prepared the ground for the objective verification of African inferiority. The superiority ascribed to 'civilized man' reduced 'savage man' to an object of pity and contempt. Whereas 'civilized man' was disciplined, guided by reason, and aware of a common good, 'savage man' lacked self-control, acted on passion, and knew only the satisfaction of individual will and appetite.[77] It is in this context that Lugard described the African as being naturally happy and thriftless, and as an excitable person who was in want of self-control, foresight, and discipline. These traits, he argued, are those of the 'child races of the world' and 'the virtues and the defects of this race-type are those of attractive children whose confidence when once it has been won is given ungrudgingly as to an older and wiser superior, without question and without envy'.[78] J. C. Smuts offered a very similar assessment of these 'child' races of the world. The African, he suggested, is good-tempered, carefree, and is easily satisfied with wine, women, and song; and, like a child, he is not burdened by past troubles and nor does he anticipate future problems. Thus, Smuts concluded that the African race 'has largely remained a child type, with a child psychology and outlook'.[79] The idea of trusteeship ordered relations between this residue of humanity, to use Lorimer's words, and their civilized guardians and teachers in so far as it expressed a standard against which the tutelage of these peoples should be judged.

---

[75] J. Lorimer, *The Institutes of the Law of Nations: A Treatise of the Jural Relations of Separate Political Communities*, vol. 1 (Edinburgh: William Blackwood and Sons, 1883), 13–16, 21, 101.

[76] Ibid. 101–58. It is worth noting that the League of Nations carried this division of humanity into the twentieth century inasmuch as the A, B, and C classes of mandated territory corresponded with Lorimer's distinction.

[77] See Cairns, *Prelude to Imperialism*, 120; and Mill, 'Civilization', 48–9.

[78] Lugard, *The Dual Mandate of Africa*, 69–72.

[79] J. C. Smuts, *Africa and Some World Problems* (Oxford: Clarendon Press, 1930), 75.

In that respect it is worth noting that even the most strident critics of empire did not disavow the value of trusteeship. John Hobson's complaint was not that empire existed, but that European trustees of civilization had failed to fulfil their obligations. Indeed, he submitted that the 'chief indictment of Imperialism in relation to the lower races consists in this, that it does not even pretend to apply to them the principles of education and of progress it applies at home'.[80] Still, he maintained that trusteeship, understood as the progress of world-civilization, constituted a valid moral reason for interfering in the lives of uncivilized peoples. Hobson's complaints about vested economic interests, and the many miscarriages of justice, racial and religious arrogance, and the horrors of the Congo Free State, did not diminish the value that attached to the idea of trusteeship. In fact, they had the opposite effect. Experience in Africa furthered the development of the idea of trusteeship by establishing its status in international law so that the condition and welfare of the world's most underdeveloped peoples became a legitimate subject of international scrutiny. And at a time when Joseph Chamberlain was busy proclaiming that 'the British race is the greatest of governing races that the world has ever seen',[81] the internationalization of trusteeship and the scrutiny it entailed loosened ever so slightly the absolute (national) grip on empire.

[80] Hobson, *Imperialism*, 237–43.

[81] J. Chamberlain, 'Speech at the Imperial Institute, 11 November 1895', in G. Bennett (ed.), *The Concept of Empire: Burke to Attlee, 1774–1947* (London: Adam and Charles Black, 1953), 315.

4

Trusteeship as an Institution of International Society

If we understand the Berlin and Brussels Acts and the experience of the Congo Free State as representing the internationalization of the idea of trusteeship, then we might understand the League of Nations mandates system as representing its institutionalization in international society. The purpose of this chapter is to examine the current of ideas from which the institutionalization of trusteeship arose out of the debates concerning the disposal of German colonies conquered during the First World War, and the subsequent compromise that resulted in the creation of the mandates system. It will become evident, then, that the mandates system stands as a response to the problem of ordering relations of Europeans and non-Europeans by reconciling the obligations of trusteeship and the search for national security in a single institutional arrangement. The victorious Allied powers divided Germany's colonial possessions amongst themselves, in no small part for reasons of national security, but in assuming administrative responsibility for these territories they also accepted the oversight of 'international machinery' to ensure that the work of civilization was being done.

War and the Old Diplomacy

The founders of the League of Nations believed, at least outwardly, that they had broken with the 'discredited' principles of nineteenth century power politics by introducing into world affairs an entirely new way of ordering the relations of states. Critics of the League of Nations, such as E. H. Carr, denounced this claim of novelty as a foolish, though well-meaning, delusion. In his seminal volume, *The Twenty Years' Crisis*, Carr thoroughly ridiculed the great aspiration of the League's most ardent supporters: the attempt to realize perpetual peace by banishing power from the relations of states and substituting in its place the liberal virtues of discussion, persuasion, and consent. Power, he confidently asserted, would be neither absent nor incidental to the League of Nations, despite its commitment to the principles of legal equality, political independence, and territorial integrity.[1] But in spite of the unrelenting force of Carr's criticism, proponents of the League of Nations were not so naïve as to believe that international organization would suddenly abolish the problem of war and thus render all states absolutely secure. Those who looked to international organization with great hope were not unaware of the centrality of power in the relations of states; rather, they believed that the exercise of power could be subjected to the constraint of law so that armed peace would give place to public right.[2] The extent to which the League of Nations marked an authentic break with the 'old diplomacy' of alliances, war, and the balance of power continues to attract scholarly attention. For example, the American historian William Keylor concludes in a recent reckoning of the League's significance that historians of the Versailles settlement have vastly exaggerated its importance.[3] What is sure, though, is that the League of Nations experiment did result in a truly novel approach to the administration of at least some of the 'subject races' of Africa, Asia, Oceania, namely those that resided in colonies that were stripped from Germany as a result of the war. The mandates system reaffirmed the principle of trusteeship enshrined in the Berlin Act; but it went further than the arrangements of Berlin in specifying procedures of international supervision to guard against the sort of maltreatment and misrule that transpired in the Congo Free State.

But colonial questions were noticeably absent from the earliest declarations of Allied war aims. In the first major statement of British war aims, Prime Minister Herbert Asquith spoke of the vindication of public right in Europe. Militarism, he declared, must be repudiated, the independence and free development of small nationalities preserved, and, in an allusion to some form of international organization, rival alliances discarded in favour of a 'real European partnership based on the recognition of equal right, and established and enforced by a common will'.[4] The vindication of public right entailed nothing less than the reversal and restitution of injury inflicted by German aggression. Indeed, Asquith's successor, David Lloyd George, recounted that the war was initially cast as a struggle on behalf of weak and

---

[1] E. H. Carr, *The Twenty Years' Crisis* (London: Macmillan, 1970), 103–4.

[2] See, for example, G. L. Dickinson, *The Choice Before Us* (New York: Dodd, Mead, and Company, 1917).

[3] W. R. Keylor, 'Versailles and International Diplomacy', in M. F. Boemeke, G. D. Feldman, and E. Glaser (eds.), *The Treaty of Versailles: A Reassessment After Seventy-Five Years* (Cambridge: Cambridge University Press, 1998), 471.

[4] 'Mr. Asquith (Prime Minister)—Speech, Dublin, September 25, 1914', *British Documents on Foreign Affairs: Reports and Papers From the Foreign Office Confidential Print*, part II, series H, vol. 4 (Frederick, MD: University Press of America, 1989), 251.

small nations against 'arrogant and aggressive militarism'.[5] On this view, the burden of war guilt rested with Germany alone; for the pacific and defensive intentions of the Allied powers stood in stark contrast with the appetite of Prussian autocracy. And the redress of wrong would be achieved, as it had been in the past, through the maintenance of the balance of power, restoration of Belgian independence, and the preservation of British naval superiority.[6] Thus, the restoration of peace in Europe would be concluded by a victorious concert of powers rather than by a league of nations.

So long as the war remained primarily a European affair, colonial questions attracted little attention. It was only after Germany's overseas empire fell to advancing Allied armies that colonial questions became a matter of great importance. At that point they could not be ignored: once the Allied powers assumed control of German colonies in Africa and the Pacific they were confronted with the problem of determining their future. But with the outcome of the war very much in doubt, Britain and its allies reached several understandings that contemplated colonial adjustments at Germany's expense. Italy was encouraged to enter the war on the side of the Allies in exchange for a pledge to treat favourably Italian colonial claims at the conclusion of the conflict.[7] And, predictably, the advantages of annexing German colonies did not escape the attention of influential members of the Imperial government. The conquest of German East Africa revived the long-held dream of establishing an uninterrupted land route connecting Egypt with the Cape of Africa. As talk of a territorial settlement gathered pace, J. C. Smuts, a member of the Imperial War Cabinet, expressed the hope that 'it will be borne in mind that East Africa gives us this through land communication from one end of the Continent to the other, but that East Africa also ensures to us the safety of the sea route around the Cape and the sea route through the Red Sea to the East'.[8] Walter Long, the Secretary of State for Colonies, also favoured a policy of annexation, albeit on the grounds of national honour. In assuring the British public that 'their struggles for these colonies had not

---

[5] D. Lloyd George, *The Truth About Peace Treaties*, vol. 2 (London: Victor Gallancz, 1938), 752.

[6] G. Egerton, *Great Britain and the Creation of the League of Nations: Strategy, Politics, and International Organization, 1914–1919* (Chapel Hill, NC: University of North Carolina Press, 1978), 36.

[7] 'Agreement between France, Russia, Britain and Italy (Treaty of London), 26 April 1915', in J. A. S. Grenville and Bernard Wasserstein (eds.), *The Major International Treaties of the Twentieth Century*, vol. 1 (London: Routledge, 2001), 64–6.

[8] 'General Smuts (Member of War Cabinet)—Speech, Savoy Hotel, May 22, 1917', *British Documents on Foreign Affairs: Reports and Papers From the Foreign Office Confidential Print*, part II, series H, vol. 4 (Frederick, MD: University Press of America, 1989), 99.

been in vain', he allowed no ambiguity in stating his view: '[l]et no man think that the colonies will ever return to German rule'.[9]

But as the war ground into an appalling human tragedy, confidence in the trusted traditions of European diplomacy came under intense fire. Members of the British pacifist, socialist, and labour movements, and especially members of the Union for Democratic Control (UDC), brought enormous pressure to bear on what they considered to be the discredited practices of the old diplomacy. These voices of dissent introduced into the discourse of world affairs a very different way of thinking about international relations. They understood world affairs as consisting in something more than the practice of statecraft—an activity reserved to the privileged few. And collectively they demanded, not merely reform, but a total repudiation of the principles, practices, and institutions of traditional diplomacy; for they believed that nothing less than the survival of civilization itself depended on a turning away from a precarious and, indeed, dangerous condition of armed peace. We must move towards a world, John Hobson insisted, in which the 'interests, capacities, and needs, not of sovereign states, but of peoples shall prevail'.[10] Only then would it be possible to think, not in terms of independent states, each existing in splendid isolation from all others, but in terms of interdependent peoples that composed a society of states, an international community, or a commonwealth of nations. Hobson's colleagues, many of whom were fellow members of the UDC, all denounced the perils of secret diplomacy, armaments, alliances, competitive rivalries, economic privilege, and what he called that 'supreme engine of international mischief', the balance of power. Henry Brailsford condemned the rivalry in armaments and alliances as indicators of 'universal insecurity', and he likened the balance of power to a hypocritical disguise for the perennial struggle for power. And E. D. Morel attacked a philosophy of militarism that regarded states as 'antagonistic units' and the folly of secret diplomacy—the greatest obstacle to the unity of humanity.[11]

However, it was probably the thought of G. Lowes Dickinson that yielded the most penetrating and lucid insights into the causes of the war. Dickinson attributed the cause of all wars to the nature of the international system itself.

---

[9] 'Mr. W. Long (Secretary of State for Colonies)—Speech, Westminster City Hall, January 31, 1917', *British Documents on Foreign Affairs: Reports and Papers From the Foreign Office Confidential Print*, part II, series H, vol. 4 (Frederick, MD: University Press of America, 1989), 98.

[10] J. A. Hobson, *Towards International Government* (New York: Garland Publishing, 1971), 164, 181.

[11] Ibid. 181; H. N. Brailsford, *The War of Steel and Gold: A Study of Armed Peace* (New York: Garland Publishing, 1971), 22–8; and E. D. Morel, 'Militarism and the Beast of the Apocalypse' and 'Secret Diplomacy', *Truth and the War* (New York: Garland Publishing, 1972), 61, 113.

With the emergence of the sovereign state, he claimed, arose an 'international anarchy' that was the fruit of political relations nurtured by fear and suspicion. And where there was neither common law nor common force, peace could be no more than a state of latent war; for an all-consuming insecurity born of armaments and militarism would always frustrate the best of intentions and thus rule out any chance of lasting peace. Hence, he concluded rather pessimistically that '[m]utual fear and mutual suspicion, aggression masquerading as defence and defence masquerading as aggression, will be the protagonists in the bloody drama; and there will be, what Hobbes truly asserted to be the essence of such a situation, a chronic state of war, open or veiled.'[12] That the cause of war was grounded in this condition of international anarchy permitted Dickinson to assign war guilt more widely than to Germany alone. He conceded that Germany was responsible for provoking the war in the immediate instance, but he asserted as well that 'the main and permanent offence is common to all states. It is the anarchy for which they are all responsible for perpetuating.'[13] This opinion was not that of a lone objector. Both Norman Angell and Morel concurred fully with Dickinson's assessment. Angell argued that the popularity of Germany's purported war guilt 'obscured the view that an inherent defect in the political mechanism of the world's life had produced the catastrophe, not merely some double dose of original sin on the part of one particular people'.[14] Morel similarly denied that Germany should be burdened with sole responsibility for the war. The only difference between German militarism and British 'navalism', he argued, was the reality of superior German organization and efficiency.[15] For these voices of dissent the war could not in any case be one of exclusive self-defence; rather it was the inevitable consequence of a world composed of sovereign states that conducted their relations according to faulty, if not fraudulent, principles of diplomacy.

Trusteeship or Annexation?

It is this universal attribution of guilt that led to a sweeping indictment of the old diplomacy, and along with it conventional thinking about the role of colonies in world affairs. Whereas Lloyd George claimed that colonial questions presented themselves only after the conquest of Germany's overseas

[12] G. L. Dickinson, *The European Anarchy* (London: George Allen & Unwin, 1916), 9–10.
[13] Ibid. 10.
[14] N. Angell, 'The International Anarchy', in L. Woolf (ed.), *The Intelligent Man's Way To Prevent War* (London: Victor Gallancz, 1933), 31.
[15] Morel, 'Militarism and the Beast of the Apocalypse', 61–7.

empire, dissenters such as Brailsford identified the very workings of the international system, the balance of power, for example, with the sort of exploitation that was often associated with the scramble for Africa. 'The struggle for a balance of power,' he wrote, 'means to-day a struggle for liberty and opportunity to use "places in the sun" across the seas'.[16] Indeed, dissenting opinion held that the competition for colonies abetted a penchant for war, as well as trampled on the rights of native peoples, extinguished their hope of development, and retarded their advancement on the road of civilization. However, these same dissenters doubted that the promise of nineteenth century liberalism, the individualist doctrines of Manchester School economics, were suitable for engaging the problems of the twentieth century. For Brailsford, the unwillingness of continental powers to compete on equal terms with 'pioneering' England, and the enthusiasm with which national governments assumed direction of their citizens' economic interests, signalled the twilight of Cobdenism. Hobson extended this criticism to argue generally that the social, political, and economic doctrines of nineteenth century liberalism were insufficiently responsive to the needs of ordinary human beings.[17]

In place of Cobdenite orthodoxy, which prescribed a policy of reform at home and retrenchment abroad, the preponderance of dissenting opinion reconciled itself to the existence of empire and to the burdens and responsibilities of alien rule. Morel, Hobson, and Brailsford did not in any way entertain the possibility that the 'subject races' of any European empire were ready for self-government. Rather, their objection to empire stemmed from a firm conviction that the economic exploitation of distant colonies was incompatible with the goal of perpetual peace. The motive of profit stood before the realization of peace. Thus, Morel argued that if the peoples of Europe were to live in peace, then dependent territories must be neutralized from European wars and the principle of the open door must be observed by all powers as contemplated by the Berlin and Brussels Acts. For he was convinced that 'so long as the European governments look upon these vast African and Asiatic territories as areas for the pursuit of privileges and monopolies, carried on behind closed doors, in favour of a microscopic fraction of their respective nationals, so long will these territories continue to be one of the prime causes of European unrest and European armaments.[18] But the object of Morel's solicitude did not stop at the achievement of peace in Europe. He conceived of no separation

---

[16] Brailsford, *The War of Steel and Gold*, 32.

[17] H. N. Brailsford, *Olives of an Endless Age: Being a Study of This Distracted World and Its Need of Unity* (New York: Harper & Brothers Publishers, 1928), 42–5; and B. Porter, *Critics of Empire: British Radical Attitudes to Colonialism in Africa 1895–1914* (London: Macmillan, 1968), 178.

[18] E. D. Morel, 'The Way Out', *Truth and the War* (New York: Garland Publishing, 1972), 262–3.

between the claims of dependent peoples and the peace of the world. Indeed, he wished to lift from the shoulders of the black man the burden imposed by contact with the white man. Morel understood the problem of colonial development, especially in Africa, as being grounded in the establishment of economic relations that were inevitable, but which did not 'entail degradation and destruction upon the African peoples, and disgrace to Europe'.[19] It is in this cardinal conviction that the idea of trusteeship took root as an alternative to the annexation of Germany's conquered colonies.

In putting forth the idea of trusteeship, Leonard Woolf asserted that: 'if anything is certain in international politics, it is that you cannot base international relations in one quarter of the world upon right and law and co-operation, and in another quarter upon economic hostility and force.'[20] He shared with other radical dissenters—the 'trouble makers' as A. J. P. Taylor called them—the view that the gradual annexation of nearly the entire African continent had resulted in wholly evil consequences; and, like Dickinson, he attributed the maltreatment of the peoples of Africa to an international system that was founded on principles of aggression, domination, and exploitative economic relations. Woolf complained that the singular pursuit of that cherished Manchester maxim, the right to sell in the dearest and to buy in the cheapest market, shattered any notion of responsibility for the rights and interests of the native races. Yet he doubted that the interests of Africa could be adequately secured by making the black man the master of his own affairs. To reverse the evil that the white man had visited upon the black man, Europeans needed to dispossess themselves of the attitude that Africa was a great estate to be exploited for economic advantage. For the plight of Africa depended on determining 'how the European State can be changed from an instrument of economic exploitation into an instrument of good government and progress, not for a few hundred white men, but for the millions of Africans'.[21] Indeed, Woolf claimed that the justification for European dominion in Africa depended on something more than the provision of law and order. It depended on the reservation of all lands for native use, the application of all revenue raised from the human and natural endowment of Africa to the advancement of the native races, and protection of the natives from the evil effects of alcohol and the ravages of European wars. And, crucially, dominion enjoined an obligation to educate the black man so that he will be able to participate in, and one day direct, his own government.[22] In sum, then, Woolf demanded nothing less than a revolution

---

[19] E. D. Morel, *The Black Man's Burden* (London: The National Labour Press, 1920), 234.
[20] L. Woolf, *Empire and Commerce in Africa: A Study in Economic Imperialism* (London: George Allen and Unwin, 1920), 356.   [21] Ibid. 354–8.   [22] Ibid. 355, 362–3.

in the way that Europe dealt with Africa: 'the belief that the State should use its power to promote the economic interests of Europeans would have to give place to the belief that its position was merely that of trustee for the native population and that its only duty was to promote the interests, political, social, and economic, of the Africans.'[23]

It is this concern for the welfare of the subject races of Africa, no less than a concern for the peace of Europe, which led to the popularity of the wartime slogan 'no annexations'. Dissenting opinion viewed the annexation of occupied German colonies as being inconsistent with an international community composed of peoples, as opposed to states, and, thereby, incompatible with the general peace of the world. But, in the end, their proposals regarding the disposal of the German colonies appeared to be less revolutionary than a demand for the extension and faithful implementation of the principles enshrined in the Berlin and Brussels Acts. For example, the UDC resolved that Britain should repudiate all claims of annexation and that '[t]ropical Africa should be neutralised under international guarantee, and absolute freedom of trade and enterprise established there.'[24] And, in a more elaborate and ambitious statement, the British Labour Party and the Trade Union Congress declared in a joint memorandum that *all* dependent territories of Africa should be administered as a single independent state according to the following principles:

(1) the open door and equal freedom of enterprise to the traders of all nations; (2) protection of the natives against exploitation and oppression, and the preservation of their tribal interests; (3) all revenue raised to be expended for the welfare and development of the African State itself; and (4) the permanent neutralisation of this African State and its abstention from participation in international rivalries or any future wars.[25]

The substance of these ideas constituted an important part of a much larger agenda that would eventually destroy the legitimacy of the old diplomacy. Indeed, A. J. P. Taylor argues that in time dissenting opinion would ultimately garner such broad acceptance that it discredited 'all traditional

---

[23] Ibid. 362.

[24] 'Union of Democratic Control—Resolutions prepared for Stockholm Conference, September 1917', *British Documents on Foreign Affairs: Reports and Papers From the Foreign Office Confidential Print*, part II, series H, vol. 4 (Frederick, MD: University Press of America, 1989), 102.

[25] 'British Labour Party and Parliamentary Committee Trade Union Congress—War Aims Memorandum, adopted Joint Conference, December 28, 1917', *British Documents on Foreign Affairs: Reports and Papers From the Foreign Office Confidential Print*, part II, series H, vol. 4 (Frederick, MD: University Press of America, 1989), 102.

diplomacy—"power politics" as the contemporary term of abuse had it'.[26] And in this achievement these dissenting voices invested considerable legitimacy in the idea of trusteeship as a way of ordering relations between the European and non-European worlds.

From the New World

The British and French governments continued to pursue a quiet policy of annexation, in spite of the growing popularity of the ideas championed by the UDC and the British Labour movement. But if dissenting opinion changed the terms of debate concerning colonial questions, then the Russian revolution and the United States' entry into the war altered them permanently. The Bolsheviks viewed the war as an undisguised imperialist contest. Lenin betrayed no doubt in his famous tract, *Imperialism, The Highest Stage of Capitalism*, that the Great War 'was imperialist (that is, an annexationist, predatory war of plunder) on the part of the both sides; it was a war for the division of the world, for the partition and reparation of colonies and spheres of influence of finance capital, etc'.[27] After publishing the secret treaties and, thereby, exposing Allied territorial ambitions, the Bolsheviks proclaimed principles of foreign relations that denounced all annexations, new and old. Peace and democracy, they declared, required recognition that all peoples must be free in the pursuit of independent development. Thus, Leon Trotsky declared that to deny the right of self-determination for all peoples, in Alsace Lorraine, Transylvania, and Bosnia and Herzegovina, as well as in India, Egypt, and Ireland, is to sanction an 'unprincipled compromise between the pretension of Imperialism and the opposition of the labouring Democracy'.[28] Members of the UDC and the British Labour movement greeted these proclamations with great enthusiasm and hope, so much so that Dickinson proclaimed that the Russian revolution, along with America's entry into the war, '[b]oth enhance, beyond all reckoning, the good prospects of civilisation'.[29]

But it was the American president, Woodrow Wilson, who represented the greatest hope of realizing a peace that repudiated the right of conquest. Morel

[26] A. J. P. Taylor, *The Trouble Makers: Dissent Over Foreign Policy, 1792–1939* (London: Hamish Hamilton, 1957), 169.

[27] V. I. Lenin, 'Imperialism, the Highest Stage of Capitalism (1916): A Popular Outline', *Lenin on Politics and Revolution*, ed. J. E. Connor (Indianapolis, IN: The Bobbs-Merrill Company, 1975), 112.

[28] L. Trotsky, 'To Peoples and Governments of Allied Countries', *The Papers of Woodrow Wilson*, vol. 45, ed. A. S. Link (Princeton, NJ: Princeton University Press, 1984), 412.

[29] Dickinson, *The Choice Before Us*, p. vii.

openly appealed to Wilson, the only man whose stature, character, and sense of right could 'save the soul of the peoples and governments of Europe'.[30] Wilson championed a 'new and more wholesome diplomacy' that would help found peace upon the collective strength of the international community—a community inclusive of all peoples in all places.[31] For he could not reconcile a world of interdependent peoples, a world in which the interests of all nations were identified with the interests of mankind, with secret counsels, antagonistic alliances, and an illusory peace afforded by the balance of power. The world had reached a point where peace depended, not on individual efforts, but on the efforts of all. No nation could contemplate a retreat into isolation: all nations were joined in one great human enterprise. Indeed, Wilson believed that '[w]e are participants, whether we would or not, in the life of the world. The interests of all nations are our own also. We are partners with the rest. What affects mankind is inevitably our affair as well as the affair of the nations of Europe and Asia.'[32] Wilson envisioned a universal world order established upon principles of right and justice. Public right must reign above the interests of individual nations, political independence and territorial integrity must be guaranteed, and steps must be taken to safeguard general peace against threats of selfish aggression. But it was Wilson's suggestion that all peoples possessed the right to choose their own government that augured most effectively against European schemes of annexation. The rights of states would have bow to the rights of peoples.

Wilson advanced these ideas while fastidiously disclaiming all pretension of national advantage: peace should avoid the vindictive treatment of the vanquished and, above all else, it should bear the hallmarks of justice and generosity. It was in this spirit which Wilson insisted that there must be peace without victory: there must be '[n]o annexations, no contributions, and no punitive indemnities'.[33] Rather, he maintained throughout the war, and in its aftermath, that the United States did not aspire to revenge, 'but only the vindication of right, of human right, of which we are only a single champion'.[34] Wilson outlined his programme for peace before a joint session of Congress on 8 January 1917, in what would come to be known as the

---

[30] E. D. Morel, 'An Appeal to President Wilson', *Truth and the War* (New York: Garland Publishing, 1972), 114.

[31] W. Wilson, 'An Address in Washington to the League to Enforce Peace', *The Papers of Woodrow Wilson*, vol. 37, ed. A. S. Link (Princeton, NJ: Princeton University Press, 1981), 114.

[32] Ibid. 114.

[33] W. Wilson, 'An Annual Message on the State of the Union, December 4, 1917', *The Papers of Woodrow Wilson*, vol. 45, ed. A. S. Link (Princeton, NJ: Princeton University Press, 1984), 196.

[34] W. Wilson, 'An Address to a Joint Session of Congress, April 2, 1917', *The Papers of Woodrow Wilson*, vol. 41, ed. A. S. Link (Princeton, NJ: Princeton University Press, 1983), 520.

'fourteen points'. In a brief but historic discourse he spoke of open diplomacy, freedom of the seas, the open door, disarmament, self-determination,
the evacuation and restoration of conquered territories, and the creation of a
general organization to guarantee the political independence and territorial
integrity of all states, great and small alike. With respect to colonial questions,
Wilson proposed in point five, an 'absolutely impartial adjustment of colonial
claims' according to the principle that in matters pertaining to sovereignty,
'the interests of the populations concerned must have equal weight with the
equitable claims of the government whose title is to be determined'.[35] In these
fourteen points Wilson articulated the principles of a 'new diplomacy' that
endeavoured to subject power to the strictures of justice and law. Indeed,
he believed that the faithful implementation of these principles would make
the world 'safe for democracy'.

Although Taylor doubted that the fourteen points speech fully restored the
moral high ground to the Allies, it caused a sensation among ordinary people
who were ever more sceptical of the professed motives and aims of their
governments. Thomas Knock describes the popular approval of the fourteen
points as approaching 'phenomenal proportions'—even Lenin hailed them
as a great advance towards peace.[36] The popularity of Wilson's cherished
principles exerted considerable pressure on European leaders, who were
apprehensive about embracing the ideological commitments of the new
diplomacy yet keen to demonstrate the righteousness of the Allied cause in a
bid to revive flagging morale at home. The cry of 'no annexations' elicited
such support that Philip Kerr, Lloyd George's private secretary, counselled
Smuts on the signal importance of avoiding statements favouring annexation
and the necessity of respecting the sensibilities of American opinion. And
Lloyd George himself came under such pressure that he felt compelled to
deliver a major address in order to allay mounting distrust of the reasons for
which so many lives had been sacrificed. He recorded in his memoirs that the
necessity of responding to pacifist propaganda dictated that '[i]t was essential
to convince the nation that we were not continuing the war merely to gain
vindictive or looting triumph, but that we had definite peace aims and that
these were both just and attainable'.[37] Thus, in an act which marked a break,

[35] W. Wilson, 'An Address to a Joint Session of Congress, January 8, 1918', *The Papers of
Woodrow Wilson*, vol. 45, ed. A. S. Link (Princeton, NJ: Princeton University Press, 1984), 534–9.
[36] T. J. Knock, 'Wilsonian Concepts and International Realities at the End of the War', in
M. F. Boemeke, G. D. Feldman, and E. Glaser (eds.), *The Treaty of Versailles: A Reassessment
After Seventy-Five Years* (Cambridge: Cambridge University Press, 1998), 115; and Taylor, *The
Trouble Makers*, 149.
[37] D. Lloyd George, *War Memoirs of David Lloyd George*, vol. 5 (London: Ivor Nicholson &
Watson, 1936), 2484.

at least publicly, with the traditional principles of European diplomacy, Lloyd George issued a peace declaration before a gathering of trade unions at Caxton Hall that paid ideological tribute to the progressive principles endorsed by the British labour movement several weeks earlier.[38]

William Roger Louis suggests that, although Lloyd George delivered the Caxton Hall address three days prior to Wilson's declaration of the fourteen points, the ideas he presented were more 'Wilsonian' than those presented by Wilson himself.[39] Lloyd George issued an unequivocal repudiation of the principles of the past. He denounced, each in its own turn, aggressive war, disregard of treaty obligations, privileged interests, the burden imposed by armaments, and all schemes of domination and conquest as repugnant to the interests and dignity of all humanity. We are fighting, he insisted, for a 'just and lasting peace', a peace that will vindicate the sanctity of treaties and the right of self-determination, and which will result in the creation of an international organization in the hope of sparing future generations the ravages of war. 'The days of the Treaty of Vienna,' he said with an air of finality, 'are long past'.[40] Colonial questions occupied no small part of these remarks. Significantly, Lloyd George proclaimed that principles for achieving peace in Europe were no less applicable in matters pertaining to Africa and Asia. Thus, he distanced himself, on account of 'new circumstances', from the secret understandings concluded at the beginning of the war; and, taking a different tack, he asserted that the disposal of conquered German colonies must be a matter of a general conference 'whose decision must have primary regard to the wishes and interests of the native inhabitants of such colonies'.[41] He then edged towards the idea of trusteeship by saying: '[t]he governing consideration, therefore, in all these cases must be that the inhabitants should be placed under the control of an administration acceptable to themselves, one of whose main purposes will be to prevent their exploitation for the benefit of European capitalists or Governments.'[42] This principle, it is worth noting, is far more exacting than Wilson's proposal for the settlement of colonial questions, a proposal that Lloyd George feared to be overly vague and susceptible to misinterpretation.

The principles contained in the Caxton Hall and Fourteen Points speeches would prove to be enormously important in shaping deliberations concerning the disposal of the German colonies at the Paris Peace Conference. Taken

---

[38] W. R. Louis, *Great Britain and Germany's Lost Colonies, 1914–1919* (Oxford: Clarendon Press, 1967), 93; and Egerton, *Great Britain and the Creation of the League of Nations*, 57–61.

[39] Louis, *Great Britain and Germany's Lost Colonies*, 97.

[40] D. Lloyd George, 'The Peace Declaration: Mr. Lloyd George's Speech to the Trade Unions, 5th January, 1918', *War Memoirs of David Lloyd George*, vol. 5 (London: Ivor Nicholson & Watson, 1936), 2520.   [41] Ibid. 2524.   [42] Ibid. 2524.

together they signalled a reasonable degree of unity respecting Allied war aims, even if they sometimes proceeded from more expedient than virtuous motives. Wilson responded to Lloyd George's declaration by praising the British Prime Minister's candour and by affirming that '[t]here is no confusion of counsel among the adversaries of the Central Powers, no uncertainty of principle, no vagueness of detail.'[43] Of the Fourteen Points, Lloyd George said that they contained nothing 'which is incompatible with the war aims already proclaimed by the British and French Governments', excepting only points pertaining to freedom of the seas and reparations.[44] Crucially, then, these professions of unity publicly aligned Allied war aims with that segment of popular opinion that rejected the right of conquest, denounced the exploitation of dependent peoples, and favoured placing these peoples under some form of internationally supervised control in order to secure their interests. And in doing so Wilson and Lloyd George erected an imposing standard against which impending negotiations concerning the disposal of Germany's colonies would be judged.

The Mandates System

While Wilson and Lloyd George gave positive effect to the idea that the control of the world's dependent peoples should take due account of their interests, the origin of that control, the source of its authority, and the principle of its administration were not at all settled or clear. Both men made much of the right of self-determination; and Lloyd George went so far as to suggest that in respect of Germany's colonies, '[t]he general principle of national self-determination is . . . as applicable in their cases as in those of occupied European territories.'[45] This commitment to self-determination did not necessarily imply political independence, representative institutions, or even organized elections; rather it implied the establishment of some form of control that would safeguard the interests and aid the advancement of the peoples residing in these territories. But the most important thinking about the form that this control should take did not, however, originate with either Wilson or Lloyd George. Wilson's first draft Covenant contained no mention of the fate of dependent peoples, perhaps surprisingly so for a man who was deeply impressed by the idea of popular sovereignty; and Lloyd George made

---

[43] Wilson, 'An Address to a Joint Session of Congress, January 8, 1918', 535.

[44] Lloyd George, *The Truth About Peace Treaties*, i. 73.

[45] Lloyd George, 'The Peace Declaration', 2524; and Louis, *Great Britain and Germany's Lost Colonies*, 6.

no attempt to articulate in concrete terms how far self-determination applied to these peoples.[46] Instead, it was Smuts, a man who openly advocated the annexation of at least a portion of Germany's colonial empire, who would decisively shape the terms of debate. Smuts laid out ideas for a new world order in a pamphlet entitled *The League of Nations: A Practical Suggestion*, in the belief that the principles of Vienna had outlived their usefulness. A properly constituted league of nations, he argued, must consist in something more than a mechanism intended to prevent the outbreak of war; it must go beyond dealing with the great calamities of international life. The arrangement that Smuts had in mind 'must become part and parcel of the common international life of states, it must be an ever visible living working organ of the polity of civilization'.[47]

Smuts believed that world peace depended fundamentally on the political arrangements that would organize Europe in the aftermath of the war. For he openly fretted that dividing the remnants of the collapsed Russian, Austrian, and Turkish empires as the spoils of war, 'in a return of the old policy of grab and greed and partitions', spelled a future of despair.[48] But he too doubted that political independence provided a viable alternative to imperial dependence. A lack of preparation all but ruled out membership in the family of nations: '[t]he peoples left behind by the decomposition of Russia, Austria, and Turkey are mostly untrained politically; many of them are either incapable of or deficient in power of self-government; they are mostly destitute and will require much nursing towards economic and political independence.'[49] The mandates system represented the middle way between annexation and anarchy; that is, between aggrandizement and the chaos Smuts believed would surely follow a premature granting of political independence. It would act as a receiver for Europe's shattered empires—as an 'heir' to a 'great estate' as he described it—that would guide these peoples along the path of progress so that one day they too would take their place in the family of nations. But the great variation in the condition of life in these territories meant that the provision of guidance 'must necessarily vary from case to case, according to the development, administrative or police capacity, and homogeneous character of the people concerned'.[50] For Smuts, peoples that disclosed some capacity for the art of self-government would require only minimal guidance from an external authority; others, on account of a heterogeneous national character, would require rather more extensive guidance.

---

[46] W. Wilson, 'Wilson's First Draft', *The Drafting of the Covenant*, vol. 2, ed. D. H. Miller (New York: G. P. Putnam's Sons, 1928), 12–15.

[47] J. C. Smuts, 'The League of Nations: A Practical Suggestion', *The Drafting of the Covenant*, vol. 2, ed. D. H. Miller (New York: G. P. Putnam's Sons, 1928), 25.   [48] Ibid. 28.

[49] Ibid. 26.   [50] Ibid. 32.

It is in this respect that the idea of self-determination applied to peoples of the non-European world. Self-determination implied granting powers of self-government and autonomy in proportion to the capacity of a people to make good use of them.[51]

But Smuts entertained no hope that a league of nations could by itself supply guidance to peoples in any state of development. He submitted that, while joint international administration worked well in regulating postal matters and the use of international waterways, when applied to the administration of underdeveloped peoples the results have been uniformly disappointing. The difficult and exacting enterprise of administering a distant territory, he argued, required a wealth of experience that only a few specially qualified states possessed.[52] Thus, he recommended that in some cases the League of Nations should delegate its authority to an appointed 'agent or mandatary' that was better placed to undertake the administration of a particular people.[53] Mandatory powers would be expected to establish conditions of equal economic opportunity for all states, limit military forces to those required for the maintenance of public order, and conduct their administration according to certain principles prescribed by the league. However, all rights of authority, control, and administration would be ultimately reserved to the League of Nations in order to ensure the faithful application of these principles. Indeed, Smuts evinced great optimism, in a spirit suggestive of the aspirations of the Berlin Act 30 years earlier, that such a mandates system would remove from world affairs an important source of European rivalry.

But Smuts conceived the mandates system, not as a means by which to secure national advantage, but as a trust in the strictest sense of the word. 'The mandatary state,' he wrote, 'should look upon its position as a great trust and honor, not as an office of profit or a position of private advantage for it or its nationals'.[54] And in order to guard against the sort of misrule that occurred in the Congo Free State, Smuts proposed a number of safeguards that went well beyond the provisions of the Berlin Act. Dependent peoples should be consulted in the nomination of their mandatory power, they should be entitled to petition the league of nations in order to seek relief of grievance, and the league of nations should seek periodic reports to ensure the faithful discharge of the trust. Moreover, he proposed that 'in case of any flagrant and prolonged abuse of this trust', the League of Nations should 'assert its authority to the full, even to the extent of removing the mandate, and entrusting it to some other state, if necessary'.[55]

---

[51] J. C. Smuts, 'The League of Nations: A Practical Suggestion', 25–9.
[52] Ibid. 30.   [53] Ibid. 32.   [54] Ibid. 32.   [55] Ibid. 31–3.

It is perhaps surprising that Smuts scarcely mentions the disposition of Germany's overseas empire in his brief, albeit far-sighted, proposal. The mandates system was meant to apply only to the territories of the Russian, Austrian, and Turkish empires. The German colonies, he argued, were 'inhabited by barbarians, who not only cannot possibly govern themselves, but to whom it would be impracticable to apply any idea of political self-determination in the European sense'.[56] Thus, after dismissing the possibility that these peoples might want to remain under German rule, he suggested their future would be best decided in accordance with the fifth of Wilson's fourteen points. In spite of the ambiguity surrounding the fate of the German colonies, and his admitted haste in putting thoughts to paper, Smuts' mandates proposal proved to be enormously influential, especially with the American president. Wilson borrowed liberally from the Smuts pamphlet as he appended to the end of his second draft covenant, and to all subsequent drafts, several 'supplementary agreements', which essentially reproduced the mandate idea. Wilson's secretary of state, Robert Lansing, recorded in a memorandum that this second draft represented an attempt to harmonize Wilson's ideas with those put forward by Smuts. The Smuts pamphlet, he recalled, 'contained the rather novel thought that the League was to be "the heir of the Empires" since Imperialism was no more. This catchy phrase sank deep into the mind of the President and impressed him with the wisdom of Smuts.'[57] In a less flattering comment, Lord Robert Cecil mocked Wilson's second draft, saying that '[i]t is almost Smuts and Phillimore combined, with practically no new ideas in it'.[58] But Wilson did not reproduce the Smuts proposal in its entirety, for his supplementary agreements differed in one very important respect: they did not mention Russia and they extended the applicability of the mandates idea to the German colonies.

The Smuts proposal also appears to have been influential with at least a segment of British opinion, even if it did not always sympathize with Wilson's stringent ideological convictions. Most British supporters of the League of Nations idea did not reject the legitimacy of the empire as such. Rather, like Smuts, they viewed the British Empire and the proposed League of Nations as resembling each other, both in principle and in purpose. Smuts

---

[56] Ibid. 28.

[57] R. Lansing, 'A Memorandum by Robert Lansing on Wilson's First "Paris draft" of the Covenant of the League of Nations', *The Papers of Woodrow Wilson*, vol. 54, ed. A. S. Link (Princeton, NJ: Princeton University Press, 1986), 3; on this subject, see also R. Lansing, *The Peace Negotiations: A Personal Narrative* (New York: Houghton Mifflin Company, 1921), 82–5; and D. H. Miller, *The Drafting of the Covenant*, vol. 1 (New York: G. P. Putnam's Sons, 1928), 40–1.

[58] Lord R. Cecil, 'From the Diary of Lord Robert Cecil, January 19, 1919', *The Papers of Woodrow Wilson*, vol. 54, ed. A. S. Link (Princeton, NJ: Princeton University Press, 1986), 152.

drew this likeness so closely that he suggested 'that where the British Empire has been so eminently successful as a political system, the league, working on somewhat similar lines, could not fail to achieve a reasonable measure of success'.[59] Thus, the principles embodied in the mandates system did not strike most British observers as differing in substance from those which guided British colonial administration. And, despite differences in ideological emphasis, the British draft covenant accepted the mandates idea, albeit in less elaborate and specific terms than its American counterpart. The cause of world peace, it recalled, imposes a 'duty incumbent upon the more advanced members of the family of nations to render help and guidance, under sanction of the League, in the development of the administration of states and territories which have not yet attained to stable government'.[60] The fulfilment of this duty included annexing to the Covenant agreements defining the responsibilities of mandatory states and, in an apparent acknowledgement of the principles enshrined in the Berlin and Brussels Acts, conventions 'dealing with arms traffic, liquor traffic, and other tutelage of backward races'.[61] The British draft covenant, and Wilson's second and third drafts in particular, bestowed considerable legitimacy on Smuts' proposed mandates system; and, together, they presented a formidable obstacle to those who held fast to the idea of annexing Germany's colonial possessions. However, while both the British and American drafts indicated at least provisional acceptance of the mandates idea, the British draft's silence on the territories to which the mandates system should apply foreshadowed a split in the negotiations at the Paris Peace Conference.

Impasse at Versailles

By the time the victorious powers gathered in Versailles to repair the peace of the world, there was little talk of leaving the Austrian, Turkish, and German empires intact. The horrors of the war, the human sacrifice and material destruction, and the popularity of the idea of self-determination precluded any real possibility of returning to pre-war territorial arrangements. The fate of the Austrian Empire did not arouse great passions as it disintegrated under the weight of its own decay. Deciding the future of the Turkish Empire was similarly unproblematic because allegations of gross misrule, especially in Armenia, convinced the peacemakers of the need to emancipate Arab and

---

[59] Smuts, 'The League of Nations', 37.
[60] 'British Draft Convention, January 20, 1919, with Notes', *The Drafting of the Covenant*, vol. 2, ed. D. H. Miller (New York: G. P. Putnam's Sons, 1928), 106.   [61] Ibid. 114.

Christian races that had suffered mightily under the Turkish boot. The crimes committed in Armenia struck Lord Cecil as being so shocking that he claimed: '[a]ny change, even the most Imperialistic annexation, would be of benefit to the people who suffered such crimes as that.'[62] Lloyd George similarly denounced Turkish rule as an abuse of trust held on behalf of civilization. The Turk, he declared, 'has been false to his trust, and the trusteeship must be given over to more competent and more equitable hands, chosen by the congress which will settle the affairs of the world'.[63] The character of Turkish rule in territories populated by Arabs and Christians was so repugnant in the eyes of the Allied powers that alternatives to the dismemberment of the Turkish Empire were very few indeed. They rejected without discussion a Turkish overture that sued for the maintenance of the territorial *status quo ante bellum*. The Grand Vizier, Damad Ferid Pasha, admitted Turkey's complicity in the commission of great crimes but maintained nevertheless that equilibrium in the east depended on the preservation of the Turkish Empire. Lord Balfour responded on behalf of the Allied governments by stating plainly that the Turkish people had shown themselves to be unfit to rule over alien races: 'the experiment has been tried too long and too often for there to be the least doubt as to its result.'[64]

While attitudes regarding the fate of the Austrian and Turkish empires disclosed no fundamental divergence of opinion, the disposition of the German colonies proved to be a far more contentious issue, inasmuch as the negotiations concerning their fate revealed a very deep rift among the peacemakers. It was at this point that Wilson's ideological convictions and his profound distrust of imperialism collided with the annexationist aspirations of the British Empire's southern dominions: Australia, New Zealand, and South Africa.[65] The difficulty in obtaining consensus on the disposal of Germany's colonial possessions followed from the long-standing British interest of imperial security, and the need to reconcile that interest with declarations in favour of a new world order founded on principles of the new diplomacy. Thus, the main problem confronting the British Empire, as Louis observes,

---

[62] Lord R. Cecil, 'Speech, House of Commons, May 16, 1917', *British Documents on Foreign Affairs: Reports and Papers From the Foreign Office Confidential Print*, part II, series H, vol. 4 (Frederick, MD: University Press of America, 1989), 405.

[63] D. Lloyd George, 'Speech, Glasgow, June 29, 1917', *British Documents on Foreign Affairs: Reports and Papers From the Foreign Office Confidential Print*, part II, series H, vol. 4 (Frederick, MD: University Press of America, 1989), 405.

[64] Quoted in D. Lloyd George, *The Truth About Peace Treaties*, vol. 2 (London: Victor Gallancz, 1938), 1011.

[65] For an overview of the Dominion's position, see H. D. Hall, 'The British Commonwealth and the Founding of the League Mandate System', in K. Bourne and D. C. Watt (eds.), *Studies in International History* (London: Longman, 1967).

was finding a way of achieving imperial security without alienating Wilson or betraying the idea of a 'Wilsonian' peace.[66] Louis contends that Britain worked towards this goal, in part, by casting opprobrium on Germany's fitness as a colonial master, even though most Britons approved of German colonial administration prior to the outbreak of war. Before then the Germans were generally highly regarded for the efficiency with which they developed their overseas territories. Indeed, they were included as members of an ascendant Anglo-Teutonic race that was gradually taking the place of declining Latin races—the French, Belgians, and Portuguese, who through misrule and cruelty were deemed to have forfeited their claim to colonial rule.[67]

The sudden popularity of portraying German colonial administration in a bad light strengthened arguments in favour of stripping Germany of its colonial possessions. Evans Lewin alleged early on in the war that Germany had failed both in its native policy and in the colonization and exploitation of its African colonies. The German colonial administrator was said to have dispensed justice unevenly, encroached upon native lands, exhibited little sympathy for the needs of native subjects, and demonstrated little ability or inclination to free himself from the inflexible methods and habits of Prussian bureaucracy from which many of these problems arose. In short, then, the German 'lacked the broader instinct of compromise, which has so frequently saved British administrators from errors that might have led to disastrous results'.[68] Reports submitted to the British Parliament seemingly confirmed Lewin's assessment, as they recorded numerous examples of German administrators treating their native subjects quite harshly. For example, E. H. M. Georges submitted a report on the state of affairs in German South West Africa that asserted:

a large amount of evidence is presented which contains irrefutable proofs of the gross ineptitude with which Germany entered upon her scheme of colonising this territory, of the callous indifference with which she treated the guaranteed rights of the native peoples established here, and of the cruelties to which she subjected those peoples when the burden became too heavy and they attempted to assert their rights.[69]

Georges added, in the same vein as Lewin, that the failure of this administration was attributable to something that the German lacked and the Englishman possessed—a special understanding of native usages and customs.[70] It is important to realize that these views were not restricted to ardent imperialists

---

[66] Louis, *Great Britain and Germany's Lost Colonies*, 7.   [67] Ibid. 35.

[68] E. Lewin, *The Germans in Africa: Their Aims on the Dark Continent and How They Acquired Their African Colonies* (New York: Frederick A. Stokes Company, 1915), 112.

[69] E. H. M. Georges, 'Report on the Natives of South-West Africa and Their Treatment by Germany', *Parliamentary Papers*, Cmd. 9146, xvii, (1918), 4.   [70] Ibid. 10.

seeking to obtain advantage at Germany's expense; nor were they limited to persons driven by a deeply held humanitarian impulse or some purely altruistic motive. George Beer, an American colonial expert who was surely not possessed of an overriding imperial interest, contended that the character and magnitude of German misrule in Africa confirmed a 'total failure to appreciate the duties of colonial trusteeship'.[71] And with this ostensible confirmation of German misrule and incompetence is was easy for Lord Cecil to declare before Parliament: 'I do not say that we attacked the conquered German African colonies in order to rescue the native from misgovernment... but, having rescued them, are you to hand them back?'[72]

Allegations of German misrule, even if it was at times disingenuous and self-serving, provided a powerful rejoinder to any suggestion that Germany's lost colonies should be returned. Germany, this argument supposed, had regressed into barbarism and, therefore, could no longer be trusted in the supervision of underdeveloped peoples. The earliest discussions concerning the disposal of the German colonies implied just that. The Germans, Lloyd George said, had been very harsh in their treatment of their native subjects and they encouraged their native troops to act in ways that 'would even disgrace the Bolsheviks'.[73] Delegates to the peace conference also dispensed with the idea of direct international rule, or what Smuts called joint international administration, in equally expeditious fashion. There was general agreement that direct or joint international administration would lead only to confusion of authority and, thus, to the wholly undesirable results obtained in the Congo and the New Hebrides.[74] The impossibility of restoration and the unsuitability of joint international control set the stage for an engaging and often acrimonious debate between Wilson, who strongly favoured some form of trusteeship, and the leaders of the southern dominions, who favoured just as strongly outright annexation. And in that respect the future of Germany's colonial possessions turned on a conflict between the obligations of trusteeship and the imperatives of national security.

New Zealand claimed Samoa, an island W. F. Massey described as being the 'key to the Pacific', in order to buttress its security. Smuts argued that German South West Africa should rightly pass to South African hands because of German intrigue in South African affairs, and on account of the natural geographical unity exhibited by the two territories. It is worth nothing that Smuts, the same man who pleaded for a peace founded on the principles of self-determination and no annexations, justified South Africa's claim by

---

[71] G. L. Beer, *African Questions at the Paris Peace Conference*, ed. L. H. Gray (New York: Macmillan, 1923), 58.　　　　[72] Cecil, 'Speech, House of Commons, May 16, 1917', 98.
[73] 'BC-10, Quai d'Orsay, January 24, 1919', *The Paris Peace Conference*, vol. 3 (Washington, DC: Government Printing Office, 1943), 718.　　　　[74] Ibid. 719, 721–7.

suggesting: 'there might be a strong case for the administration of the other German possessions in Africa by a mandatory,' but that South West Africa did not represent such a case.[75] But it was the Australian Prime Minister, W. M. Hughes, who spoke most forcefully in support of annexation. In staking a claim to the largest of Germany's Pacific islands, Hughes said that Australia could not be at peace so long as New Guinea was in the hands of a superior power, be it a European power or the League of Nations. The Pacific islands, he continued, 'encompassed Australia like a fortress' and were consequently 'as necessary to Australia as water to a city'.[76] Hughes then went on to question the wisdom and desirability of the mandatory principle itself. Past experience convinced him of the superiority of direct rule. He dismissed popular opinion set against annexation as being fundamentally misplaced. Australia, he countered, fought alongside the democracies of Europe and America in a great struggle against militarism and for liberty; and, like other responsible democracies, it would not tolerate the exploitation of under-developed peoples subject to its rule. Thus, Hughes summarized the Australian claim to New Guinea by asserting: 'Australia had governed New Guinea; New Guinea was essential to the safety of Australia; Australia was a democracy; the Australians were on the spot; Australia knew what New Guinea wanted far better than any League of Nations.'[77]

Acceptance of the mandates idea seemed to be very much in doubt when France indicated its support of the arguments articulated by Hughes and Massey, and its principal author, Smuts. Mr Simon agreed that the disadvantages of a mandates system outweighed the disadvantages of annexation. Thus, he declared that he had come that day to speak in favour of annexation, the only policy he believed that would 'accomplish the double object of every colonial government worthy of the name, namely, the development of the country and the effective protection of the natives during the period required for their development toward a higher plane of civilization'.[78] The frankness with which Simon presented the French position provoked disappointment in Wilson, who observed that thus far the deliberations amounted to an unambiguous repudiation of some form of internationally supervised trusteeship. The world, he reminded the Conference, would surely interpret the annexation of German colonial possessions as a crude partition of the spoils of conquest. Partition would surely entail a denial of the new

[75] 'BC-10' and 'BC-13', *The Paris Peace Conference*, 722–3, 726, 751.

[76] 'BC-10', *The Paris Peace Conference*, 720–1.

[77] 'BC-12, Quai d'Orsay, January 27, 1919', *The Paris Peace Conference*, vol. 3 (Washington, DC: Government Printing Office, 1943), 746–7.

[78] 'BC-14, Quai d'Orsay, January 28, 1919', *The Paris Peace Conference*, vol. 3 (Washington, DC: Government Printing Office, 1943), 761.

diplomacy and the hope of a new world order founded on principles of right and justice. And such a settlement, Wilson feared, would be disastrous: 'it would make the League of Nations impossible, and they would have to return to the system of competitive armaments with accumulating debts and the burden of great armies.'[79] Wilson would not accept a return to the practices of the past; for he understood the work of the Conference as charting a wholly new course, one devoid of historical precedent. Indeed, he demanded an entirely new arrangement that embraced the principle of trusteeship, uncorrupted by the impulse of annexation, and which repudiated the dubious principles of Vienna once and for all.

In spite of Wilson's insistence that the Conference accept 'the genuine idea of trusteeship', disagreement over the disposal of the German colonies centred on means rather than ends. For Wilson, trusteeship consisted in 'the development of the country for the benefit of those already in it, and for the advantage of those who would live there later'.[80] At no point, though, did any member of the Conference disavow this obligation. Hughes and Massey in particular declared themselves to be in favour of, and fully committed to, the obligations of trusteeship. Hughes did not equivocate when he said Australia would agree to requirements respecting the well-being of native peoples; for '[i]t was reasonable and fair that the rights of the natives should be insisted upon'.[81] Likewise, Massey made every effort to assure the American president that New Zealand was committed to ruling dependent peoples assigned to its jurisdiction in the spirit that Wilson advocated. And he offered as proof New Zealand's putative success in ruling the Maoris in claiming that annexation would satisfy the obligations of trusteeship by aiding 'the education of the native races, not only in secular matters, but also in the principles of Christianity, which he believed were necessary for the welfare of all nations'.[82] The French were no less earnest in professing their commitment to the obligations of trusteeship. Simon noted that dependent peoples subject to French rule possessed the same rights as French citizens, they enjoyed representation in the French Chamber, and their system of local government did not differ in principle from the government of France. The world need not fear that annexation might lead to exploitation and maltreatment of native peoples, he continued, for all great powers recognized that the obligations of trusteeship entailed nothing less than the maintenance of peace, the provision of education, and protection against the evils inflicted by alcohol and firearms. Indeed, Simon asserted that the time of rapacious

---

[79] Ibid. 766.   [80] 'BC-12', *The Paris Peace Conference*, 740.
[81] 'BC-10, Quai d'Orsay, January 24, 1919', *The Papers of Woodrow Wilson*, vol. 54, ed. A. S. Link (Princeton, NJ: Princeton University Press, 1986), 252.
[82] 'BC-13' and 'BC-18', *The Paris Peace Conference*, 751–2, 798.

exploitation had already passed and that all great powers 'considered their colonies as wards entrusted to them by the world'.[83]

Faced with Wilson's unyielding resistance, Lloyd George presented a compromise in the hope of reconciling what were for the Conference conflicting obligations. In an attempt to convince the Conference that acceptance of the mandates idea would not entail significant deviation from accepted principles of colonial administration, he pointed out that

there was no large difference between the mandatory principle and the principles laid down by the Berlin Conference, under which Great Britain, France, and Germany held many of their colonies. This Conference had framed conditions about the open door, the prohibition of the arms and liquor traffic, which resembled those President Wilson had in view in many respects, except that no external machinery had been provided for their enforcement.[84]

The compromise that eventually won the support of the British dominions took as a point of departure this experience, in order to fashion a resolution that endeavoured to satisfy the demands of security as well as those of trusteeship. Thus, the Conference resolved that the welfare of the peoples of the German and Turkish Empires should be 'entrusted to advanced nations who by reason of their resources, their experience or their geographical position, can best undertake the responsibility, and that this tutelage should be exercised by them as mandatories on behalf of the League of Nations'.[85]

Owing to the different degrees of development that these peoples disclosed, it was also decided that the responsibilities of the mandatory powers should vary in accordance with the particular conditions of the territories in question. Hence the resolution established three categories of mandates: (1) former Turkish territories that were granted provisional recognition of independence, subject to the receipt of administrative advice and assistance; (2) former German territories in Central Africa that were administered according to principles that approximated those contained in the Berlin Act; and (3) territories that were administered as integral parts of a mandatory power on account of their sparse population, small size, distance from centres of civilization, or geographical contiguity to that power.[86] The creation of this third category, the 'C' mandates, which applied to New Guinea, Samoa, and South West Africa, satisfied the demand for security by granting a degree of

---

[83] 'BC-14', *The Paris Peace Conference*, 760–1.

[84] 'BC-13, Quai d'Orsay, January 24, 1919', *The Papers of Woodrow Wilson*, vol. 54, ed. A. S. Link (Princeton, NJ: Princeton University Press, 1986), 310–11.

[85] 'Draft Resolutions in Reference to Mandatories', *The Paris Peace Conference*, vol. 3 (Washington, DC: Government Printing Office, 1943), 795.

[86] Ibid. *The Paris Peace Conference*, 795–6.

control that differed only slightly from that exercised over a formal colony. Thus, Hughes, satisfied by this degree of control, finally conceded that 'he did not feel justified in opposing the views of President Wilson and those of Mr. Lloyd George, beyond the point which would reasonably safeguard the interests of Australia'.[87]

Trusteeship or Deception?

Even though the dominions did not agree fully with the fundamental premise of Lloyd George's compromise—they never disowned their preference for annexation—acceptance of the mandates system marked a definite triumph for Wilson and for the idea of trusteeship. David Hunter Miller, a member of the American delegation, recorded in his diary that Wilson had hoped for a more ambitious resolution, but that the President nevertheless concurred with his view that the resolution represented a great achievement.[88] Indeed, the resolution formed the basis of what would become Article 22 of the League of Nations Covenant. Wilson said of a draft of this article that the peacemakers had finally put an end to territorial aggrandizement and to the exploitation of the world's most disadvantaged peoples. For we have come to recognize, he submitted to the Conference,

in the most solemn manner that the helpless and undeveloped peoples of the world, being in that condition, put an obligation upon us to look after their interests primarily before we use them for our interest, and that in all cases of this sort hereafter it shall be the duty of the League to see that the nations which are assigned as the tutors and advisors and directors of those peoples, shall look to their interests and to their development before they look to the interest and material desires of the mandatory nation itself.[89]

It is in this spirit that Article 22 declares:

To those colonies and territories ... not yet able to stand by themselves under the strenuous conditions of the modern world, there should be applied the principle that the well-being and development of such peoples form a sacred trust of civilisation and that securities for the performance of this trust should be embodied in this Covenant.[90]

[87] 'BC-17, Quai d'Orsay, January 30, 1919', *The Paris Peace Conference*, vol. 3 (Washington, DC: Government Printing Office, 1943), 786.
[88] D. H. Miller, 'From the Diary of David Hunter Miller', *The Papers of Woodrow Wilson*, vol. 54, ed. A. S. Link (Princeton, NJ: Princeton University Press, 1986), 379.
[89] 'Plenary Session of the Peace Conference, February 14, 1919', *The Drafting of the Covenant*, vol. 2, ed. D. H. Miller (New York: G. P. Putnam's Sons, 1928), 564.
[90] 'Covenant Text in the Treaty of Versailles', *The Drafting of the Covenant*, vol. 2 (New York: G. P. Putnam's Sons, 1928), 737.

With these words the founders of the League of Nations took a momentous step beyond the idea of trusteeship that the European powers had enshrined in the Berlin and Brussels Acts. Not only did they affirm that the well-being of subject peoples constituted a legitimate subject of international scrutiny, they also erected what was often referred to as 'international machinery' to ensure the faithful performance of the obligations of trusteeship.

These obligations were enumerated in specific mandate treaties, which established in international law the responsibilities of particular mandatory powers, and in several related international agreements. All mandated territories were to enjoy freedom of conscience and of all forms of worship, subject to requirements of public order and morals; and missionary societies were permitted to operate freely irrespective of affiliation or nationality. Additional responsibilities were specified in accordance with a territory's state of development, that is, in terms that corresponded roughly with James Lorimer's division of humanity into civilized, barbarian, and savage peoples.[91] Mandatory powers were vested with few additional administrative duties in the 'A' mandates, the former territories of the Turkish Empire, outside of the conduct of foreign relations. In contrast, the rather extensive obligations imposed upon mandatory powers in the 'B' mandates, the former German colonies in Central Africa, were noteworthy in so far as they very closely reflected the obligations enshrined in the Berlin and Brussels Acts. Mandatories in these territories were responsible for establishing freedom of commerce; preventing or regulating abuses such as slavery and the slave trade, the arms and liquor traffic, forced and compulsory labour; and they were prohibited from constructing military fortifications. Responsibilities in the controversial 'C' mandates, which included South West Africa, New Guinea, and Samoa, differed from the 'B' mandates only to the extent that mandatory powers were under no obligation to maintain the open door. And in both classes of mandate, 'B' and 'C', supervising powers were obliged to 'promote to the utmost the material and moral well-being and the social progress of its inhabitants'.[92]

Many of these responsibilities were clarified in general instruments of international law and were extended to apply to parts of Asia and to nearly the entire continent of Africa. But the extension of these responsibilities did not result in wholly new agreements; rather, at the first meeting of the

[91] See J. Lorimer, *The Institutes of the Law of Nations: A Treatise of the Jural Relations of Separate Political Communities*, vol. 1 (Edinburgh: William Blackwood and Sons, 1883), 100–1.

[92] G. Schwarzenberger, *Power Politics: A Study of International Society* (New York: Frederick A. Praeger, 1951), 652–60; the mandate treaties are reprinted in the appendices of Q. Wright, *Mandates Under the League of Nations* (Chicago: University of Chicago Press, 1930), 593–621.

Permanent Mandates Commission, members set out to regulate the traffic in firearms and liquor, and, significantly, to revise sections of the Berlin and Brussels Acts.[93] They agreed to prohibit the export of arms and ammunition to parts of Asia, including Transcaucasia, Persia, and the Arabian peninsula, and to the entire continent of Africa, except for Algeria, Libya, and South Africa. They similarly agreed to prohibit the importation, distribution, sale, and possession of spirituous liquors in sub-Saharan Africa, again, except for South Africa.[94] In revising the Berlin and Brussels Acts, contracting parties reaffirmed principles that included the establishment of complete economic equality in territories comprising the Congo basin and freedom of navigation on the Congo and Niger rivers, and on all of their tributary waterways. They also pledged that they would 'continue to watch over the preservation of the native populations and to supervise the improvement of the conditions of their moral and material well-being', including the suppression of slavery, the promotion and protection of religious, scientific, and charitable institutions, and the guarantee of freedom of conscience and the free exercise of religious faith.[95]

This rather elaborate codification of the obligations of trusteeship did not impress all who were interested in such matters. Many newspaper editors, even those that had expressed sympathy and desire for a Wilsonian peace, interpreted the mandates system as a thinly disguised division of the spoils.[96] Members of the Labour movement, the various peace societies, and the UDC also greeted the mandates system with suspicion, if not open disappointment. Brailsford asked why the mandatory principle, which asked that civilized nations conduct themselves honourably towards backward peoples, should not be generalized and applied to all subject peoples of the world. For the only defence of white rule in Africa, he argued, consisted in a trust undertaken by the imperial powers 'on behalf of the whole civilised world, in the interests of the natives'.[97] Dickinson regarded no section of the Covenant as more important than Article 22, but he complained bitterly about the

[93] A. Walworth, *Wilson and His Peacemakers: American Diplomacy at the Paris Peace Conference, 1919* (New York: W. W. Norton & Company, 1986), 486; and Wright, *Mandates Under the League of Nations*, 219.

[94] 'Treaty of St. Germain, September 10, 1919 and Convention Relating to the Liquor Traffic in Africa, and Protocol', reprinted in Beer, *African Questions at the Paris Peace Conference*, 483–506.

[95] 'Convention Revising the General Act of Berlin, February 26, 1885, and the General Act and Declaration of Brussels, July 2, 1890', reprinted in Beer, *African Questions at the Paris Peace Conference*, 507–14.

[96] Louis, *Great Britain and Germany's Lost Colonies*, 139–42; and Walworth, *Wilson and His Peacemakers*, 78.   [97] Brailsford, *Olives of an Endless Age*, 339.

disingenuous spirit with which the Allied governments implemented it. They were no less enamoured with the profit of crude economic exploitation, he charged, than they were at the start of the war. Indeed, he lamented that 'the Covenant of the League can never be anything more than a piece of solemn hypocrisy' so long as their 'real' interests remained fixed on securing oil, phosphate, and other raw materials.[98] Even Robert Lansing, a member of the American peace delegation, meted out harsh criticism. He doubted, as did Hughes and Massey, that the mandates system afforded any peculiar advantage over the traditional practice of annexation; for '[i]n actual operation,' he said, 'the apparent altruism of the mandatory system worked in favour of the selfish and material interests of the Powers which accepted the mandates'.[99]

The implementation of the mandates system did not of course pass without controversy or defect. For example, the inhabitants of the 'A' mandates were not consulted in the nomination of supervising powers, even though Article 22 stipulated that 'the wishes of these communities must be a principal consideration in the selection of the Mandatory'.[100] Critics of the Palestine mandate argued that the establishment of a Jewish national home, as required in the mandate treaty, conflicted with the principle that the inhabitants' interests must be the first and primary concern of mandatory rule. Likewise, the French were alleged to have made a mockery of the mandatory principle by reserving its right to press natives under its supervision into military service. Other complaints centred on the fact that the mandates system did not always contribute to peaceful development. Armed rebellion erupted in Mesopotamia, Syria, and South West Africa; and violence frequently disrupted life in Palestine as Jews and Arabs fought over immigration policy. In more remote and undeveloped territories the guarantees and protections afforded by the mandates system were poorly understood, if understood at all, by native peoples. They seldom made use of their right of petition, and they seemed to make no distinction between the imperial authority under which they once lived and the League appointed authority that succeeded imperial control.[101]

These guarantees and protections did not in any case render mandatories or the Mandates Commission immune from the same questions that beset colonial administrators. Should mandatory rule be direct or indirect? To

---

[98] G. L. Dickinson, *Causes of International War* (New York: Garland Publishing, 1972), 92–101.   [99] Lansing, *The Peace Negotiations*, 156–7.

[100] Wright, *Mandates Under the League of Nations*, 62; and 'Covenant Text in the Treaty of Versailles', 737.

[101] Wright, *Mandates Under the League of Nations*, 62, 72, 92–5, 578; and Dickinson, *Causes of International War*, 94.

what extent should administrators seek to preserve native customs and institutions? Or should the traditions of native life be swept away in favour of the progressive enlightenment of civilized life? One member of the Commission, D. F. W. Van Rees, declared his preference for direct rule by saying: 'the least perfect European administration was one hundred times better than a purely native administration.'[102] Lord Lugard, who was also a member of the Commission, responded by saying that such a view was contrary to the idea that mandated peoples were to be prepared to stand alone. With respect to native customs, Kunio Yanaghita suggested that while mandatory governments agreed that repugnant native practices ought to be abolished without delay, those which were not impediments to progress should be left in undisturbed. And Freire d'Andrade argued that since the moral education and development of native peoples 'must take scores of years, or even centuries,' they should not be permitted to idle in the meantime.[103] Similar debates took up questions concerning land use, health, labour, education, and language of instruction; and in each cases we encounter the voices of Charles Grant, James Mill, T. B. Macaulay, Thomas Munro, David Livingstone, and, of course, Lord Lugard.

Quincy Wright aptly described the creation and implementation of the mandates system, and the debates to which it gave rise, as 'mutilated in details, sullied by the spirit of barter, delayed in confirmation, and minified by the mandatories'.[104] But in spite of obvious defects and shortcomings, the mandates system experienced a considerable degree of acceptance and success. Wright observed that with few exceptions the League Council implemented most of the Commission's recommendations and that it diligently scrutinized the confirmation of mandates in order to ensure their conformity with the intent of Article 22. To this evidence he added that mandatory powers were not negligent in forwarding petitions of complaint, answering questions about their administration, or providing annual reports as stipulated in the mandate treaties. Mandatories sometimes complained of the expense incurred in administering mandated territories, but they did not question the fundamental principle that the interests of native inhabitants were the foremost concern of their administration.[105] Thus, it is no exaggeration to say that the mandatory powers, not to mention the League's general membership, regarded the mandates system as a reasonable success.

---

[102] Quoted in Wright, *Mandates Under the League of Nations*, 244.
[104] Ibid. 63.
[103] Ibid. 242–54.
[105] Ibid. 98, 580.

Novelty and Tradition

In the mandates system, the peacemakers at Versailles invented a new way of ordering the relations of European and non-European peoples. Critics, of which there were many, derided the League experiment as a self-serving disguise, which shrouded beneath a thin veneer of hypocrisy the operation of the selfish, pernicious, and, indeed, dangerous principles of the old diplomacy. A despondent Smuts, fearing that the chance for a new world order had been lost, complained that instead of a Wilsonian peace, the world would be presented with a 'reactionary Peace—the most reactionary since Scipio Africanus dealt with Carthage'.[106] And in what is perhaps the most famous polemic attacking the Versailles settlement, John Maynard Keynes suggested that an intellectually feeble Wilson had been hoodwinked by vastly more skilled European statesmen into accepting a wholly inadequate peace. For Keynes, the stakes of diplomacy were obvious:

[p]rudence required some measure of lip service to the "ideals" of foolish Americans and hypocritical Englishmen; but it would be stupid to believe that there is much room in the world, as it really is, for such affairs as the League of Nations, or any sense in the principle of self-determination except as an ingenious formula for rearranging the balance of power in one's own interests.[107]

But the League of Nations surely represented something more than a deceptive and ingenious formula meant to obscure the practice of power politics. Alfred Zimmern described the League of Nations, not inaccurately, as consisting in something more than a convenient mechanism of power politics: 'it represents a great political ideal'.[108] And the authors of the Versailles settlement certainly worked out that ideal in the very imperfect world of human relations. The fact that it became somewhat tarnished does not impute its authenticity.

The same may be said of the mandates system. Wright was not mistaken when he said that the system was not a 'product of disinterested juristic thought nor of detached scientific investigation but was a compromise invented by the Versailles statesmen to meet an immediate political dilemma'.[109] In reaching this compromise, it is true, most states remained fixed on the all important search for security. The minutes of the deliberations indicate that much. But, in seeking security, the men who gathered at

---

[106] J. C. Smuts, 'To M.C. Gillett, 19 May 1919', *Selections from the Smuts Papers*, vol. 4, eds. W. K. Hancock and J. Van Der Poel (Cambridge: Cambridge University Press, 1966), 171.

[107] J. M. Keynes, *The Economic Consequences of the Peace* (New York: Harper Torchbooks, 1920), 33.

[108] A. Zimmern, *The Third British Empire* (Oxford: Oxford University Press, 1934), 95.

[109] Wright, *Mandates Under the League of Nations*, 3.

Versailles gave positive effect to the principle that the pursuit of national interests could not entail the exploitation or neglect of 'backward' peoples. They were obliged as well to attend to their well-being so that they too might one day join the family of nations. Thus, above all else, the mandate system afforded these peoples protection from tyranny. The machinery and procedures that were created to ensure the orderly and just performance of these obligations represented a truly novel system, which found its origin in international law rather than in national sovereignty. Under the mandates system 'backward' peoples became subjects of international law; and because they were endowed with rights established in international law, they, or a third party, could appeal directly to the League for relief of grievances. Thus, Wright concluded:

While ordinarily rights under international law vest only in states, it appears that the mandated peoples have a status, withdrawing them from the sovereignty of any state and giving them the opportunity to invoke the direct protection of the League, which makes it not inappropriate to speak of them as enjoying rights under international law correlative to the duties imposed by the mandates upon the mandatories for their benefit.[110]

Although the mandates system marks a most important development in the administration of subject peoples, the principles in which it was grounded are anything but novel. In fact, what is striking is the extent to which the mandates system reflects the assumptions and principles of British colonial administration. The graduated understanding that emerged in nineteenth century British Africa lies at the very centre of Article 22 and the mandates system generally. But the fundamental moral claim of Article 22 reaches further back to the thought of Edmund Burke and the idea that political power ought to benefit those people that are subject to it. Thus, the mandates system discloses a lineage that runs from Burke, through the Berlin and Brussels Acts, to the Kenya White Paper of 1923. Perhaps it should come as no surprise, then, that Smuts was fond of comparing the British Empire and the League of Nations. In proposing the mandates idea, Smuts suggested that 'the British Empire was the nearest approach to the league of nations'.[111] Alfred Zimmern did not mistake the continuity of these ideas; for he understood the mandates system as the constitutional form of earlier theories of colonial government, which obtained their justification in the idea of trusteeship. 'This conception,' he wrote, ' has been implicitly in British colonial policy at least since the time of Burke's indictment of Warren Hastings; but its international consecration carries it a long stage further than that exemplified either in the Pronouncement of August 1917 or in the Kenya White Paper'.[112]

---

[110] Ibid. 457, 473–4.   [111] Smuts, 'The League of Nations', 36.
[112] Zimmern, *The Third British Empire*, 21.

5

The Destruction of the Legitimacy of Trusteeship

The place and purpose of trusteeship in the post-Second World War world order aroused passions and suspicions that were no less pronounced than those which threatened to disrupt the peace negotiations at Versailles two decades earlier. These tensions, which divided the United States and Great Britain in particular, emanated from a fundamental disagreement over the purpose of trusteeship and its relation to the future of empire in world affairs. British commentators on empire tended to interpret the idea of trusteeship in the context of an imperial tradition that dated back to Edmund Burke's interest in the affairs of the East India Company. They invoked trusteeship as a principle against which to judge colonial administration and, therefore, understood the tutelage of dependent peoples as a justification of empire. Americans, who were born of a very different colonial and political experience, were a great deal less inclined to see trusteeship as a justification of empire than as an alternative to the perpetuation of empire. In this chapter I want to interrogate the claims that structured the terms of this debate, how they shaped the purpose of trusteeship as contemplated in the Charter of the United Nations, and the ideas upon which the anti-colonial movement seized in order to destroy the legitimacy of trusteeship in international society.

The Atlantic Charter and the Future of Empire

The divide that separated American and British attitudes towards trusteeship during the Second World War is most clearly evident in their respective responses to the Atlantic Charter. Winston Churchill and Franklin Roosevelt outlined in this historic declaration their hope for a world in which all peoples would enjoy equal economic opportunity and access to raw materials, free and unhindered use of the seas, improved labour standards and social security, a more equitable distribution of wealth, and, significantly, the right 'to choose the government under which they will live'.[1] In this better, more

---

[1] 'The Atlantic Charter, August 14, 1941', in H. S. Commager (ed.), *Documents of American History* (New York: Appleton-Century-Crofts, 1948), 636.

humane world, the use of force would give place to mutual cooperation and power would be subjected to principle; for only then, that is, when right, justice, and the rule of law reigned supreme, would all humanity be able to live their lives in peace and in freedom from fear and want. Indeed, the peoples who aspired to this sort of world constituted, as Roosevelt put it, 'a great union of humanity' whose collective hopes had been 'given form and substance and power through a great gathering of peoples now known as the United Nations'.[2] The Atlantic Charter very quickly came to be regarded as a document of signal importance. Less certain, though, and more contentious to be sure, was its precise meaning in respect of how Roosevelt's great union of humanity might be realized. Churchill's wartime memoirs indicate that the greatest difficulty in negotiating the Atlantic Charter had to do with provisions relating to freedom of trade and access to raw materials.[3] But it appears as if no one anticipated how the right of self-determination, the right of peoples to choose their own government, would ignite an impassioned debate about the future of empire in world affairs. It is in this debate that we encounter two contending notions of trusteeship: one that understood trusteeship as integral to the maintenance of empire, and another which understood trusteeship as an alternative to empire.

That the Atlantic Charter might be interpreted as implying a general right of self-determination did not go unnoticed in Parliament or in the territories of the dependent empire. For instance, the Governor of Burma observed that the Burmese people will ask if the Atlantic Charter is to apply equally to all nations; and, he cautioned, if they are told that they are to be excluded from this great charter of liberty because they are subjects of the British Empire 'they will have quite a lot to say about British justice, and so forth'.[4] The Colonial Office, which generally regarded any endorsement of self-determination as being unnecessarily dangerous, maintained that the diversity of the empire simply precluded the establishment of self-governing institutions in most dependent territories. Considerations of imperial security rendered the idea of self-government unthinkable in some of these territories; in others, a general state of underdevelopment ruled out the possibility of self-government, at least for sometime; and in still others,

[2] See 'Joint Declaration by United Nations, Washington, January 1, 1942' and 'Franklin D. Roosevelt, President: Message to Prime Minister Churchill Commemorating the First Anniversary of the Atlantic Charter, August 14, 1942', in L. W. Holborn (ed.), *War and Peace Aims of the United Nations: September 1, 1939–December 31, 1942* (Boston: World Peace Foundation, 1943), 1, 108.
[3] W. Churchill, *The Grand Alliance* (Boston: Houghton Mifflin Company, 1950), 433–42.
[4] Quoted in D. J. Morgan, *Guidance Towards Self-Government in British Colonies, 1941–1971*, vol. 5 (London: Macmillan, 1980), 2.

settler and native had not yet worked out arrangements of public life that would permit the establishment of self-governing institutions. In short, the Colonial Office deemed most, if not all, of these territories as being unfit 'to stand by themselves under the strenuous conditions of the modern world', to use the language of Article 22 of the League of Nations covenant.[5] And the peoples residing in these territories could hope for no more than some form of limited self-government, under the watchful eye of imperial authority, even though they were not barred entirely from participating in the political life of the Empire. Political development had to respect British principles of good colonial government, and, like the progressivist outlook of Lord Lugard's indirect rule and the League of Nations mandates system, it had to proceed in accordance with the situation and circumstances of particular territories.[6]

Most members of the British government considered the constitutional development of the British Empire as presenting a problem quite separate from that of restoring the sovereign rights of conquered peoples in Europe. Churchill moved to dispel any confusion about the right of self-determination and its application to British territories by stating: 'At the Atlantic Meeting, we had in mind, primarily, the restoration of the sovereignty, self-government and national life of the States and nations of Europe now under the Nazi yoke, and the principles governing any alterations in the territorial boundaries which may have to be made.'[7] Indeed, Churchill rejected without hesitation the suggestion that the principle of self-determination contained in the Atlantic Charter could be applied indiscriminately to the territories of the British Empire. These territories, he argued, must be permitted to evolve gradually and according to established principles of British colonial administration; and adherence to the Atlantic Charter did not alter the general course of their political, economic, and social development. Thus, constitutional development would proceed in India, as promised in the Declaration of August 1940, just as it would, in time, proceed elsewhere in the Empire. In drawing this rather sharp distinction between the affairs of Europe and the affairs of the British Empire, Churchill did not repudiate the principles of the Atlantic Charter as being alien to the principles of British colonial administration; rather, he understood both sets of principles as

---

[5] 'Covenant Text in the Treaty of Versailles', in D. H. Miller (ed.), *The Drafting of the Covenant*, vol. 2 (New York: G. P. Putnam's Sons, 1928), 737.

[6] W. R. Louis, *Imperialism at Bay, 1941–1945: The United States and the Decolonization of the British Empire* (Oxford: Clarendon Press, 1977), 126–9.

[7] W. S. Churchill, 'Speech to the House of Commons, Atlantic Meeting with President Roosevelt, September 9, 1941', in L. W. Holborn (ed.), *War and Peace Aims of the United Nations: September 1, 1939–December 31, 1942* (Boston: World Peace Foundation, 1943), 211.

being born of the same high ideals of human freedom and justice.[8] But this attempt to allay confusion about the Atlantic Charter and its application to the British Empire amounted to little more than a reaffirmation of a tradition of trusteeship that fixed the interests and well-being of dependent peoples as the principal concern of colonial administration.[9] And in acknowledging this end as the overriding, though not singular, rationale of British colonial administration, Churchill wielded the idea of trusteeship as the ultimate justification of empire.

The American government understood the idea of trusteeship as disclosing a very different justification, in part because of a pervasive and historic mistrust of imperialism. Roosevelt made no secret of his dislike of imperialism, even the imperialism of allies united in the struggle against totalitarianism. He found nothing to admire in the French Empire as he believed that corrupt and oppressive rule had done nothing to improve the lot of French colonial subjects. At the Tehran Conference of 1943, he expressed that much to Churchill and Stalin when he said that the inhabitants of Indo-China were, as a consequence of French rule, worse off than had they been left to their own devices. And he made it known, even if this charge of misrule was not entirely true, that he did not wish to see the French Empire restored to its former status at the end of the war. Thus, he suggested that it was better to place the whole of Indo-China under a trusteeship system, in order to prepare its people for independence within a specified period of time, than return it to French rule.[10]

Roosevelt held the British Empire in higher esteem, but the emergency in India in 1942 seemed to confirm his view that British power presented a very real danger to the achievement of general world peace. His fear of British power followed from an appraisal of imperialism that rather closely approximated the positions taken by Woodrow Wilson and Leonard Woolf 25 years earlier. The colonial system, he confided in his son Elliot, supplied dangerous incentives for war and exploited the natural wealth of dependent territories without ever making a commensurate and reciprocal investment in the development of that territory's inhabitants.[11] This indictment of imperialism was no less

---

[8] Ibid. 210–11.

[9] Morgan, *Guidance Towards Self-Government in British Colonies*, 4.

[10] 'Roosevelt–Stalin Meeting, November 28, 1943, 3 P.M., Roosevelt's Quarters, Soviet Embassy', *Foreign Relations of the United States: The Conferences at Cairo and Tehran, 1943* (Washington, DC: Government Printing Office, 1961), 485; and Louis, *Imperialism at Bay*, 27–47.

[11] Louis, *Imperialism at Bay*, 226; L. Woolf, *Empire and Commerce in Africa: A Study in Economic Imperialism* (London: George Allen and Unwin, 1920); and 'BC-14, Quai d'Orsay, January 28, 1919', *The Paris Peace Conference*, vol. 3 (Washington, DC: Government Printing Office, 1943), 766.

pronounced in the attitudes of Roosevelt's most important political rivals. Wendell Willkie, a prominent member of the Republican Party, openly rebuked '[t]hose who sneer when it is suggested that freedom and self-government can be brought to all men' and who feel that underdeveloped peoples 'must be ruled perpetually by some nation's colonial imperialism'.[12] The dependent peoples of the world, he argued, are alive physically, intellectually, and spiritually; and they have awakened to take their rightful place in the world. Indeed, they are, he proclaimed, 'resolved, as we must be, that there is no more place for imperialism within our own society than in the society of nations. The big house on the hill surrounded by mud huts has lost its awesome charm.'[13]

Margery Perham, one of the most thoughtful and informed commentators on the British Empire, attributed this profound and sometimes exaggerated suspicion of imperialism to the legacy of American revolutionary experience. Of this peculiarly American habit of thought, she wrote: '[t]he British are guilty of a sin called Empire. They committed it against the American people until these broke clear of British control to become a nation. The Americans are innocent of such guilt. They thus are in a moral position to condemn Britain as they watch her continuing in her way of sin against other people.'[14] American critics of imperialism were no less certain about how best to remedy the noxious, not to mention dangerous, effects of this sin as they typically regarded the Atlantic Charter as a blueprint for a world based upon the values of liberty, justice, and fraternity. Cordell Hull, Roosevelt's Secretary of State, expressed the substance of this view when he described the Charter as a 'statement of basic principles and fundamental ideas and policies that are universal in their practical application'.[15] Of course not all Americans were comfortable in this opinion. Walter Lippmann denounced the Atlantic Charter as dangerously Wilsonian, in style and in substance, and feared that the pursuit of a perfect moral order, the universal society, would end only in confusion, disorder, and paralysis. 'We shall collaborate best,' he wrote, 'if we start with the homely fact that their families and their homes, their villages and lands, their countries and their own ways, their altars, their flags, and their hearths—not charters, covenants, blueprints, and generalities—are

[12] W. L. Willkie, 'Republican Presidential Candidate, 1940: Report to the People (Broadcast) after Return from Middle East, Russia and China, New York, October 26, 1942', in L. W. Holborn (ed.), *War and Peace Aims of the United Nations: September 1, 1939–December 31, 1942* (Boston: World Peace Foundation, 1943), 657.   [13] Ibid. 653.

[14] M. Perham, 'African Facts and American Criticism', *Colonial Sequence, 1930 to 1949* (London: Methuen & Co, 1967), 250.

[15] C. Hull, 'Comment on the Atlantic Charter, Press Conference, Washington, August 14, 1941', in L. W. Holborn (ed.), *War and Peace Aims of the United Nations: September 1, 1939–December 31, 1942* (Boston: World Peace Foundation, 1943), 45.

what men live for and will, if it is necessary, die for'.[16] But neither Roosevelt nor Hull harboured the illusion that defeating the forces of totalitarianism and implementing the Atlantic Charter would bring about a perfect world in one easy step. They did believe, however, as did most Americans, that a better world could be fashioned out of the principles enshrined in the Charter—principles that were 'true' for all peoples in all places—provided that they and other like-minded nations approached the problem with sufficient determination. Indeed, Roosevelt asserted that the Atlantic Charter expressed an ideal 'so clear-cut that it is difficult to oppose in any major particular'.[17]

This belief in the universal applicability of the Atlantic Charter is especially pronounced in the American-inspired Draft Declaration by the United Nations on National Independence, which affirmed that the 'Atlantic Charter sets forth certain fundamental principles and purposes, applicable to all nations and to all peoples'.[18] Most contentious, though, was language that would have made it the duty of all colonial powers to advance, in cooperation with the United Nations, the political, economic, social, and educational development of the dependent peoples charged to their care. And to these peoples, those not yet 'qualified' to assume the responsibilities of self-governing peoples, the Draft Declaration contemplated granting 'such measure of self-government as they are capable of maintaining in the light of the various stages of their development toward independence'.[19] The ultimate end of this programme of development was stated repeatedly and unequivocally: full and complete independence.

Although the United Nations never adopted the Draft Declaration, indeed the British deplored the document as being wholly unacceptable, it brought into focus the peculiarly American attitude that harnessed trusteeship to the engine of liberty. As is typical of this view, Hull believed that '[t]he spirit of liberty, when deeply embedded in the minds and hearts of the people, is the most powerful remedy for racial animosities, religious intolerance, ignorance, and all the other evils which prevent men from uniting in a brotherhood of truly civilized existence.'[20] Trusteeship was therefore little more than a means by which to spread

[16] W. Lippmann, *U.S. War Aims* (Boston: Little, Brown, and Company, 1944), 182.

[17] F. D. Roosevelt, 'Atlantic Charter, Message to Congress, August 21, 1941', in L. W. Holborn (ed.), *War and Peace Aims of the United Nations: September 1, 1939–December 31, 1942* (Boston: World Peace Foundation, 1943), 45.

[18] 'Declaration by the United Nations on National Independence', in H. A. Notter (ed.), *Postwar Foreign Policy Preparation, 1939–1945* (Washington, DC: US Government Printing Office, 1949), 470.   [19] Ibid. 471.

[20] C. Hull, 'Address on "The War and Human Freedom,"' July 23, 1942', in L. W. Holborn (ed.), *War and Peace Aims of the United Nations: September 1, 1939–December 31, 1942* (Boston: World Peace Foundation, 1943), 103; and C. Hull, *The Memoirs of Cordell Hull*, vol. 2 (New York: Macmillan, 1948), 1238, 1305.

the spirit of (American) liberty to dependent peoples in an attempt to rid the world of these and other evils. It is in this context that Roosevelt understood the idea of trusteeship as an integral part of a just and peaceful future world order: trusteeship would promote the enjoyment of liberty throughout the world and bolster chances for peace by bringing about the speedy end of empire.[21]

The Reform of Empire

Harsh and none too diplomatic American criticism, as well as shocking military setbacks, did not deter Churchill from stubbornly defending the integrity of the British Empire and its place in world affairs. In one of his most memorable speeches of the war, he declared defiantly: 'Let me...make this clear, in case there should be any mistake about it in any quarter: we mean to hold our own. I have not become the King's First Minister in order to preside over the liquidation of the British Empire.'[22] But in being determined to hold their own, British officials found themselves in the uncomfortable position of having to subject their methods of colonial administration and their justification of empire to the scrutiny of others.

Churchill complained bitterly that most Americans, including Roosevelt, failed to grasp the fundamental character of the British Empire, and, consequently, that they typically engaged questions of empire 'in terms of the thirteen colonies fighting George III at the end of the eighteenth century'.[23] But the litany of abuses recorded in Thomas Jefferson's Declaration of Independence did not register with Churchill or with the British public, the greater part of which tended to view the Empire as a source of pride and as a force for peace, freedom, and justice. Rather, defenders of empire imputed less virtuous motives to American criticism than a dogged passion for liberty. Some protested that the Americans possessed little experience in colonial affairs and that in their ignorance they were intruding into matters they did not properly understand. Others alleged that the Americans wished to undermine Britain's place in the world in order to establish for themselves an informal empire to pursue their economic interests.[24] However, pride,

[21] Louis, *Imperialism at Bay*, 147.

[22] W. Churchill, 'Address Made at Dinner for the Lord Mayor after the Landing of American and British Troops in North Africa, London, November 10, 1942', in L. W. Holborn (ed.), *War and Peace Aims of the United Nations: September 1, 1939–December 31, 1942* (Boston: World Peace Foundation, 1943), 264.

[23] W. S. Churchill, *The Hinge of Fate* (Boston: Houghton Mifflin Company, 1950), 219.

[24] 'A Public Declaration of Colonial Policy: The Viceroy to Secretary of State for India, 2 January 1943, CO 323/1858/9057B', in A. N. Porter and A. J. Stockwell (eds.), *British Imperial Policy and Decolonization, 1938–64*, vol. 1 (London: Macmillan, 1987), 135–40; and Louis, *Imperialism at Bay*, 247.

misconception, and ambition notwithstanding, American criticism rendered British officials acutely attuned to the way in which outsiders perceived the Empire, especially during the early years of the war. Hence the Viceroy of India, conscious of the importance of American opinion, advised in early 1943 that 'we must take account of misunderstandings, jealousies, and prejudices on the part of the United States of America, and that it would not be wise to leave our colonial record merely (?to) (?speak) for itself. We must (?therefore) be prepared to cultivate it both by indirect propaganda and to some extent by endeavouring to establish a common front with the United States of America in regard to it'.[25]

But criticism did not always emanate from without, for British colonial experience disclosed a well-established tradition of critical self-examination that dated back to late eighteenth century India. It was in this context that Perham asked if the citizens of Great Britain could reasonably expect colonial subjects, who had endured social and political segregation, and personal humiliation and neglect, to stand alongside their European masters in times of war. However, it would be some compensation, she went on to suggest, if the harsh lessons of defeat 'stirred us to read those passages in the writing on the wall which refer to our colonial empire, and which warn us to infuse a new energy into its administration and to achieve a new and more intimate and generous relationship with its peoples.'[26] The editors of *The Times* agreed. After the humiliating fall of Singapore in February 1942, they called for a sober reckoning of empire: 'by common consent the old order in the colonial government has been exposed to a searching challenge'.[27] Out of this earnest, if not disconcerting, examination emerged a rather different relation between Britain and its colonial dependencies. It was no longer possible to justify the continuation of imperial dominion by merely invoking the genius of British colonial administration. Improvements in education, health, and agriculture may have been the result of wise policy, but development through much of the Empire often proceeded fleetingly for want of adequate investment. It is in that respect that the Colonial Development and Welfare Act of 1940 is of particular significance, as Malcolm MacDonald argued before the House of Commons, since '[i]t establishe[d] the duty of taxpayers in this country to contribute directly and for its own sake towards the development in the widest sense of the word of the colonial peoples for whose good government the taxpayers of this country are ultimately

---

[25] 'A Public Declaration of Colonial Policy', 135.

[26] M. Perham, 'Capital, Labour and the Colour Bar', *Colonial Sequence, 1930 to 1949* (London: Methuen & Co, 1967), 231.

[27] 'The Colonial Future, *The Times* Leader, 14 March 1942', reprinted in M. Perham, *Colonial Sequence, 1930 to 1949* (London: Methuen & Co, 1967), 231.

responsible'.[28] From then on British officials would no longer be exposed to charges of insincerity—that colonial administration involved little more than uttering deceptive platitudes. Indeed, MacDonald endeavoured to impress upon his colleagues in parliamentary debate that voting in favour of the Act, in the darkest and most desperate of times, when the very fate of civilization was being decided on the European continent, would signal Britain's solemn promise to 'promote the well-being of our fellow subjects in the Empire overseas'.[29]

The emergence of a refined and elaborated idea of trusteeship called 'partnership' substantially redefined relations within the British Empire. Partnership took as its defining cue Viscount Cranborne's belief that there was no reason why colonial development should not proceed as it did in Canada, Australia, New Zealand, and South Africa. In time other colonies would grow-up like the 'white dominions' to be self-governing nations, equal in political status to Britain, that were fully responsible for their own affairs. And while these immature colonies might assume a different territorial configuration, for example, territories might be rearranged to form more coherent political units, Cranborne left no doubt that their diverse populations were all 'moving along the same road'.[30] Partnership expressed a relationship less permanent than that implied in periodic affirmations of the idea of trusteeship. The word 'trustee', as Colonial Secretary Oliver Stanley once put it, 'is rather too static in its connotation and that we should prefer to combine with the status of trustee the position also of partner'.[31] Thus, partnership presupposed an empire that consisted in something more than an agglomeration of isolated peoples that shared no more in common than the authority to which they were subject; it implied a dynamic and ever changing empire composed of a great family of peoples, some less developed, and others more so, that would eventually evolve into a commonwealth of self-governing nations united in common sympathy and allegiance to the British Crown. Crucially, then, partnership also suggested that colonial peoples should not expect to live out their lives as permanent wards of an imperial guardian in that it proposed 'the relationship which should exist

---

[28] M. MacDonald, 'Colonial Development and Welfare Bill: Speech in the House of Commons, 21 May 1940', in A. N. Porter and A. J. Stockwell (eds.), *British Imperial Policy and Decolonization, 1938–64*, vol. 1 (London: Macmillan, 1987), 97.

[29] MacDonald, 'Colonial Development and Welfare Bill', 94–5; and Louis, *Imperialism at Bay*, 101.

[30] Viscount Cranborne, 'Lord Privy Seal: Speech to the House of Lords during Debate on Colonial Policy, December 3, 1942', in L. W. Holborn (ed.), *War and Peace Aims of the United Nations: September 1, 1939–December 31, 1942* (Boston: World Peace Foundation, 1943), 271.

[31] O. Stanley, 'Extracts from a Speech by the Secretary of State for the Colonies in the House of Commons, 13 July, 1943', in A. N. Porter and A. J. Stockwell (eds.), *British Imperial Policy and Decolonization, 1938–64*, vol. 1 (London: Macmillan, 1987), 156.

between the United Kingdom and those dependent territories which were emerging to self-government'.[32]

If this programme of reform meant anything it gave practical effect to L. S. Amery's suggestion, made in the midst of the controversy regarding the interpretation of the Atlantic Charter, that the object of British colonial administration was the 'development of self-governing institutions to the fullest practicable extent within the British Empire'.[33] Thus, it could be said that the American insistence on colonial independence rested upon a false premise. The Empire, as the British would have it, consisted in a family of more or less developed peoples. But this familial analogy did not mean, as Harold MacMillan argued, that colonial peoples were like fruit on a tree that would, when ripe, fall to the ground. Colonial peoples, he argued, might be child-like in their characteristics and stage of development, but they should not be expected to 'necessarily grow up, wish to start upon their own, and separate themselves from their parents'.[34] The chief distinction, then, between American and British attitudes towards colonial questions was intelligible in the difference between independence, on the one hand, and self-government on the other. Indeed, Lord Hailey noted that the principal difficulty with Cordell Hull's infamous Draft Declaration by the United Nations on National Independence was its 'insistent repetition of the term "independence"'.[35] Even considered and persistent critics of empire, such as Norman Angell, objected to this insistence on complete independence as a deceptive and indeed foolhardy impossibility. He too believed that the Americans had misinterpreted the lessons of their political history to mean that the extension of liberty to all peoples would sweep away evil in whatever form it may arise. The citizens of Great Britain, he argued, would better direct their energies towards cultivating a political ideology that was more in tune with the facts of the modern world. However, Angell did not think of independence, and the heady slogans of nineteenth century liberalism, as being in consonance with these facts: '[p]eaceable, everyday life in the modern world depends on

[32] Lord Hailey, *An African Survey: A Study of Problems Arising in Africa South of the Sahara*, rev. edn. (London: Oxford University Press, 1957), 193.

[33] Quoted in Morgan, *Guidance Towards Self-Government in British Colonies*, 2.

[34] H. Macmillan, 'The War Effort and Colonial Policy: Speech by the Under-Secretary of State for the Colonies in the House of Commons, 24 June 1942', in A. N. Porter and A. J. Stockwell (eds.), *British Imperial Policy and Decolonization, 1938–64*, vol. 1 (London: Macmillan, 1987), 119.

[35] Lord Hailey, 'Note on "Draft Declaration by the United Nations on National Independence", by H. C. Hull, 5 May 1943', in A. N. Porter and A. J. Stockwell (eds.), *British Imperial Policy and Decolonization, 1938–64*, vol. 1 (London: Macmillan, 1987), 154.

co-operation; independence in any absolute sense makes co-operation impossible.'[36]

Although Angell repeatedly referred to facts that were said to be peculiar to the conditions of the modern world, his allusion to a commonwealth of peoples, an arrangement premised on the idea of interdependence rather than on independence, is anything but a curiosity of the mid-twentieth century. That some colonies might one day direct their own affairs is certainly intelligible in T. B. Macaulay's hope for India. The native inhabitants of India, he asserted, might have been enfeebled by 'political and religious tyranny', but with proper (European) instruction they might one day demand European institutions for themselves and assume direct responsibility for their own affairs'. And the arrival of that day, Macaulay proclaimed, 'will be the proudest day in English history'.[37] The idea of a commonwealth of peoples is explicitly evident in J. C. Smuts' proposals relating to the establishment of the League of Nations. Smuts argued that the British Empire, an association he described as 'the nearest approach to the league of nations', expressed an ideal of association founded, not on subordination or compulsion from above, but on the consent of the governed.[38] Of course, Macaulay and Smuts were each in his own way rather vague and incomplete in outlining the substance of their views. For instance, Smuts did not mean, nor did he intend, for native Africans to consent to their government. But two decades later the imperial ideal of which he spoke had been extended to embrace the whole of the British Empire. Smuts shared the prevalent British belief that the day of the small independent state had passed and that the future would see larger groupings joined by a common history and shared experience. He could point to no better example of the future mode of world organization than the British Commonwealth, an association he put forward as 'a precedent and a prototype for the larger world association now in the process of formation'.[39] For within the framework of the Commonwealth 'uncivilized' peoples would enjoy, as they were capable, freedom, equality, justice, and all else for which the Commonwealth stood.

---

[36] N. Angell, 'The Commonwealth Idea: Past and Future', *United Empire*, 44/4 (1953), 149–50.

[37] T. B. Macaulay, *The Works of Lord Macaulay* (London: Longman's, Green, and Co., 1879), 142. See also Morgan, *Guidance Towards Self-Government*, 2–3; and Louis, *Imperialism at Bay*, 125–6.

[38] J. C. Smuts, 'The League of Nations: A Practical Suggestion', in D. H. Miller (ed.), *The Drafting of the Covenant*, vol. 2 (New York: G. P. Putnam's Sons, 1928), 36.

[39] J. C. Smuts, 'A Vision of the Future, Pretoria, June 12, 1941', in L. W. Holborn (ed.), *War and Peace Aims of the United Nations: September 1, 1939–December 31, 1942* (Boston: World Peace Foundation, 1943), 344.

It is with this notion of self-government that the defenders of the British Empire replied to the American demand for colonial independence. Through strident American criticism, and a no less strident British response, this debate about the future of the world's colonial peoples did not devalue the currency of the idea of trusteeship. The British would continue to be wary of unwanted American interference in imperial affairs; still, they did not rule out the possibility of international cooperation on questions of empire. A world made smaller by advances in transport and communications only sharpened the need for mutual cooperation; for many of the world's problems, as Stanley argued, those relating to questions of security, economics, transport, and health, 'transcend the boundaries of political units' and were common to all.[40] Thus, the British proposed establishing regional commissions, composed of colonial and other regional powers, to discuss common problems as they might arise. However, they were absolutely set against any alteration of the administrative arrangements for colonial territories: 'Mother countries should remain exclusively responsible for the administration of their colonies and interference by others should be avoided.'[41] The Americans were not averse to the idea of regional commissions, but they contemplated a much more ambitious regimen of accountability and supervision. Both Hull's Draft Declaration and the American Draft Constitution of International Organization recommended placing all colonial peoples and territories under a formal system of trusteeship in order to prepare them, politically, economically, and socially, for full independence. What the Americans had in mind is especially evident in Article 12 of the Draft Constitution:

To those non-self-governing territories which are inhabited by peoples not yet able to stand by themselves, the principle of trusteeship shall be applied in their governance in accordance with which the welfare of the inhabitants and the general interests of other peoples shall be assured under the authority and supervision of the International Organization.[42]

While the British rejected out of hand the suggestion that an international organization would possess supervisory powers over its colonial empire, it is

[40] O. Stanley, 'Speech on International Cooperation in Colonial Affairs to the House of Commons, July, 13, 1943', in L. W. Holborn (ed.), *War and Peace Aims of the United Nations: From Casablanca to Tokio Bay: January 1, 1943–September 1, 1945* (Boston: World Peace Foundation, 1948), 432.

[41] J. C. Smuts, 'Article on the British Colonial Empire, December 28, 1942', in L. W. Holborn (ed.), *War and Peace Aims of the United Nations: September 1, 1939–December 31, 1942* (Boston: World Peace Foundation, 1943), 349; and Stanley, 'Speech on International Cooperation in Colonial Affairs', 432.

[42] 'Draft Constitution of International Organization', in H. A. Notter (ed.), *Postwar Foreign Policy Preparation, 1939–1945* (Washington, DC: US Government Printing Office, 1949), 481.

important to note that this disagreement was one over matters of form, not of principle. If anything, this disagreement placed the idea of trusteeship on more secure footing, but it was expressed in two distinct and contending forms: imperial trusteeship and international trusteeship.

For all of their differences, the two sides were not divided on the basic assumption of trusteeship, namely that most colonial peoples were incapable of managing their own affairs and that their preparation for independence or self-government, whichever the case may be, would be a gradual undertaking. Thus, in a telling remark regarding unrest in India, Amery said: 'Mr. Gandhi may view with complacency the prospect of the present government quitting India and leaving her to anarchy. But no responsible man who looks ahead, whether in India or here, or in America, would deliberately acquiesce in a course which would mean ruin to India.'[43] British officials were united in their belief that without sufficient development in all aspects of public life, the promise of self-government would be a meaningless gesture. Indeed, Harold Macmillan argued that the colonies are poor and backward, not because of misrule, exploitation, or neglect, but because they are just beginning their journey on the road to self-government. Stanley agreed in saying that development in the colonies must proceed according to their particular circumstances rather than according to a fixed schedule or a universal blueprint.[44]

This gradualist approach is no less pronounced in American trusteeship proposals. For example, Hull's Draft Declaration supposed that while some colonial peoples were well advanced along the road leading to independent national status, 'the development and resources of others are not yet such as to enable them to assume and discharge the responsibilities of government without danger to themselves and to others.'[45] It would therefore be the duty of controlling powers to tutor these not yet capable peoples in all aspects of public life. Moreover, they should be granted a share of government, as they were able to make good use of such powers, and protected from exploitation as they moved onwards to independence. Thus, in the end, both the Americans and the British accepted the fundamental incompetence of these dependent peoples to direct their own affairs. Clement Attlee conveyed just this sentiment by saying: 'No doubt, the time may come when even the most

---

[43] L. S. Amery, 'Speech on India Delivered to the American Outpost, London, May 6, 1943', in L. W. Holborn (ed.), *War and Peace Aims of the United Nations: September 1, 1939–December 31, 1942* (Boston: World Peace Foundation, 1943), 421.

[44] O. Stanley, 'Address on the Colonial Empire and Trusteeship Delivered before the Foreign Policy Association, New York City, January 19, 1945', in L. W. Holborn (ed.), *War and Peace Aims of the United Nations: From Casablanca to Tokio Bay: January 1, 1943–September 1, 1945* (Boston: World Peace Foundation, 1948), 554; and Macmillan, 'The War Effort and Colonial Policy', 120–4.   [45] 'Declaration by the United Nations on National Independence', 471.

backward of our Colonies [will] also become adult nations. But at present they are children and must be treated as such.'[46]

Trusteeship and the Charter of the United Nations

The Charter of the United Nations contains both the American and the British conceptions of trusteeship. However, before delegates assembled in San Francisco, in April 1945, to draft the Charter, the main outlines of post-war arrangements of trusteeship began to take shape at the Yalta Conference two months earlier. At Yalta, Churchill, Roosevelt, and Stalin agreed that trusteeship would apply only to: '(a) existing mandates of the League of Nations; (b) territories detached from the enemy as a result of the present war; (c) any other territory which might voluntarily be placed under trustee-ship.'[47] But in order to convince Churchill to agree to further consultations on the subject, Edward Stettinius, Hull's successor as Secretary of State, assured the Prime Minister that his government did not wish to subject the territories of the British Empire to formal machinery of international super-vision, but only those mandated territories for which Japan had been respons-ible. Churchill made it abundantly clear that 'under no circumstances would he ever consent to forty or fifty nations thrusting their interfering fingers into the life's existence of the British Empire'.[48] However, in agreeing to a formula that placed existing mandates under an international trusteeship system, Churchill, perhaps unwittingly, subjected territories under British authority— the British mandates—to a system that would almost certainly entail some form of international supervision. For the rather innocuous formula agreed at Yalta permitted the establishment in the Charter of both the American idea of international trusteeship and the British idea of imperial trusteeship. But more than that, according to William Roger Louis, 'the Yalta endorsement of the American concept of trusteeship helped to set the colonial world on a different course towards self-determination, independence, and fragmentation'.[49]

---

[46] C. Attlee, 'A Public Declaration of Colonial Policy, 14 January 1942', in A. N. Porter and A. J. Stockwell (eds.), *British Imperial Policy and Decolonization, 1938–64*, vol. 1 (London: Macmillan, 1987), 142.

[47] 'Protocol of the Proceedings of the Crimea Conference', *Foreign Relations of the United States: The Conferences at Malta and Yalta, 1945* (Washington, DC: Government Printing Office, 1955), 977.

[48] 'Sixth Plenary Meeting, February 9, 1945, 4 P.M., Livadia Palace', *Foreign Relations of the United States: The Conferences at Malta and Yalta, 1945* (Washington, DC: Government Printing Office, 1955), 844.   [49] Louis, *Imperialism at Bay*, 464.

Principles of trusteeship are enshrined in Chapters XI and XII of the Charter. Chapter XI, the Declaration Regarding Non-Self-Governing Territories, is itself an amalgamation of principles found in the Berlin and Brussels Acts, the Kenya White Paper, and Article 22 of the League of Nations covenant. Thus, Article 73 of Chapter XI stipulates:

Members of the United Nations which have or assume responsibilities for the administration of territories whose peoples have not yet attained a full measure of self-government recognize the principle that the interests of the inhabitants of these territories are paramount, and accept as a sacred trust the obligation to promote to the utmost, within the system of international peace and security established by the present Charter, the well-being of the inhabitants of these territories.[50]

To this end, administering powers were charged with the duty of protecting these peoples against abuse, ensuring their political, economic, social, and educational advancement, and, after taking account of their political aspirations, assisting them in the development towards self-government, as the circumstances of each territory permit. Moreover, they were obliged to transmit regularly to the Secretary General, 'for informational purposes', technical information relating to the economic, social, and educational conditions in territories for which they are responsible.[51] The intent of this Declaration conforms most closely to British proposals that professedly followed along the lines of Article 22: 'the primary objective of any trusteeship system is the well-being of the inhabitants of territories which are not yet able to stand by themselves.'[52] And in this respect the British made no distinction in scope of application, as administrative status did not determine the obligations of trusteeship and had no bearing on the discharge of these obligations. Thus, a territory falling outside the trusteeship formula adopted at Yalta was, on the British view, no less deserving of an administration guided by the policy of trusteeship than one that did not. The Australian proposal accepted the substance of this position by declaring: '[a]ll members of the United Nations responsible for the administration of dependent territories recognise in relation to them the principle of trusteeship.'[53]

---

[50] 'Charter of the United Nations', in A. Roberts and B. Kingsbury (eds.), *United Nations, Divided World* (Oxford: Clarendon Press, 1993), 519.   [51] Ibid. 520.

[52] 'United Kingdom Draft of Chapter for Inclusion in United Nations Charter, Doc. 2 G/ 26 (d), May 6, 1945', *Documents of the United Nations Conference on International Organization*, vol. 3 (London: United Nations Information Organizations, 1945), 611.

[53] 'Amendments to the Dumbarton Oaks Proposals Submitted on Behalf of Australia, Doc. 2 G14/(1), May 5, 1945', *Documents of the United Nations Conference on International Organization*, vol. 3 (London: United Nations Information Organizations, 1945), 548.

While the colonial powers accepted the universality of trusteeship, they did not mean to subject their own dependent territories to a system of international supervision. The French deemed trusteeship as being applicable only to existing mandates and to territories detached from enemy states as a consequence of the war. In fact, the French delegate felt compelled to state that nothing under consideration by the Trusteeship Committee shall authorize the United Nations to 'intervene in matters which are essentially within the domestic jurisdiction of any state'.[54] The British were also decidedly against any extension of international supervision to territories falling outside the Yalta formula. Principles of trusteeship, they argued, should be detailed in the Charter along the broadest lines possible; and the elaboration of rigid and exact obligations, applicable to all cases and in all circumstances, should be avoided in favour of flexibility because, too often, the circumstances of particular situations frustrate even the most enlightened and well-intentioned policies.[55] Surely the wisdom of this approach is perhaps no better confirmed than in the unhappy history of the Congo Free State.

But in admitting the universality of trusteeship, the British delegation drew a very clear distinction between 'the *principle* of trusteeship which should guide Colonial Powers in the administration of their dependent territories (and should therefore be of universal application) and the creation of a special system of international *machinery*, to apply to certain specified territories' [emphasis in original].[56] This crucial distinction illuminates the essential character of trusteeship that is enshrined in Chapter XI. The Declaration Regarding Non-Self-Governing Territories is a statement of general principles and purposes that are applicable to all dependent territories. Still, the Declaration consists in something more than its name might imply. Chapter XI is not, as Hans Kelsen argues, a unilateral declaration that depends on the conclusion of individual trusteeship agreements; it imposes obligations of international law that are no less binding than other parts of the Charter.[57] However, provisions relating to international accountability and supervision are not included among the obligations of the Declaration. Thus, Chapter XI is intelligible, not in terms of international trusteeship, but in terms of the

---

[54] 'International Trusteeship System: French Preliminary Draft', Doc. 2 G/26 (a), May 5, 1945', *Documents of the United Nations Conference on International Organization*, vol. 3 (London: United Nations Information Organizations, 1945), 605; and 'Report of the Rapporteur of Committee II/4, Doc. 1115 II/4/44 (1)(a), June, 20, 1945, *Documents of the United Nations Conference on International Organization*, vol. 10 (London: United Nations Information Organizations, 1945), 622.   [55] 'United Kingdom Draft of Chapter', 611.

[56] Ibid. 611.

[57] H. Kelsen, *The Law of the United Nations: A Critical Analysis of Its Fundamental Problems* (London: Stevens & Sons, 1951), 553–4.

British tradition of imperial trusteeship. And in that respect Chapter XI is substantively not unlike the Berlin Act.

Whereas Chapter XI expresses the idea of imperial trusteeship, Chapter XII, which establishes the United Nations Trusteeship System, reflects more closely the American ideal of international trusteeship, in so far that it creates a much more ambitious system of international administration and supervision. This part of the Charter applied to those territories included in the Yalta formula, and, like Chapter XI, it is directed towards furthering international peace and security, promoting the political, economic, social, and educational advancement of the inhabitants of trust territories, and ensuring equal treatment in social, economic, and commercial matters for all members of the organization. To these objectives Article 76 adds respect for human rights and fundamental freedoms, and, significantly, 'progressive development towards self-government *or* independence as may be appropriate to the particular circumstances of each territory and its peoples' [emphasis added].[58] Chapter XII also obliges administering authorities to make an annual report to the General Assembly, and it empowers the United Nations to receive petitions and to dispatch its own missions in order to observe, first-hand, conditions in trust territories. However, the most important innovation of the Trusteeship System is the distinction drawn between strategic and non-strategic trust territories. Article 82 states: 'There may be designated, in any trusteeship agreement, a strategic area or areas which may include part or all of the trust territory.'[59] Strategic trust territories, as opposed to non-strategic trust territories, are not subject to the administrative and supervisory functions performed by the Trusteeship Council or the General Assembly. Article 83 places all of these functions at the disposal of the Security Council. But designating a territory as a strategic trust does not in any way relieve an administering authority from fulfilling obligations enumerated in Article 76. The framers of the Charter took care in stating in Article 83 that '[t]he basic objectives set forth in Article 76 shall be applicable to the people of each strategic area.'[60]

The stress that the Trusteeship System and, for that matter, the Declaration Regarding Non-Self-Governing Territories, places on furthering international peace and security warrants special attention. At first glance it seems as if the emphasis placed on international peace and security represents a clear

[58] 'Charter of the United Nations', 520.

[59] Ibid. 522. The Pacific islands mandate held by Japan was the only territory designated a strategic trust. The United States assumed administrative responsibility for these islands under the United Nations trusteeship system. See C. E. Toussaint, *The Trusteeship System of the United Nations* (London: Stevens & Sons Limited, 1956), 71, 452.

[60] 'Charter of the United Nations', 522.

break with past practice. And in one sense it does. Whereas the Berlin Act and the mandates system neutralized territories in order to remove them from the tensions and rivalries of the great powers, Article 84 of the Charter stipulates that '[i]t shall be the duty of the administering authority to ensure the trust territory shall play its part in the maintenance of international peace and security.'[61] Thus, administering authorities are empowered to utilize the resources of a trust territory, not only for local defence and the maintenance of law and order, but in discharging duties that arise from the decisions of the Security Council and duties that pertain to the general purpose of the organization.[62] Indeed, Duncan Hall argues that historians have exaggerated the extent to which humanitarianism and liberal idealism account for the establishment of mandates and trust territories. They are, he argues, 'largely by-products of the working of the state system of the world, of the political relations of the powers, and thus factors in the balance of power.'[63] But the framers of the Charter were no more concerned about security than the framers of the Berlin Act or the League Covenant. Rather, they believed that the war in general, and Japan's violation of mandate agreements in particular, rendered neutralization less effective than integrating trust territories into a comprehensive system of international peace and security.

We might expect something different of a world devoid of moral principle and one ruled by the narrow dictates of realpolitik, but the principles of trusteeship were affirmed at every opportunity when confronted by the imperatives of strategic necessity. But it is a mistake of considerable proportion to suggest that the Trusteeship System, and the Charter in general, subordinates the well-being of dependent peoples to a narrow argument of security. Indeed, a member of the American delegation to the San Francisco Conference declared that '[i]t was his Government's attitude that international peace and security and the welfare of dependent peoples, constituted twin objectives which could not be separated.'[64] It is in this spirit that Roosevelt refused to yield to the argument of security when the War Department and United States Navy demanded the annexation of the Japanese mandated islands in the Pacific, just as Woodrow Wilson refused to bow to the argument of security when discussing the disposal of German colonies at Versailles. Roosevelt replied to the suggestion that the United States must exercise

---

[61] Ibid. 522.   [62] Toussaint, *The Trusteeship System of the United Nations*, 55.

[63] H. D. Hall, *Mandates, Dependencies, and Trusteeship* (London: Stevens & Sons, 1948), 8.

[64] 'Summary of Fourth Meeting of Committee II/4, Doc. 310 II/4/11, May 15, 1945', *Documents of the United Nations Conference on International Organization*, vol. 10 (London: United Nations Information Organizations, 1945), 440; see also Hull, *The Memoirs of Cordell Hull*, 1639.

absolute power over the Pacific islands by saying: the Joint Chiefs of Staff must 'realize that we have agreed that we are seeking no additional territory as a result of this war'.[65] There is in fact no evidence in the proceedings of the San Francisco Conference to suggest that the United States perceived a contradiction between the maintenance of international peace and security and the well-being and advancement of dependent peoples. For the American delegation generally regarded the steady progression of dependent peoples towards self-government or independence as a requisite condition of world peace. And it is in that conviction that a member of the American delegation submitted: 'the objectives of the Organization with regard to the welfare of dependent peoples applied in strategic areas as well as in other areas under trust.'[66]

The Trusteeship System should not be viewed as expressing a narrow set of interests related exclusively to either security or welfare; nor should it be viewed as an isolated arrangement that is separate from the principles and purposes expressed elsewhere in the Charter, the most important of which relate to the problem of war and the conditions of peace. Rather the Trusteeship System is, as Roosevelt had hoped, an integral part of the United Nations Organisation and is closely related to the obligations enshrined in Chapter XI. The principles contained in Chapter XI apply to non-self-governing territories and to trust territories alike. Kelsen points out that, where the obligations arising out of Chapter XI overlap with those contracted in Chapter XII, it is not necessary to enumerate them a second time in individual trusteeship agreements.[67] The Trusteeship System does not express a separate set of principles but is rather a part of the existing international law of trusteeship. Thus, the creation of the United Nations and the Trusteeship System did not alter, diminish, or otherwise void the obligations enshrined in the Berlin and Brussels Acts in the territories to which they were applicable, namely the Conventional Basin of the Congo River. And where these treaties were not in force, many, if not all, of the obligations contained therein were incorporated in individual trusteeship agreements. Indeed, the Trusteeship Agreement of Somaliland stipulated in Article 3 that the administering authority, in this case Italy, shall:

control the traffic in arms and ammunition, opium and other dangerous drugs, alcohol and other spirituous liquors; prohibit all forms of slavery, slave trade and

[65] Quoted in Louis, *Imperialism at Bay*, 373, 483.

[66] 'Summary of Fourth Meeting of Committee II/4, Doc. 310 II/4/11, May 15, 1945', *Documents of the United Nations Conference on International Organization*, vol. 10 (London: United Nations Information Organizations, 1945), 440.

[67] 'Report of the Rapporteur of Committee II/4', 608; Kelsen, *The Law of the United Nations*, 632; and Toussaint, *The Trusteeship System of the United Nations*, 214.

child marriage; apply existing international conventions concerning prostitution; prohibit all forms of forced or compulsory labour, except for essential public works and services, and then only in time of public emergency with adequate remuneration and adequate protection of the welfare of the workers; and institute such other regulations as may be necessary to protect the inhabitants against any social abuses.[68]

The heritage of these obligations is at once obvious and unmistakable, for they nearly mirror those contained in the Berlin and Brussels Acts.

Louis argues, in assessing the achievements of the United Nations Trusteeship System, that the colonial settlement of 1945 represents a modest advance over that of 1919, even though Cordell Hull, one of the most fervent believers in the promise of trusteeship, described it as constituting a 'material improvement' over the mandates system.[69] But, notwithstanding the defects and achievements of the Trusteeship System and of the colonial settlement in general, the negotiations that resulted in the Trusteeship System and the Declaration Regarding Non-Self-Governing Territories provide the first glimpse of an ideological divide that would eventually destroy the legitimacy of trusteeship. At San Francisco, the United States abandoned its historic support of colonial independence and, to the delight of the colonial powers, placed the weight of its influence behind the principle of self-government. Harold Stassen explained this rather sudden reversal by accepting fully the position advanced by the colonial powers: self-government might lead to independence though not necessarily so. Moreover, he praised the virtue of self-government, in a way that would have surely pleased Norman Angell, as being better suited to the interdependent world of the future than outdated ideas of nineteenth century national independence.[70] To Charles Taussig this qualified endorsement of independence amounted to nothing less than a total repudiation of the ideals championed by Roosevelt, who had passed away just before the San Francisco Conference convened. But in the end, the force of Stassen's arguments prevailed over what he dismissed as the philosophically perfect, but practically flawed, principle of independence that Taussig and others so deeply cherished. Stassen publicly defended American support of self-government, at the expense of independence, since it was the only principle that would gain the assent of all the great powers. Privately, though, he fretted that the universal application of independence would be productive of disorder that might adversely affect American interests.

[68] 'Trusteeship Agreement for the Territory of Somaliland Under Italian Administration', *Yearbook of the United Nations, 1950* (New York: Department of Public Information, 1951), 803.   [69] Louis, *Imperialism at Bay*, 532; and Hull, *The Memoirs of Cordell Hull*, 1238.
[70] Louis, *Imperialism at Bay*, 534–5.

Indeed, he demanded to know if his colleagues were prepared to accept the full consequences of universal independence: did they mean to include Puerto Rico and Hawaii in their project of emancipation?[71]

A growing suspicion of the Soviet Union also induced a sense of caution in the American delegation. In particular, Soviet amendments to American trusteeship proposals that included a reference to the self-determination of dependent peoples in order to 'expedite the achievement by them of the full national independence' evoked considerable alarm.[72] Hence, to most Americans, the prospect of breaking up the British Empire for the cause of liberty suddenly appeared to be less inviting. But a group of small states exposed the difficulty of the American position by siding, at least on the question of independence, with the Soviet Union. A member of the Mexican delegation conceded the desirability of self-government but asserted never-theless that 'independence should be conceded whenever a self-governing people had unmistakably expressed its wish for complete liberation'.[73] The Philippine delegation concurred: 'self-government might express the ultim-ate happiness for some peoples. Other peoples, however, might find the ultimate happiness in independence, and the Charter should not bar this avenue to happiness for such peoples.'[74] With the unwillingness of small states to accept anything but independence, and the American abandonment of independence as the only goal of imperial trusteeship, passed the hope of an orderly liquidation of empire. But the colonial powers confronted a dilemma of a different sort: '[w]ith the motley international assembly now becoming a reality, Stanley pointed out that this meddlesome band would "seek outlet for its energies in quite undesirable directions".'[75] And indeed they would.

---

[71] Louis, *Imperialism at Bay*, 535–41.

[72] 'Amendments of the Soviet Delegation to the United States Draft on Trusteeship System, Doc. 2 G/26 (f), May 11, 1945', *Documents of the United Nations Conference on International Organization*, vol. 3 (London: United Nations Information Organizations, 1945), 618; and 'Summary of Fourth Meeting of Committee II/4, Doc. 310 II/4/11, May 15, 1945', *Documents of the United Nations Conference on International Organization*, vol. 10 (London: United Nations Information Organizations, 1945), 441.

[73] 'Summary Report of Fifth Meeting of Committee II/4, Doc. 364 II/4/13, May 17, 1945', *Documents of the United Nations Conference on International Organization*, vol. 10 (London: United Nations Information Organizations, 1945), 446.

[74] 'Summary Report of Fifteenth Meeting of Committee II/4, Doc. 1090 II/4/43, June 19, 1945', *Documents of the United Nations Conference on International Organization*, vol. 10 (London: United Nations Information Organizations, 1945), 562.

[75] Louis, *Imperialism at Bay*, 524.

The End of Empire

Oliver Stanley's anxiety proved to be well founded as anti-colonial powers directed their energies towards the destruction of empire and, along with it, the legitimacy of trusteeship. The history of decolonization, though well documented, is no less contested than the history of European expansion in Africa and Asia. Historians have variously stressed the importance of changes in the balance of power, the economic exhaustion induced by the war, and the role of national liberation movements as factors in hastening the end of empire. Others, mainly of the Marxist persuasion, assert that colonialism never ended and that colonial powers merely substituted economic dominion for political dominion.[76] I am not interested in deciding, which of these accounts is on balance most persuasive; nor am I interested in providing an alternative account of the history of decolonization. The writing of history is best left to historians. But when the events of decolonization are examined in the context of trusteeship two arguments stand out as being especially noteworthy: the violation of trust and the right of self-determination.

Colonial peoples are apt to tell the story of decolonization quite differently than the way in which the colonial administrator might tell it. Arnold Toynbee suggests that in order to appreciate the experience of the colonized we must enter into the world of the Bengali in India, the Ashanti in Africa, and the Arab of the Levant. Their rendering of history is likely to be punctuated by accounts of aggression, conquest, enslavement, deportation, and alien rule. For these peoples the sacred trust, and the protections afforded in declarations of colonial policy and in various instruments of international law, too often resulted in maltreatment, forced labour, racial segregation, and loss of land, culture, and economic livelihood. Indeed, these peoples could only look on with cynicism as their colonial masters spoke of the white man's burden. They are apt to remind all who ask, not of their advancement at the hand of a benevolent, humane, and enlightened colonial ruler, but of their encounter with the West, the 'arch-aggressor of modern times'.[77] It is in this context that Jawaharlal Nehru denounced an (British) authoritarian government that enfeebled the people of India by ignoring their interests and those of humanity. But more than anything else he objected to the arrogance of a ruling caste enthroned by the supposed superiority of race. To endure the exclusionary polices of racialism 'in one's own country', he wrote from a prison cell during the

[76] For a summary of these arguments, see A. N. Porter and A. J. Stockwell, 'Introduction', *British Imperial Policy and Decolonization, 1938–64*, eds. A. N. Porter and A. J. Stockwell (London: Macmillan, 1987), 4–7.

[77] A. Toynbee, *The World and the West* (New York: Oxford University Press, 1953), 1–4.

war, 'is a humiliating and exasperating reminder of our enslaved condition.'[78]
Julius Nyerere similarly regarded colonial policies as having excluded
Tanzanians from political, economic, and social benefits that were the right of
all peoples and all nations; and he too denounced racialism, in even stronger
terms, as constituting 'an aggression against the human spirit, as colonialism
is the result of a past aggression against a people and a territory'.[79]

In characterizing colonial rule in these terms, both Nehru and Nyerere
advanced the claim that the European administrator, missionary, trader,
planter, and soldier had inadequately attended to the interests and well-being
of peoples for whom they were responsible; that is to say, European colonial
masters had failed in their self-proclaimed role as trustees of civilization.
Kwame Nkrumah, whose unyielding indictment of empire best discloses the
major premise of this argument, understood empire as the creature of selfish
economic interest whereby the laws of economy, the discipline imposed by
markets, and the appetite of capital and finance compelled the inevitable and
necessary partition of Africa. Colonies existed to serve the narrow interests of
their European masters: they supplied a boundless source of raw materials,
furnished markets for European manufactures, and provided outlets for the
disposal of surplus capital.[80] Nkrumah argued that this unbridled pursuit of
national economic advantage betrayed nothing but a brutal story of domination and exploitation. Africans were thus mere tools of European enrichment: they toiled in mines and on plantations, while 'progressive' colonial
administration kept the people of Africa in a depressed state of poverty,
disease, and mass illiteracy. And when they dared to organize themselves,
to assert their rights and protest their mistreatment, they were persecuted
and imprisoned as threats to peace and public order.[81] For Nkrumah,
the 'true' character of colonialism exposed the complete and utter moral
bankruptcy of trusteeship and all ideas related to it. He disparaged the many
promises of protection and guardianship that were enshrined in the Berlin
Act, the League of Nations covenant, and the United Nations charter, as
platitudinous camouflage meant to disguise the exploitative nature of imperialism; for '[b]eneath the "humanitarian" and "appeasement" shibboleths of
colonial governments, a proper scrutiny leads one to discover nothing but
deception, hypocrisy, oppression, and exploitation'.[82] Trusteeship was just
another cruel and disingenuous device with which to oppress colonial peoples.

[78] J. Nehru, *The Discovery of India* (New York: The John Day Company, 1946), 294, 486.

[79] J. Nyerere, 'At the United Nations General Assembly', *Freedom and Development: A Selection from Writings and Speeches, 1968–1973* (Oxford: Oxford University Press, 1973), 208.

[80] K. Nkrumah, *Towards Colonial Freedom: Africa and the Struggle Against World Imperialism* (London: Heinemann, 1962), 1–6.   [81] Ibid. 35.

[82] Nkrumah, *Towards Colonial Freedom*, xvi.

It might be tempting to dismiss Nkrumah's account of colonialism as empty rhetoric or as a gross distortion of the actual events that distinguished Africa's encounter with the West. But even if allegations of deception and oppression were shown to be factually untrue, his principal claim—that violation of trust rendered European colonial masters unfit to rule—is amply supported in international history. Edmund Burke charged the East India Company, and Warren Hastings in particular, with ruling as the worst sort of despot. The Company's agents waged aggressive wars, they broke solemn promises, and they abused their power in order to enrich themselves while providing nothing that might benefit the subjects for whom they were responsible. In short, Burke alleged that the Company had abused its trust and, therefore, forfeited its right to rule; for 'it is the very essence of every trust to be rendered *accountable*, and even totally to *cease* when it substantially varies from the purposes for which alone it could have a lawful existence [emphasis in original]'.[83] The British government invoked a similar argument in 1908 when it withheld recognition of Belgium's annexation of the Congo Free State, which had been ostensibly founded and subsequently recognized for the purpose of promoting civilization and other humane and benevolent ends. During the First World War, observers on both sides of the Atlantic agreed that evidence of gross misrule confirmed that the Germans were unfit to take on the obligations expected of a civilized power. In place of rapacious German rule, the victorious powers accepted Smuts' idea, whereby cases of 'flagrant and prolonged' abuse of trust would oblige the proposed league to assert its authority to the full, 'even to the extent of removing the mandate, and entrusting it to some other state, if necessary'.[84] And 25 years later the United States appealed to this principle as reason for placing the Japanese Pacific Islands mandate under the supervision of the Trusteeship System: '[i]n utter disregard of the mandate, Japan used the territories for aggressive warfare, in violation of the law of nations... This, under international law, was a criminal act; it was an essential violation of the trust, and by it Japan forfeited the right and capacity to be the mandatory of the islands'.[85]

---

[83] Burke, 'Speech on Mr. Fox's East India Bill, December 1, 1783', *The Works of the Right Honourable Edmund Burke*, vol. 2 (Boston: Little, Brown, and Company, 1899), 439.

[84] See 'Foreign Office to Mr. Lamont, May 29, 1912', Correspondence Respecting the Affairs of the Congo, February 1913, Cmd. 6606 lix (1912–13), 22; E. H. M. Georges, 'Report on the Natives of South-West Africa and Their Treatment by Germany', *Parliamentary Papers*, 1918, Cmd. 9146, xvii, (1918), 4; G. L. Beer, *African Questions at the Paris Peace Conference*, ed. L. H. Gray (New York: Macmillan, 1923), 58; and Smuts, 'The League of Nations', 32.

[85] Quoted in Toussaint, *The Trusteeship System of the United Nations*, 88; see also 'Final Text of the Communiqué, Cairo Conference', *Foreign Relations of the United States: The Conferences at Cairo and Tehran, 1943* (Washington, DC: Government Printing Office, 1961), 448–9.

If it is the essence of every trust to be held accountable, and international practice seems to suggest that it is, then criticism of empire consists in something more than idle commentary. It provides evidence in an ongoing referendum on the justification of imperial dominion. Indeed, the grievances about which Nehru, Nyerere, and Nkrumah complain, while often dismissed as being unrealistic, exaggerated, and self-serving, find at least implicit support in European criticism of empire, and especially in the writings of Richard Cobden, John Hobson, G. Lowes Dickinson, Leonard Woolf, and Margery Perham. For example, Perham denied that Britain had plundered the continent of Africa and built a great empire on the backs of its people; and she understood the word 'trusteeship' as conveying a sincere aspiration and the word 'colonialism' as consisting in something more than a term of abuse. But she also had the courage to admit that '[l]ike all other imperial powers we expanded by force and like them we have in the process committed our crimes.'[86] British colonial administrators, she observed, were sometimes slow, neglectful, and unimaginative; and the European money economy and Christian education time and again frayed the fabric of indigenous society while leaving little in its place. Moreover, pernicious myths of racial superiority precluded the realization of a common imperial citizenship and at the same time sustained stratified societies based on the fundamental inequality of peoples. Thus, to be black was to be despised, pitied, and humiliated; for 'European rulers of Africa believed that Africans were not only almost immeasurably inferior to themselves in development but were inherently, permanently inferior as a race'.[87] But when Africans and Asians demanded rectification of these grievances, when they expressed their wish to be treated no differently than civilized, white Europeans, they were branded as extremists. And yet these African extremists demanded only what American extremists demanded at the end of the eighteenth century: equal rights of citizenship. Indeed, A. W. Benn observed that an African extremist was 'a man who believes that the Africans are entitled to the same full social, political and economic rights as the white man'.[88]

For the African or Asian who wished to escape a condition of servitude and tutelage, the charge that European colonial rulers failed to fulfil their obligations as trustees of civilization provided a powerful argument in support of

[86] M. Perham, 'Our Task in Africa', *Colonial Sequence, 1930 to 1949* (London: Methuen & Co., 1967), 147.

[87] M. Perham, *The Colonial Reckoning* (London: Collins, 1961), 15, 33–9; and Perham, 'African Facts and American Criticism', 254.

[88] A. W. Benn, 'Speech on Colonial Policy in the House of Commons, 2 November 1959', in A. N. Porter and A. J. Stockwell (eds.), *British Imperial Policy and Decolonization, 1938–64*, vol. 2 (London: Macmillan, 1987), 516.

their claim of independence. But this argument did not discredit the idea of trusteeship itself; it merely undermined the justification of the means by which colonial powers attempted to carry out their obligations. The argument of self-determination achieved something quite different: self-determination rendered trusteeship an unsustainable practice by definition. The chief supposition of this argument, the belief that the 'subjection of peoples to alien subjugation, domination and exploitation constitutes a denial of fundamental human rights...and is an impediment to the promotion of world peace and co-operation', is disclosed in the decisions of a succession of conferences, the most noteworthy being the Bandung Conference of 1955, and in the activities of the United Nations General Assembly.[89] Acceptance of this proposition irreversibly altered the terms of debate, for peace and prosperity no longer depended on the provision of a gradual political, economic, social, and moral education, but on the speedy granting of independence. Dependent peoples would, as a matter of right, no longer be forced to endure the opprobrium of racial segregation and discrimination; nor would they be consigned to a position of permanent inferiority in all aspects of public life. Instead, they would be free to choose their own government, empowered to seek their own livelihood, and at liberty to decide the ends of their collective lives. Indeed, the peoples of Africa and Asia would be able to reclaim their dignity as human beings: independence would bring salvation.

This claim of a right of self-determination, so far as trusteeship is concerned, is not without precedent. Self-determination is implied in the British practice of colonies acceding to dominion status, Article 22 of the League Covenant, and Articles 73 and 76 of the United Nations Charter; and, as well, self-determination is mentioned in the Charter as one of the purposes of the United Nations. The duties that attach to the right of self-determination, though not clearly stated in positive international law, are evident in the decisions of the General Assembly. In Resolution 421 (V) the General Assembly charged the Commission on Human Rights with the task of studying the means by which all peoples would enjoy self-determination; and in Resolution 545 (VI) it resolved that any future covenant on human rights should be drafted so that '[a]ll peoples shall have the right of self-determination'.[90] Accordingly, Article 1 of the International Covenant on Civil and Political Rights of 1966 states: '[a]ll peoples have the right of self-determination.

---

[89] 'Final Communiqué of the Bandung Conference, 24 April 1955', in N. Frankland (ed.), *Documents on International Affairs, 1955* (Oxford: Oxford University Press, 1958), 433.

[90] General Assembly Resolution 421 (V), *Yearbook of the United Nations, 1950* (New York: United Nations Department of Public Information, 1951), 530; and quoted in *Yearbook of the United Nations, 1952*, 439.

By virtue of that right they freely determine their political status and freely pursue their economic, social and cultural development.'[91] The right of self-determination is again affirmed in Resolution 637 A (VII), which declares what is enshrined in the Final Communiqué of the Bandung Conference: 'the right of peoples and nations to self-determination is a prerequisite to the full enjoyment of all fundamental human rights'.[92] And Resolution 2621 (XXV) declares, in even stronger language, that colonialism is a crime and reaffirms the right of all colonial peoples to self-determination and their 'inherent right... to struggle by all necessary means' to secure freedom and independence.[93] The principles embodied in these resolutions presupposed a normative shift whereby independence became an unqualified right and colonialism an absolute wrong.[94]

But the most important and celebrated statement in what would come to be known as the law of decolonization is found in General Assembly Resolution 1514 (XV): The Declaration on the Granting Independence to Colonial Countries and Peoples. In affirming the supreme value of self-determination, this landmark resolution declared that the denial of independence precluded the full enjoyment of fundamental human rights and that colonialism itself, no matter how enlightened, impeded the realization of world peace. Keeping people in a state of dependence inflicted a grievous injury on the sanctity of their human dignity. Thus, the great achievement of Resolution 1514 was that it established the principle that dependent peoples were entitled to determine their own destiny without preconditions of any sort: '[i]nadequacy of political, economic, social or educational preparedness should never serve as a pretext for delaying independence.'[95] This unequivocal repudiation of any test of preparedness dealt a fatal blow to the legitimacy of trusteeship: the right of self-determination transformed trusteeship into nothing less than a crime against humanity. The idea that a people could

---

[91] 'International Covenant on Civil and Political Rights, 1966', in I. Brownlie (ed.), *Basic Documents on Human Rights*, 3rd edn (Oxford: Clarendon Press, 1992), 125. The International Covenant on Economic, Social, and Cultural Rights, 1966, contains the same article pertaining to self-determination. See Brownlie, *Basic Documents on Human Rights*, 114.

[92] 'General Assembly Resolution 637 A (VII)', *Yearbook of the United Nations, 1952* (New York: United Nations Department of Public Information, 1953), 445; and 'Final Communiqué of the Bandung Conference', 433.

[93] 'General Assembly Resolution 2621 (XXV)', *Yearbook of the United Nations, 1970* (New York: United Nations Department of Public Information, 1972), 707.

[94] R. Jackson, *Quasi-States: Sovereignty, International Relations and the Third World* (Cambridge: Cambridge University Press, 1990), 85.

[95] 'Declaration on the Granting of Independence to Colonial Countries and Peoples, 1960', in I. Brownlie (ed.), *Basic Documents on Human Rights*, 3rd edn (Oxford: Clarendon Press, 1992), 29.

be deprived of their right to independence on account of inferior race, false religion, decaying culture, despotic government, and repulsive habits, customs, and traditions no longer had any place in world affairs. For newly independent members of international society generally agreed that '[t]he Trusteeship System has not justified itself anywhere and should be buried together with the entire colonial system, which is an anachronism.'[96] Significantly, then, decolonization abolished the distinction upon which the idea of trusteeship depended. There were no more 'child-like' peoples that required guidance in becoming 'adult' peoples: everyone was entitled by right to the independence that came with adulthood. Thus, it no longer made any sense to speak of a hierarchical world order in which a measure of development or a test of fitness determined membership in the society of states.

With the acceptance of Resolution 1514, by the unambiguous vote of 89 to 0 with 7 abstentions, an entire approach to understanding and organizing world affairs suddenly seemed to be hopelessly out of date. Decolonization signalled an historic change in the criteria that determined membership in the society of states. Whereas membership in international society prior to decolonization admitted the conditional reasoning of trusteeship, post-colonial international society excluded all considerations of efficacy, utility, and ability. Thus, it became possible for dependent peoples to argue with great effect that '[a]lien rule, no matter how benevolent or paternalistic, inhibits the free development of peoples, saps their creative energies and deprives them of their national self-respect and dignity. Foreign domination can never be a substitute for independence.'[97] This argument obtained legal standing in Security Council Resolution 183 (1963), in so far as it acknowledged formally 'the interpretation of self-determination laid down in General Assembly resolution 1514 (XV).'[98] The discourse of 'fitness' was therefore no longer intelligible in international life. Thereafter, Portugal, the European power most determined to retain the trappings of empire, could no longer plead its case by invoking its centuries of colonial experience. The right of self-determination disallowed, by definition, all arguments that invoked considerations of skill or achievement. Champions of the British Empire were likewise stripped of their most potent defence, for it was impossible to argue, as did W. M. Macmillan, that African nationalists consistently underrated the complexities of independence; that they confronted burdens imposed by

[96] United Nations General Assembly, 926th Plenary Meeting, 28 November 1960, United Nations General Assembly Official Records, A/PV 926, 1000–1.

[97] United Nations General Assembly, 927th Plenary Meeting, 29 November 1960, United Nations General Assembly Official Records, A/PV 927, 1011.

[98] United Nations Security Council, S/RES/183 (1963).

adult responsibilities for which they were not prepared; and that they 'demand, but have not yet learnt the full meaning of, equality'.[99]

Africans and Asians advanced their cause, and thereby rejected the legitimacy of trusteeship, by invoking the irreducible value of freedom. Indeed, Mr Alemayehou, the Ethiopian representative to the United Nations, articulated the fundamental claim of this argument just before the General Assembly adopted Resolution 1514:

But if, in spite of all, the question would be to choose between freedom with all its attendant economic difficulties and internal conflicts on the one hand, and the maintenance of colonial rule with all its attendant subjugation, exploitation, degradation and humiliation, and so on, on the other, I would right away and unequivocally say that the peoples, all peoples, under colonial rule prefer poverty in freedom to wealth in slavery, and they will definitely prefer fighting in freedom to peace in slavery.[100]

Freedom is of supreme value, even more so than personal welfare, even if it means placing one's self in danger in order to escape the humiliation of subjugation. It is in this context that anti-colonial powers mounted a sustained assault on South Africa's claims in respect of one of the most difficult of all colonial questions—the mandate of South West Africa. The General Assembly deployed both arguments against trusteeship, the right of self-determination and the violation of trust, in rejecting South Africa's attempt to assimilate the mandate. In Resolution 2145 (XXI) it affirmed that 'the people of South West Africa have the inalienable right to self-determination, freedom, and independence' and then declared the revocation of South Africa's mandatory rights because it failed 'to fulfil its obligations in respect of the administration of the Mandated Territory and to ensure the moral and material well-being and security of the indigenous inhabitants of South West Africa'.[101] The General Assembly's decisions in respect of South West Africa only confirmed what was already obvious: trusteeship was no longer a recognized and accepted practice of international society. For the force of these arguments smashed the props that sustained the legitimacy of trusteeship, not only in South West Africa, but in nearly all the world's non-self-governing territories.

---

[99] 'General Assembly Resolution on Territories Under Portuguese Administration, Adopted 14 December 1962', in D. C. Watt (ed.), *Documents on International Affairs, 1962* (Oxford: Oxford University Press, 1971), 893; United Nations General Assembly, 926th Plenary Meeting, 989; and W. M. Macmillan, 'African Growing Pains', *United Empire*, 44, 3 (1953), 104.

[100] United Nations General Assembly, 928th Plenary Meeting, 30 November 1960, United Nations General Assembly Official Records, A/PV 928, 1021.

[101] 'General Assembly Resolution 2145 (XXI)', *Yearbook of the United Nations, 1966* (New York: United Nations Department of Public Information, 1968), 605–6.

Human Equality and the Illegitimacy of Trusteeship

On 3 February 1960, British Prime Minister Harold Macmillan said before the South African Parliament: '[t]he wind of change is blowing through this continent and, whether we like it or not, this growth of national consciousness is a political fact. We must all accept it as a fact, and our national policies must take account of it.'[102] But what sort of idea did this wind of change carry, and why did it so effectively destroy the legitimacy of trusteeship? African and Asian nationalists seemed to object most strenuously to their status as political, economic, social, cultural, and racial unequals; and their subsequent estrangement from their European masters culminated in an unrelenting and unequivocal demand for absolute equality. They demanded their own state in which to make their own decisions about their own political, economic, and social future. Thus, Africans and Asians objected to alien rule in no small part because it was premised upon conditions of inequality.

In asserting their demand for equality Africans and Asians certainly revolted against their colonial masters, but they did not reject the West as such. Rather, their encounter with the West, while marked by many instances of aggression, humiliation, and degradation, is also an immensely successful story of making the ideas of the West their own. Hedley Bull describes this revolt against the West as having been:

conducted, as least ostensibly, in the name of ideas or values that are themselves Western, even if it is not clear in all cases that these ideas are exclusively or uniquely Western: the rights of states to sovereign equality, the rights of nations to self-determination, the rights of human beings to equal treatment irrespective of race, their rights to minimum standards of economic and social welfare.[103]

Africans and Asians succeeded in destroying the legitimacy of trusteeship, and empire along with it, by turning the ideas of the West against the West; and no idea is more important in that regard than obtaining recognition of the right to makes one's own decisions by one's own lights. It is this idea that secures the good of self-determination. The idea of self-determination implies that the good life is possible when actions are freely chosen in relation to human needs, desires, values, and interests; and it recognizes, as Elie Kedourie summarized what he took to be the great insight of Immanuel

---

[102] H. Macmillan, 'The Wind of Change: Speech to Both Houses of the Parliament of the Union of South Africa, Cape Town, 3 February 1960', in A. N. Porter and A. J. Stockwell (eds.), *British Imperial Policy and Decolonization, 1938–64*, vol. 2 (London: Macmillan, 1987), 525.

[103] Bull, 'The Revolt Against the West', in H. Bull and A. Watson (eds.), *The Expansion of International Society* (Oxford: Clarendon Press, 1984), 222.

Kant's thought, that the 'good will, which is the free will, is also the autonomous will'.[104] Trusteeship rules out the notion of autonomous will. Europeans acted on behalf of Africans and Asians that were deemed (by Europeans) to be incapable of self-direction on account of some sort of political, economic, religious, or racial defect. Hence dependent peoples were treated as immature children, as opposed to mature adults, that did not properly understand the conditions of their own happiness. Self-determination destroyed this manner of thinking to the extent that it requires recognition of the equality of all who lay claim to it. Indeed, Michael Oakeshott argues that the right of self-determination depends fundamentally on principle of reciprocal recognition: '[t]o deny the right of self-determination to others is to remove the foundation upon which a man claims it for himself.'[105]

Armed with the ideas of the West, equality being foremost among them, the colonial peoples of Africa and Asia mounted a determined and ultimately successful assault on the legitimacy of trusteeship. Indeed, A. W. Benn reminded members of the House of Commons in 1959 that the origin of African 'extremism' is found in British universities and in the British Parliament itself, for 'here in this Chamber is the greatest revolutionary inspiration of the lot. If we can do it, why cannot they do it?' For what impressed him most about the new leaders of Africa was what 'they had in common with everyone in this country and with the famous leaders of the last century who sought to bring equal political, economic and social rights to the working class in Britain'.[106] The claim of equality also precluded the implementation of a proposal for establishing a 'second tier' membership for African colonies in the British Commonwealth, because it would be rightly interpreted as sustaining relations of subordination. Subsequent events proved that all British colonies, no matter how small, poor, and otherwise marginal, were entitled, not only to full and equal membership in the Commonwealth, but to full and equal membership in the society of states as well. Africans and Asians asserted their claim of equality at the United Nations by holding colonial powers accountable to their own standards. They quoted Abraham Lincoln, Woodrow Wilson, the Atlantic Charter, and they invoked the ideals of the American and French revolutions. They too claimed the rights of men. Egyptians asked if the colonial powers had forgotten 'that a great American said: "... that all men are created equal, that they are endowed by their Creator with certain inalienable rights, that among these are life, liberty and

---

[104] E. Kedourie, *Nationalism* (London: Hutchinson University Library, 1971), 24.

[105] M. Oakeshott, in *Morality and Politics in Modern Europe* ed. S. R. Letwin (New Haven, CT: Yale University Press, 1993), 60.

[106] Benn, 'Speech on Colonial Policy in the House of Commons', 516–7.

the pursuit of happiness"'; and Ghanaians similarly argued: '[t]he writings of Rousseau, Jefferson, Marx, Thomas Paine, Machiavelli and other political thinkers have had their influence. Thus, everywhere in Africa, Africans demand freedom, equality, and justice.'[107] The principal justification of trusteeship, that colonial peoples were not competent to direct their own affairs, simply could not withstand the blows inflicted by these arguments. Europeans found themselves unable to reply in any meaningful way because they could not claim the rights of men for themselves and at the same time withhold them from the men of Africa and Asia. And so the legitimacy of the idea of trusteeship succumbed to the legitimacy of the idea of universal human equality.

---

[107] United Nations General Assembly, 929th Plenary Meeting, 30 November 1960, United Nations General Assembly Official Records, A/PV 929, 1047.

6

The New Paternalism

On 1 November 1994, the United Nations Trusteeship Council voted to suspend operations after Palau, the last remaining trust territory, attained independence. The idea of trusteeship expressed in Chapter XI of the United Nations charter is scarcely more relevant as only a handful of non-self-governing territories, most of which are marginal in size, location, and importance, remain subject to its provisions. Indeed, the international law of trusteeship has, for the most part, fallen into disuse for the same reason that it is no longer necessary to interpret declarations of colonial policy in order to obtain insight into the obligations of trusteeship. The sovereign state has emerged out of decolonization as the supreme form of political organization in post-colonial international society—an international society in which dominions, colonies, principalities, free cities, and, of course, mandates and trust territories, have all but vanished. To the person who is unacquainted with these historic forms of political association, trusteeship is likely to appear as a remote and obscure practice of the past. We now live in what is truly a universal society of states. But the ostensible failure of this post-colonial project, the fact that the promise of peace and prosperity held out by independent statehood is too often betrayed by appalling violence and absolute poverty, has reinvigorated interest in trusteeship as a way of responding to problems of international disorder and injustice. Thus, the purpose of this chapter is threefold. First, I want to examine the principal dilemma of decolonization that has resulted in a renewed interest in trusteeship. Second, I want to consider this renewed interest in trusteeship in the context of international involvement in administering Bosnia and Herzegovina, Kosovo, and, until recently, East Timor. Third, and by way of conclusion, I want to reflect upon the normative implications that a resurrected practice of trusteeship carries for a society of states that is premised on the juridical equality of all its members.

The False Promise of Post-Colonial Independence

Just before the Constituent Assembly of India adopted the state's newly drafted constitution in 1949, B. R. Ambedkar reminded his colleagues of the implications of sovereign statehood: '[i]ndependence is no doubt a matter of joy. But let us not forget that this independence has thrown on us great responsibilities. By independence, we have lost the excuse of blaming the British for anything going wrong. If hereafter things go wrong, we will have nobody to blame except ourselves.'[1] In these brief and unusually candid words we are able to detect the supreme dilemma of decolonization: independence held out the promise of emancipation, but entailed a frightening risk of failure. This promise of emancipation, deliverance from poverty, ignorance, and oppression, conceives states as public arrangements which afford groups of human beings an opportunity to pursue and, if they are successful, to live the good life. Independence endows a group of people with the right to build a state of their own, a state directed towards the realization of ends that are of their own choosing, rather than ends that are chosen for them. Human beings make choices, which are usually flawed and imperfect in some way, in relation to particular and divergent beliefs about what is thought to be right, good, and desirable. But the ends they cherish rarely, if ever, constitute a harmonious whole. Indeed, our world is a study of difference; it is a world conspicuous for a diversity of ideas and values that move human beings to action. Most human beings agree in the abstract that it is good to be just, but there is little agreement amongst them about what it means to be just in particular situations. Thus, what may be desirable, advantageous, pleasurable, sublime, or virtuous to one person may be anything but those things to someone else. And it is independence, and all the responsibilities it entails, that permits human beings to strive for ends that are distinctly their own.

The hazards of independence did not fail to impress Ambedkar, who proved to be prophetically correct when he also warned his colleagues that with independence 'there is a great danger of things going wrong'.[2] Indeed, things have gone very badly wrong in a frighteningly large number of states that emerged out of the ashes of empire. One of the distinctive features of post-colonial international society is the problem of failed states, that is, states in which evidence of the good life is largely, if not totally, absent. The category 'failed states' does not, however, include all underdeveloped states: poverty, disease, and lack of education are not by themselves sufficient to make a state a failed state. The poor, the diseased, and the ignorant are no less responsible for acting civilly than the rich, the well, and the educated.[3] And, in fact, most do. Rather, failed states are typically distinguished by a type of

---

[1] Government of India, *The Constituent Assembly Debates: Official Report, 14-11-1949 to 26-11-1949*, vol. 11 (New Delhi: Lok Sabha Secretariat, undated), 980.   [2] Ibid. 980.

[3] R. Jackson, *The Global Covenant: Human Conduct in a World of States* (Oxford: Oxford University Press, 2000), 295.

violence which, according to K. J. Holsti, is initiated in the absence of formal declarations of belligerents, prosecuted in lieu of established and accepted codes of international conduct, and concluded in want of negotiated settlements. These so-called wars of the third kind obliterate the distinction between civilian and soldier, and, consequently, they visit disproportionate destruction upon the innocent and the unarmed. Wars of the third kind are predominantly affairs of attrition, terror, and psychological actions against civilians; for they 'involve civilians as both combatants and victims, [and] their main legacy after killing and maiming is the waves of refugees they create'.[4] Thus, in failed states, authority, right, and law count for little as disputes are settled according to the dictates of necessity and the unbridled assertion of power. The activity of politics is an elusive and all too infrequent engagement in public life as tolerance, compromise, and accommodation give place to absolutism, coercion, and violence. Failed states are, then, in Robert Jackson's words, states that 'cannot or will not safeguard minimal *civil* conditions for their populations: domestic peace, law and order, and good governance [emphasis in original]'.[5] Daily life in these states is a sordid tale of endemic civil war, gross human rights abuses, and absolute poverty.

The false promise of independence calls to mind arguments that once justified trusteeship as a way of responding to problems that are today associated with failed states. The difficulty with independence, as Margery Perham understood it, was that most colonial territories lacked many of the attributes of coherent and viable communities, the most important being the existence of a notion of community—civic, natural, or otherwise. These societies were politically weak, economically impoverished, socially divided, and their populations ignorant of the obligations of citizenship and unfamiliar with the workings of modern government. This general condition of backwardness, Perham argued, presented the greatest obstacle to the granting of independence.[6] For those who wished for an orderly transformation of empire, and surely Perham would be included among them, the granting of independence could not be separated from an estimate of ability. Conducting the affairs of state required a type of wisdom and experience that is acquired slowly and only in the practice of doing things. Even the most sympathetic voices in support of colonial independence maintained, as did Arthur Creech Jones, that the extension of 'political freedom is an indifferent objective if the economic basis for the operation of that freedom is not properly laid'.[7] For

---

[4] K. J. Holsti, *The State, War, and the State of War* (Cambridge: Cambridge University Press, 1996), ch. 2.   [5] Jackson, *The Global Covenant*, 296.

[6] M. Perham, *The Colonial Reckoning* (London: Collins, 1961), 26.

[7] A. C. Jones, 'The Labour Party and Colonial Policy 1945–51', in A. C. Jones (ed.), *New Fabian Colonial Essays* (London: Hogarth Press, 1959), 25.

independence to mean anything, for it to contribute something valuable, it must be subjected to a test of ability. Thus, the best for which the inadequately prepared could hope was a graded status under the watchful eye of a supervising trustee. To proceed any other way would be to embark upon an uncertain journey fraught with danger. Indeed, Perham warned with great prescience in 1945 that if the colonies were 'cut loose, they would presumably be set up as very weak units under an experimental world organization'.[8]

It is certainly true that places like Afghanistan, Angola, Burma, the Congo, Cambodia, East Timor, Liberia, Rwanda, Sierra Leone, Somalia, and the Sudan have been in recent years extraordinarily dangerous places in which to live.[9] But the desperate conditions that are the hallmark of daily life in these places should not be confused with being peculiarly African or Asian. The atrocities committed in the Balkans ought to dispel the notion that the moral and material achievements of Western civilization have rendered Europe immune to the sort of wanton destruction that might justify trusteeship. Failed states are creatures of a normative shift that precipitated decolonization and which, subsequently, became entrenched in international law. Thus, the world's most destitute states, and the patterns of violence to which they give rise, are sustained in a rather perverse way by the constitutive norms of international society. Sovereign equality, political independence, territorial integrity, and non-interference help ensure the survival of what are otherwise unviable states.[10] Prior to decolonization, membership in international society depended upon a state's ability and willingness to fulfil the obligations of statehood. Only these so-called civilized states were entitled to membership in international society. Passion and violence, the hallmarks of barbarism, excluded 'uncivilized' peoples from membership because they were to the nineteenth century mind incapable of respecting the law of nations. Hence, John Stuart Mill argued that barbarians were fit only to be conquered and subjugated to foreign rule.[11] James Lorimer, a nineteenth century international lawyer, similarly argued that barbarian and savage societies, inasmuch as they are unable to perform the duties of statehood, were entitled only to partial or human recognition because they could not be trusted to perform the duties of civilized nations. These societies, he maintained, were populated

---

[8] M. Perham, 'Education for Self-Government', *Colonial Sequence, 1930–1949* (London: Methuen & Co., 1967), 267.

[9] See E. W. Nafziger, F. Stewart, and R. Vayrynen (eds.), *War, Hunger, and Displacement: The Origins of Humanitarian Emergencies* (Oxford: Oxford University Press, 2000).

[10] For a detailed explication of this argument, see R. Jackson, *Quasi-States: Sovereignty, International Relations and the Third World* (Cambridge: Cambridge University Press, 1990).

[11] J. S. Mill, 'A Few Words on Non-Intervention', in G. Himmelfarb (ed.) *Essays on Politics and Culture*, (Gloucester, MA: Peter Smith, 1973), 377–78.

by child-like races, and the relation between 'inferior races and superior races, if such there be, is that of perpetual pupilarity and guardianship'.[12]

This practice of the past is nowhere more evident than in the Charter of the United Nations, which stipulates in Article 4(1) that the membership of the organization shall be comprised of states that are 'able and willing' to carry out the obligations of the Charter.[13] However, this criterion of membership is today little more than legal fiction since the law of decolonization established that denial of independence precluded the full enjoyment of fundamental human rights and that colonialism itself, no matter how enlightened, impeded the realization of world peace. Independence by right resulted in the creation of a class of states that were entitled to full and unqualified membership in the society of states, but lacked working institutional arrangements, relied disproportionately upon international assistance, and whose existence was underwritten by the moral justification of self-determination.[14] That some states more closely resemble Hobbes' state of nature raises searching questions about the justification of sovereign statehood. The law of contemporary international society is well equipped to deal with domestic disorder that threatens the general peace; but in lieu of a threat to international peace and security, a situation that would oblige the Security Council to act, international law is rather poorly equipped to respond to the problems presented by failed states. It is with this dilemma in mind that Mervyn Frost argues that '[a] self-respecting free state is one that is recognized as such by other such states'.[15] The act of granting recognition is therefore concerned with the realization of an autonomous state that is fundamental to the well-being of its citizens; and granting recognition to a (failed) state, one that cannot fulfil its domestic or international obligations, enjoins an activity of learning so that it might develop into a 'fully competent member' of international society. Thus, if the autonomy of one state depends on the autonomy of all others, then people residing in failed states cannot be left to sort out their problems on their own. Rather, steps must be taken so that they do not compound their mistakes; they must be educated, tutored, and guided in the aspects in which they are deficient, '[j]ust as social workers attempt to educate inadequate parents to the responsibilities of parenthood'.[16]

---

[12] J. Lorimer, *The Institutes of the Law of Nations: A Treatise of the Jural Relations of Separate Political Communities*, vol. 1 (Edinburgh: William Blackwood and Sons, 1883), 101–33, 158.

[13] 'Charter of the United Nations', in A. Roberts and B. Kingsbury (eds.), *United Nations, Divided World* (Oxford: Clarendon Press, 1993), 502.   [14] Jackson, *Quasi-States*, 169.

[15] M. Frost, 'What Ought to be Done about the Condition of States?' in C. Navari (ed.), *The Condition of States: A Study in Normative Political Theory* (Milton Keynes: Open University Press, 1991), 195.

[16] Ibid. 195; M. Frost, *Ethics in International Relations: A Constitutive Theory* (Cambridge: Cambridge University Press, 1996), 146–55; and Jackson, *The Global Covenant*, 300–1.

While Frost edges towards the idea of trusteeship when he suggests that failed states should be educated in becoming legitimate members of international society, Peter Lyon goes one step further in suggesting that pronouncements of the death of trusteeship may have been premature. The weak and disadvantaged peoples of the world, he observes, continue to be disproportionately affected by persistent disorder, warfare, human misery, and acute shortages of welfare. And while he concedes that any attempt to resurrect trusteeship is sure to evoke unhappy memories of colonialism, he maintains nonetheless that 'a UN trusteeship would almost certainly be an improvement on the anarchical condition of the several quasi-states the world has now'.[17] Indeed, the events of post-colonial international society seem to have vindicated the views of Margery Perham rather than those of Kwame Nkrumah. It is in this respect that Ronald Robinson's claim, made in 1965, rings especially true: '[t]he problems of trusteeship were the problems of power, of the responsibilities of the strong towards the weak. The unequal distribution of political and economic power in the world, which was the fundamental basis of colonialism, has not been suddenly abolished by the accession of most colonies to political independence.'[18] This view is no less true today than it was at the onset of decolonization. Independence, and its central assumption that self-determination is an indispensable prerequisite of peace, security, and welfare, has been for some people just as dangerous as Ambedkar feared. And, consequently, Lyon's defence of trusteeship raises a question of signal importance: is there once again a place for trusteeship in world affairs?

Innovation and Convention

The proposition that there is a place for trusteeship in contemporary world affairs is most frequently argued in the context of three cases: Bosnia and Herzegovina, East Timor, and Kosovo. These territories are conspicuous for administrative arrangements that grant to the United Nations and other international organizations sweeping authority to conduct the day-to-day affairs of government. Missions undertaken by the United Nations in particular, missions that are typically subsumed under the rubric of international, interim, or transitional administration, are often described as being 'unprecedented',

---

[17] P. Lyon, 'The Rise and Fall and Possible Revival of International Trusteeship', *The Journal of Commonwealth and Comparative Politics*, 31/1 (1993), 105–7.

[18] K. Robinson, *The Dilemmas of Trusteeship: Aspects of British Colonial Policy Between the Wars* (London: Oxford University Press, 1965), 93.

'novel', or 'unique'. The Report of the Panel on United Nations Peace Operations (Brahimi Report) conveys just this sentiment in asserting that the interim administration in Kosovo (UNMIK) and the now defunct transitional administration in East Timor (UNTAET) present 'challenges and responsibilities that are unique among United Nations field operations'.[19] But international involvement in the administration of a disputed territory or failed state does not in and of itself bear the mark of innovation. The League of Nations administered the Free City of Danzig from 1920–1939, the Colombian district of Leticia from 1933–1934, and the German Saar Basin for a period of 15 years as part of the compensatory reparations imposed by the Treaty of Versailles. The United Nations too is not without experience in the field of international administration: the Congo, Irian Jaya, and South West Africa (Namibia) have all been in varying degrees objects of United Nations administration that predate the responsibilities undertaken in the Balkans and East Timor.[20]

If the name 'international administration' is to mean anything substantive, if it is to impart anything more than the current state of academic and journalistic jargon, then it must consist in something more than traditional peace operations. Ensuring security, monitoring cease-fires, disarming paramilitary groups, promoting human rights, facilitating truth and reconciliation, and providing technical assistance for institutional and economic development are all related and relevant to international administration, but they do not individually or collectively imply an activity that is distinguishable from conflict resolution, peacekeeping, and peace-building.[21] Rather, the missions in Kosovo and East Timor, and to a lesser extent in Bosnia and Herzegovina, are said to be innovative because of the extraordinary executive and legislative powers enjoyed by international administrators who are in no way directly accountable to the people over whom they exercise these powers. For example, UNMIK Regulation 1 vests in the office of the Special Representative of the Secretary-General '[a]ll legislative and executive authority with respect to Kosovo, including the administration of the judiciary'.[22] A nearly identical

---

[19] 'Report of the Panel on United Nations Peace Operations (Brahimi Report)', United Nations General Assembly/Security Council, A/55/305-S/2000/809, 13. For similar opinions, see J. Chopra, 'The UN's Kingdom in East Timor', *Survival*, 42/3 (2000), 29; M. J. Matheson, 'United Nations Governance of Postconflict Societies', *American Journal of International Law*, 95/1 (2001), 79; B. Kondoch, 'The United Nations Administration of East Timor', *Journal of Conflict and Security Law*, 6/2 (2001), 246; and S. Chesterman, 'East Timor in Transition: Self-determination, State-building and the United Nations', *International Peacekeeping*, 9/1 (2002), 46.

[20] See R. Wilde, 'From Danzig to East Timor and Beyond: The Role of International Territorial Administration', *The American Journal of International Law*, 95/3 (2001), 583–606.

[21] For an overview of United Nations peace operations, see the Brahimi Report, 2–3.

[22] UNMIK, 'Regulation No. 1999/1, On the Authority of the Interim Administration in Kosovo, 25 July 1999', UNMIK/REG/1999/1, section 1.

regulation that clarified the extent of UNTAET's authority afforded no greater facility for local accountability: the Special Representative there was charged to 'consult and co-operate closely with the representatives of the East Timorese people'.[23] In these territories law is promulgated rather than enacted. The Special Representative is empowered to appoint persons at all levels of government and to remove them should they act in a manner that is inconsistent with the principles and purpose of the mission. And the legitimacy of these arrangements is underwritten, not by the consent of the governed, but by the will of the Security Council—the only institution to which the Special Representative is accountable.

In Bosnia and Herzegovina, the Office of the High Representative created by the Dayton Peace Agreement is similarly empowered to promulgate law and to remove elected officials, even those of the highest rank, who are judged to be in violation of the Peace Agreement or the terms of its implementation. The extent of this authority is laid bare in Paddy Ashdown's inaugural address upon assuming the duties of High Representative in May 2002: 'I have concluded that there are two ways I can make my decisions. One is with a tape measure, measuring the precise equidistant position between three sides. The other is by doing what I think is right for the country as a whole. I prefer the second of these.'[24] In these words it is possible to detect a rather pronounced and perhaps paradoxical distrust of democratic politics. Value is ascribed to democracy in part because individual human beings are thought to be the best judges of their own interests. The people of Bosnia and Herzegovina are told that they must extinguish the chauvinist fires of nationalism and they are urged to choose leaders of hope rather than fear, in a thinly veiled reference to the deadly politics of ethnic conflict. Only then will they enjoy a stable and prosperous democratic society and accede fully to the European family of nations. But should they fail in this enterprise and elect officials who are corrupt or who are hostile to the idea of a multi-ethnic democratic state, it is then the solemn duty of the High Representative to make the 'right' choice on their behalf by removing the offending party from office. Hence, Ashdown professes that it is not his job to 'interfere in elections', but he leaves no doubt that he will use the exceptional powers of his office if they can be made to serve what he conceives to be the interests of the people as a whole.[25]

It is breadth of authority and the degree of interference that international administration entails, not only in Bosnia and Herzegovina, but in Kosovo

---

[23] UNTAET, 'Regulation No. 1999/1, On the Authority of the Transitional Administration in East Timor, 27 November 1999', UNTAET/REG/1999/1, section 1.

[24] P. Ashdown, 'Inaugural Speech by Paddy Ashdown, the New High Representative for Bosnia and Herzegovina', Office of the High Representative Press Office, 27 May 2002. For commentary, see D. Chandler, 'Bosnia's New Colonial Governor', *Guardian*, 9 July 2002.

[25] See Ashdown 'Inaugural Speech'.

and East Timor as well, that is said to be unique. Indeed, '[n]o operations,' the Brahimi Report says of UNMIK and UNTAET, 'must set and enforce the law, establish customs services and regulations, set and collect business and personal taxes, attract foreign investment, adjudicate property disputes and liabilities for war damage, reconstruct and operate all public utilities, create a banking system, run schools and pay teachers and collect the garbage'.[26] Yet, for all the ostensible innovation that contemporary international administration is claimed to represent, there seems to be an abundance of confusion about the juridical status of the territories that are or have been subject to such arrangements. For example, David Chandler describes Bosnia and Herzegovina as an international protectorate that is subordinate to a High Representative whose authority is more akin to that of a colonial governor.[27] In the wake of NATO's intervention in Kosovo, former American Deputy Secretary of State Strobe Talbott saw fit to describe Kosovo's present status as that of a 'ward of the international community'.[28] Jarat Chopra, a former member of the transitional administration in East Timor, has described UNTAET as approximating something like a 'pre-constitutional monarch in a sovereign kingdom'.[29] And in view of each of these cases, in what seems to be an attempt to answer Lyon's call for the revival of trusteeship, Richard Caplan suggests that a new form of trusteeship is now 'a reality in all but name'.[30] But these associations—protectorate, sovereign kingdom, and trusteeship—and the authorities that rule them—colonial governor and pre-constitutional monarch—disclose distinct and mutually exclusive identities. A sovereign kingdom is neither a protectorate nor a ward, and the activity of ruling as a monarch, pre-constitutional or otherwise, is not the same as the activity of ruling as a colonial governor. The postulates in which these constitutions and offices are intelligible presuppose particular beliefs about how public life should be carried out and they specify the terms of participation in a particular association, as well as the nature of authority that is peculiar to that association. Thus, it is impossible to confirm the 'reality' of a resurrected practice of trusteeship on account of the extraordinary executive and legislative powers exhibited in cases that are in fact constitutionally different.

These constitutional differences, which obscure crucial distinctions if left unexamined, demand further scrutiny if we are to acquire an adequate understanding of trusteeship in contemporary international society. For

---

[26] Brahimi Report, 13.   [27] Chandler, 'Bosnia's New Colonial Governor'.
[28] S. Talbott, 'The Balkan Question and the European Answer', Address at the Aspen Institute, Aspen, Colorado, August 24, 1999, 5.
[29] Chopra, 'The UN's Kingdom in East Timor', 29.
[30] R. Caplan, 'A New Trusteeship?: The International Administration of War-torn Territories', *Adelphi Paper, No. 341* (London: IISS, 2002), 7.

example, in arguing that at present Bosnia and Herzegovina more closely resembles an international protectorate than what is commonly understood as a sovereign state, Chandler observes that the internationally directed attempt to establish a viable multi-ethnic democratic state has rendered meaningless the notion of self-government.[31] What began as a one-year period of transition that was to be terminated in September 1996 has been since extended indefinitely. NATO remains seized with the task of providing security in a country where substantial portions of the population demonstrate a pronounced reluctance, if not outright unwillingness, to live peacefully alongside one another. The Organization for Security and Co-operation in Europe (OSCE) continues to exercise extensive supervisory powers over the electoral process, including the adoption of rules and regulations pertaining to registration, participation, and enforcement. And, all along, the notoriously vague language of the Dayton Agreement has been read in the broadest terms possible, thereby enlarging further the international role in public life and marginalizing, by the same proportion, local authorities and institutions. Indeed, the extent to which the population of Bosnia and Herzegovina has been excluded from public life leads Chandler to conclude that the internationally supervised political reconstruction of Bosnia and Herzegovina is evocative of the 'White Man's Burden' that provided such a powerful justification of nineteenth century empire.[32] But this attempt to trade on the paternal discourse of empire, which embraced trusteeship in a righteous mission of civilization ordained by divine providence, is in this particular context misleading because it mistakes a condition of independence for one of dependence.

The people of Bosnia and Herzegovina are not, in the tradition of imperial trusteeship, members of a primitive society, devoid of reason and child-like in habit and development, who must be coerced for their own good until they understand and are able to realize the conditions of their own happiness. The international presence in Bosnia and Herzegovina is coercive to be sure; but that alone is not enough to satisfy the criteria of trusteeship, much less extinguish the independence of a sovereign state. Bosnia and Herzegovina is a member of the society of states and it is, if the United Nations charter is to be taken seriously, the legal equal of each of the other members of that society, no matter how militarily weak, economically poor, and socially fractured it might be. And as a member of the society of states, it is expected, like all others, to conduct its foreign relations according to the fundamental principles of that association. Thus, the juridical status that is our concern, namely sovereign statehood, leaves no other conclusion than Bosnia and Herzegovina

---

[31] D. Chandler, *Bosnia: Faking Democracy After Dayton*, 2nd edn. (London: Pluto Press, 2000), 64.   [32] Ibid. 3, 34–65.

is fully, as opposed to nominally, independent, despite protestations to the contrary. Indeed, it is not possible, at least so far as international practice is concerned, to be constitutionally independent and at the same time constitutionally dependent. Sovereign statehood, and the independence that is its necessary consequence, refers to a 'legal, an absolute, and a unitary condition'.[33] Thus, the vast international presence in Bosnia and Herzegovina, which is commonly mistaken for the type of juridical dependence implied by trusteeship, is less intelligible in the paternal discourse of empire than in the concept of civil freedom that Rousseau puts forth in *The Social Contract*. On this view, freedom consists in human beings obeying law that they have made themselves; and such a condition of freedom is realized when appetite gives way to duty so that they are obedient to their own will for the good of all. But Rousseau submits that, because there can be no guarantee that these duties will be observed, it may be necessary, lest the compact from which their freedom arises be in vain, 'to compel a man to be free'.[34] It is in this spirit that the people of Bosnia and Herzegovina have subjected themselves to the authority of the High Representative—the 'final authority in theater'[35] regarding the interpretation of law that they have made for themselves. In other words, the international administrative arrangements established by the Dayton Agreement represent, not the horizon of innovation, but the stolid convention of an international treaty, joining legally and, therefore, authoritatively equal parties in an exchange of promises, that is legitimated by the principle of consent.

The transitional administration that guided East Timor to independent statehood was established, not by an international treaty that expressed the will of parties to whom particular administrative arrangements shall apply, but by Security Council resolution 1272 (1999), which endowed UNTAET 'with overall responsibility for the administration of East Timor'.[36] But lost in the dinned enthusiasm for a world of innovation, the many pronouncements that the international presence in East Timor heralds either the resurrection of trusteeship or a unique experiment in protecting distressed civilians, is a rather more conventional account of United Nations involvement in that once troubled territory. In short, the juridical status that is so crucial to understanding the international role in bringing East Timor to independence, and

---

[33] A. James, 'The Practice of Sovereign Statehood in Contemporary International Society', in R. Jackson (ed.), *Sovereignty at the Millennium* (Oxford: Blackwell Publishers, 1999), 40.

[34] J. J. Rousseau, 'The Social Contract', *Social Contract: Essays by Locke, Hume, and Rousseau* (Oxford University Press, 1971), 179–84.

[35] 'General Framework Agreement for Peace in Bosnia and Herzegovina, Annex 10', *U.S. Department of State Dispatch*, 7/supplement 1, (1996).

[36] United Nations Security Council Resolution 1272 (1999), S/RES/1272 (1999).

to understanding trusteeship in contemporary international society generally, is intelligible in the well-established law of decolonization. Prior to achieving independent statehood, East Timor enjoyed the status of non-self-governing territory as contemplated in Chapter XI of the United Nations charter, a status confirmed in General Assembly resolution 1542 (XV), which rejected Portugal's claim that as a so-called Overseas Province, East Timor constituted an integral part of Portugal.[37] Indonesia's invasion and subsequent annexation of East Timor in 1975–1976 in no way altered this status: members of the United Nations, save Australia, refused to recognize the Indonesian claim in respect of East Timor. Indeed, the General Assembly repudiated the legitimacy of Indonesia's action by affirming in a succession of resolutions the inalienable right of the East Timorese population to determine their collective future in accordance with the principles contained in General Assembly resolution 1514 (XV). The Security Council concurred and called upon member states in resolutions 384 (1975) and 389 (1976) 'to respect the territorial integrity of East Timor as well as the inalienable right of its people to self-determination in accordance with General Assembly resolution 1514 (XV)'.[38]

Of particular importance is the fact that both the General Assembly and the Security Council continued to regard Portugal as the legitimate administering power in East Timor even though it exercised no effective control there whatsoever. In doing so they refused to accept the view expressed by Australian Minister of Foreign Affairs Andrew Peacock, on recognizing Indonesia's de facto incorporation of East Timor in January 1978, that annexation 'is a reality with which we must come to terms'.[39] So long as East Timor remained a non-self-governing territory, a territory that had not achieved a full measure of self-government as specified in General Assembly resolution 1541 (XV), the obligations of trusteeship expressed in Chapter XI were applicable. Thus, the East Timorese people possessed an inalienable right to self-determination, as is recognized in every relevant United Nations resolution pertaining to East Timor, but they did not possess the concomitant authority to realize the substance of that right. In other words, independence could not be merely declared; it had to be granted. It is in this respect that the

[37] 'Transmission of Information Under Article 73e of the Charter', United Nations General Assembly Resolution 1542 (XV), A/RES/1542 (1960).
[38] United Nations Security Council Resolution 384 (1975), S/RES/384 (1975); and United Nations Security Council Resolution 389 (1976), S/RES/389 (1976). The General Assembly's first resolution on the question of East Timor, which reflects the general basis of all subsequent resolutions, was Resolution 3485 (XXX), A/RES/3485 (1975).
[39] Quoted in International Court of Justice, 'Case Concerning East Timor (Portugal *v.* Australia)', 30 June 1995, 11.

5 May Agreements, which provided for the aptly named 'popular consultation' that led to the resolution of the East Timor question, are instructive.[40] The East Timorese people were not a party to the Agreements; they were objects of an agreement between Indonesia and Portugal. They were to be consulted, through a United Nations supervised popular ballot, on accepting or rejecting a special autonomous status within the Indonesian republic, but they possessed no authority to negotiate the terms of that consultation or the modalities of its implementation. Portugal, the legitimate authority in East Timor, represented those interests on their behalf. And failing acceptance of Indonesia's offer, that authority would be ceded, not to the East Timorese people, but to the United Nations, which would, again on their behalf, initiate the transition towards independence that began with creating the trusteeship conducted by UNTAET.[41] In that respect, the constitutional basis as well as underlying justification of the United Nations conducted trusteeship in East Timor is suggestive of convention rather than innovation. As a trusteeship falling within the meaning of Chapter XI, in what is an instance of decolonization, it is accommodated fully within the existing framework of international society. And in that respect East Timor provides little insight into the future of trusteeship in world affairs, because it belongs to a category that is for the most part historically exhausted.

The only contemporary example of international administration that sustains the claim of innovation is that of Kosovo. In fact, the international administration conducted by UNMIK is problematic in every way that the UNTAET is not. Of course, similarities abound. The international presence in Kosovo is charged (as was the mission in East Timor) with maintaining law and order, protecting human rights, performing basic administrative functions, and overseeing the development of democratic institutions. And the authority granted to UNMIK in Security Council resolution 1244 (1999),

---

[40] An overview of the 5 May Agreements and subsequent United Nations involvement in East Timor may be found in 'Question of East Timor, Progress Report of the Secretary-General', United Nations General Assembly, 13 December 1999, A/54/654; on East Timor generally, see I. Martin, *Self-determination in East Timor: The United Nations, the Ballot, and International Intervention* (London: Lynne Rienner, 2001).

[41] 'Agreement Between the Republic of Indonesia and the Portuguese Republic on the Question of East Timor (5 May Agreements)', reprinted in Martin, *Self-determination in East Timor*, 141–3. The results of the consultation were as follows: 78.5% against, 21.5% in favour, with 98.6% of registered voters participating. In accordance with the 5 May Agreements, Portugal announced on 20 October 1999 its intention to relinquish its authority in East Timor to the United Nations once the Security Council authorised UNTAET. The United Nations deemed formal Indonesian acceptance of the results as unnecessary since it did recognize not the legitimacy of the occupation of East Timor. See J. Chopra, 'Introductory Note to UNTAET Regulation 13', *International Legal Materials*, 39 (2000), 937.

as a report of the Secretary-General makes clear, is just as broad as the 'overall responsibility' enjoyed by UNTAET: 'UNMIK is the only legitimate authority in Kosovo'.[42] But UNMIK is not, like UNTAET, legitimized by the obligations of trusteeship that apply to non-self-governing territories and which are laid down in Chapter XI; nor is it legitimized by an international treaty, sanctioned by the consent of the contracting parties, as is the case in Bosnia and Herzegovina. Rather, international administration in Kosovo is the result of a controversial, if not dubious, use of force that obtained retroactive assent from the Security Council in the form of resolution 1244. Indeed, the most sympathetic of assessments of NATO's war in Kosovo are inclined to concede, as does the Independent International Commission on Kosovo (IICK), that the intervention 'was illegal but legitimate'.[43] Of course, scholarly interest in Kosovo tends to converge on this putative gap between legality and legitimacy in order to ask questions about a presumptive right of humanitarian intervention. But lost in this enterprise is any sustained attempt to think through what comes after humanitarian intervention and the type of argument that is required to justify those arrangements. Crucially, resolution 1244 transfers supreme civil authority in Kosovo from the Federal Republic of Yugoslavia to the United Nations, with the effect of transforming what was once a part of a sovereign state into a de facto trust territory supervised by UNMIK. In that respect, Talbott is right to describe Kosovo as a ward that 'goes about the business of rebuilding itself under the day-in, day-out protection and supervision of a consortium of global and regional organizations'.[44] We might also agree that NATO's intervention, although legally suspect, put an end to a type of oppression that is wholly inconsistent with the principles and purposes of the United Nations charter. That said, the international administration in Kosovo stands outside the normative framework of international society because it is an arrangement of power rather than one of law.

---

[42] United Nations Security Council, 'Report of the Secretary-General on the United Nations Interim Administration Mission in Kosovo', 23 December 1999, S/1999/1250, para. 35; and United Nations Security Council Resolution 1244 (1999), S/RES/1244 (1999). For an overview of the authority and competencies of UNMIK, see 'Report of the Secretary-General on the Interim Administration Mission in Kosovo', 12 July 1999, S/1999/779, para. 35–42.

[43] Independent International Commission on Kosovo, *Kosovo Report: Conflict, International Response, Lessons Learned* (Oxford: Oxford University Press, 2000), 4. The British Foreign Affairs Select Committee reached a similar conclusion. See Government of Great Britain, 'Fourth Report from the Foreign Affairs Committee, Session 1999–2000, HC 28-1', 7 June 2000. For detailed discussion of NATO's intervention in Kosovo and on humanitarian intervention in general, see N. Wheeler, *Saving Strangers: Humanitarian Intervention in International Society* (Oxford: Oxford University Press, 2000).

[44] Talbott, 'The Balkan Question and the European Answer', 5.

This arrangement of power runs up against deeply ingrained injunctions against all forms of constitutional dependence internationally. Indeed, the practice of post-colonial international society has been guided by the belief that accession to independent statehood entails passage through a one-way door that affords no return to a state of dependence. And trustee-ship, as the law of decolonization makes clear, could be justified only as a transition to independence, and a speedy one at that, rather than as a reversion to dependence. It was no longer possible to argue that founding and maintaining political society required a degree of virtue, knowledge, and skill in order to conduct the affairs of public life. The political, eco-nomic, and social conditions of backwardness that once justified trustee-ship now formed the basis of an unconditional claim to membership in the society of states.[45] Independence became a categorical right and dependence a categorical wrong. This presumption against trusteeship is also evidenced in the United Nations charter, which in Article 78 unambiguously stipulates: '[t]he trusteeship system shall not apply to territories which have become Members of the United Nations, relationship among which shall be based on respect for the principle of sovereign equality.'[46]

Kosovo is not, of course, administered as part of the trusteeship system outlined in Chapters XII and XIII, but, presumably, informal arrangements of trusteeship, such as those that have been established in Kosovo, are no less susceptible to the moral opprobrium that attaches to this prohibition. It is in this respect that the international presence in Kosovo is truly innovative. The people of Kosovo, Albanian and Serb alike, have been forcibly deprived of their independence and have been made wards of the United Nations. This conclusion should not, however, be misconstrued to cast doubt on the sincerity of NATO's motives in Kosovo; nor should it be misconstrued as an apology for Slobodan Milosovic's oppressive regime. But if we were to express Kosovo's present status in the paternal language of empire, we would say that it is analogous to a political child that is being prepared, under the United Nations' watchful eye, for the adulthood that comes with constitutional independence. Indeed, UNMIK represents not merely the resurrection of trusteeship, but the resurrection of the nineteenth century practice of making dependencies out of territories whose domestic arrangements and practices fall outside the bounds of something called 'civilization'.

[45] R. Jackson, *Quasi-States*, 26–49, 85.   [46] 'Charter of the United Nations', 521.

The New International Legitimacy

This resurrection of trusteeship and the notion of civilization in which it is intelligible must be situated, if its implications are to be made clear, in the broader context of an emerging notion of international legitimacy expressed in terms of human rights, democracy, and free market economy. An account of this standard of legitimacy is most ambitiously put forward by Francis Fukuyama in his provocative volume, *The End of History and the Last Man*. Fukuyama's reading of history suggests that fascism, communism, and various manifestations of neo-Marxism have been proven to be dead-ends and, consequently, that capitalism and liberal democracy have prevailed in the global market place of ideas. Capitalism, he contends, is the world's only viable mode of economic organization. The inevitable victory of capitalism is ensured by its handmaiden, modern natural science; for only capitalism is capable of producing the wealth, prosperity, and technological advances that are necessary to satisfy human desires. Indeed, he submits, in a thought that is evocative of T.B. Macaulay's notorious deprecation of Hindu and Arabian knowledge, that 'Islamic "science" was incapable of producing the F-4 fighter-bombers and Chieftain tanks required to defend Khomeini's Iran from ambitious neighbours like Iraq'.[47] It is modern natural science that 'guides us to the gates of the Promised Land of liberal democracy' and it is democracy's ability to satisfy man's yearning for recognition as a man, free and equal to all others. Democracy, then, is the 'only coherent political aspiration that spans different regions and cultures around the globe'.[48] Thus, Fukuyama argues that the liberal state is a universal association in which membership is accorded on the basis of being recognized as a human being rather than as a member of a particular group. And because the liberal state embodies values that not only recognize, but also protect, the dignity of human personality—what we normally call human rights—he concludes by saying: 'modern liberal democratic world . . . is free of contradictions'.[49]

This absence of contradiction anchors the claim that capitalism, liberal democracy, and human rights have triumphed over all rival forms of economic, political, and social organization. The implications for world affairs that follow from this claim are for Fukuyama equally obvious and certain.

[47] F. Fukuyama, *The End of History and the Last Man* (New York: Avon Books, 1993), pp. xv–xvi, 76, 90; and T. B. Macaulay, 'T. B. Macaulay's Minute on Education', in C. H. Philips (ed.), *The Correspondence of Lord William Cavendish Bentinck, Governor-General of India, 1828–1835* (Oxford: Oxford University Press, 1977), 1406–7.

[48] Fukuyama, *The End of History and the Last Man*, pp. xiii, xv.   [49] Ibid. 139.

The same universal and homogeneous state, that is, the liberal state, which abolishes relations of inequality within societies, can be expected to abolish relations of inequality between them as well. Democracies, by their nature, are disinclined to question each other's legitimacy that is conferred in an act of mutual recognition not unlike that which Frost describes. And democracies are similarly disinclined towards domination and aggrandizement on account of their common love of universal equality and rights. So beneficial are the effects of democracy that Fukuyama claims: '[t]he argument then is not so much that liberal democracy constrains man's natural instincts for aggression and violence, but that it has fundamentally transformed the instincts themselves and eliminated the motive for imperialism.'[50] Thus, the onward march of liberal democracy will ultimately see the end of imperialism, and all other forms of domination and exploitation, as a force in world affairs. In a world in which democracy flourishes, human beings will be free to think, communicate, innovate, and create; and they will be able to realize their material desires and to satisfy their need for recognition. It is these characteristics, which are inherently good and desirable, that leads Fukuyama to conclude: 'the United States and other democracies have a long-term interest in preserving the sphere of democracy in the world, and in expanding it where possible and prudent.'[51]

The sort of world that Fukuyama champions is most firmly entrenched in Europe, that is, a new Europe that has moved beyond a dark past of totalitarianism and total war. The idea of the new Europe, the values, principles, and codes of conduct that order relations within the European family of nations, is evident in a succession of agreements and declarations, the most important of which follow from the Helsinki Final Act of 1975. At Helsinki, thirty-five states agreed to a set of principles related to questions of security, disarmament, and economic, scientific, environmental, and humanitarian co-operation, which included a re-statement of their respect for sovereign equality, the non-use of force, territorial integrity, and the peaceful settlement of disputes. Of particular significance is their pledge to promote and encourage human rights and fundamental freedoms, 'all of which,' they declared, 'derive from the inherent dignity of the human person and are essential for his free and full development'.[52] The intent and meaning of this pledge is further elaborated in the Document of the Copenhagen Meeting of 1990: 'pluralistic democracy and the rule of law are essential for ensuring respect for all human rights and fundamental freedoms, the development of human contacts and

---

[50] Fukuyama, *The End of History and the Last Man*, p. 263.   [51] Ibid. 245, 280.

[52] 'Final Act of the Helsinki Conference', in I. Brownlie (ed.), *Basic Documents on Human Rights*, 3rd edn. (Oxford: Clarendon Press, 1992), 393–5.

the resolution of other issues of a related humanitarian character.'[53] The idea of the new Europe is predicated on the belief, the same belief that underwrites Fukuyama's claims, that human rights and democracy are fundamental and necessary conditions of peace. Indeed, this belief holds that 'respect for human rights and fundamental freedoms and the development of societies based on pluralistic democracy and the rule of law are prerequisites for progress in setting up the lasting order of peace, security, justice and cooperation that they seek to establish in Europe'.[54]

The idea of the new Europe is discerned in full relief in the Charter of Paris of 1990. In this declaration, signatory states reaffirm their commitment to the principles enshrined in the Helsinki Final Act and pledge to work towards realizing a family of like-minded nations that share in common a fundamental respect for the sanctity of human personality. They regard democracy, which is legitimized by the will and the consent of the people, as being founded on respect for the human person and the rule of law. Only democracy can safeguard freedom of expression, tolerance of minorities, and equality of person. Thus, parties to the Charter agree to 'build, consolidate and strengthen democracy as the only system of government of our nations'.[55] Democracy is also accepted as a necessary condition of material prosperity and welfare, in the belief that economic progress is impossible where individual human beings are not free and autonomous. In the absence of democratic institutions and free economic intercourse, social and economic progress remains a distant and remote aspiration. Thus, adherents to the Charter declare, in support of economic liberty, that 'economic co-operation based on market economy constitutes an essential element of our relations and will be instrumental in the construction of a prosperous and united Europe'.[56] Indeed, the Charter of Paris is justified principally by the belief that a Europe built upon human rights, democracy, and economic liberty is destined to be a Europe whole, free, and prosperous.

Although Europe has moved furthest along the road of Fukuyama's universal history, the principles that constitute the new Europe are in evidence elsewhere in international society. For example, both the Organization of American States and the Organization of African Unity (the successor of which is the newly created African Union) have adopted regionally specific treaties pertaining to the promotion of human rights. The OAS resolved in

---

[53] 'Document of the Copenhagen Meeting of the Conference on the Human Dimension of the CSCE, 1990', in I. Brownlie (ed.), *Basic Documents on Human Rights*, 3rd edn. (Oxford: Clarendon Press, 1992), 455.   [54] Ibid. 455.

[55] 'The Charter of Paris for a New Europe, 1990', in I. Brownlie (ed.), *Basic Documents on Human Rights*, 3rd edn. (Oxford: Clarendon Press, 1992), 474.   [56] Ibid. 481.

1991 that any 'irregular interruption of the democratic political institutional process or of the legitimate exercise of power by the democratically elected government in any of the Organization's members states' is a matter of direct concern to all members of the organization.[57] It has since adopted an Inter-American Democratic Charter that establishes a 'right to democracy' and an 'obligation to promote and defend it', in the belief that democracy is an indispensable condition of the enjoyment of human rights, elimination of discrimination, environmental stewardship, and economic, social, and cultural development generally.[58] The universalization of the principles of the new Europe is also discernible in the now fashionable theory of human security. The United Nations Human Development Report of 1994 first popularized the term *human security* by suggesting:

Human security is a child who did not die, a disease that did not spread, a job that was not cut, an ethnic tension that did not explode in violence, a dissident who was not silenced. Human security is not a concern with weapons—it is a concern with human life and dignity.[59]

The Commission on Global Governance invoked this idea to suggest that 'the international community needs to make the protection of people and their security an aim of global security policy'.[60] On this view, a proper understanding of security should be founded on the sanctity of human dignity, so that it refers to a people-centred approach that includes chronic threats such as hunger, disease, repression, and grave disruptions of ordinary life. The rights of states, then, are justified solely by the benefit they confer on the governed and by their continuing consent and democratic representation. Thus, the Commission seems to accept the central premise of the Charter of Paris: promoting and protecting human rights is the 'first responsibility of government'.[61]

---

[57] Organization of American States, 'Representative Democracy', Resolution Adopted at the Fifth Plenary Session of the Organization of American States, 5 June 1991, AG/RES. 1080 (XXI-O/91).

[58] Organization of American States, 'Inter-American Democratic Charter', Adopted at the Twenty-Eighth Special Session of the OAS General Assembly, September 11, 2001, AG/doc. 8 (XXVIII-E/01). For further discussion and evidence of a growing sense of entitlement to democracy, see G. Fox and B. Roth, 'Democracy and International Law', *Review of International Studies*, 27/3 (2001), 327–52; and the text of the 'Final Warsaw Declaration: Toward a Community of Democracies', Warsaw, Poland, 27 June 2000.

[59] United Nations Development Programme, *Human Development Report, 1994* (New York: Oxford University Press, 1994), 22.

[60] Report of the Commission on Global Governance, *Our Global Neighbourhood* (Oxford: Oxford University Press, 1995), 82.   [61] 'The Charter of Paris', 475.

Human security differs in several important ways from the theory of national security that in the twentieth century dominated both the theoretical and practical understanding of security. Human security entails a commitment to democratic development, and to ensuring quality of life and equity for all human beings. It also recognizes the elementary importance of 'human rights and fundamental freedoms, the right to live in dignity, with adequate food, shelter, health and education services, and under the rule of law and good governance'.[62] Thus, above all else, human security is concerned with the protection of the individual; for the ethics of human security do not allow us to remain detached from, or indifferent to, human suffering on account of deeply ingrained injunctions against interfering in the domestic affairs of sovereign states. Human security means safety for people before safety for states.[63] The rights of states must not be permitted to impede action intended to secure safety of people; and the justification of national security must not be accepted, as it has been historically, as a reason for pre-empting human rights, fundamental freedoms, and democratic government. Indeed, human security seeks to establish the principle that that national security is not an end in itself; and following from this principle is the further claim, advanced by the International Commission on Intervention and State Sovereignty (ICISS), that when a state is unable or unwilling to protect its population 'it becomes the responsibility of the international community to act in its place'.[64]

This notion of 'international community' asserts the superiority of a particular conception of the good life, a conception mediated by the values of human security and the new Europe, over the procedural rights and duties that are associated with classical international society: sovereign equality, territorial integrity, non-interference, and the non-use of force. On this view, the society of states consists in a unified enterprise that is concerned with securing common advantage; and the good life within that society consists solely and exclusively in respect for human rights, democratic governance, and free market economy. It is this idea of unity and exclusivity that prefigures

[62] L. Axworthy, Notes for an Address by the Honourable Lloyd Axworthy, Minister of Foreign Affairs, to the 51st General Assembly of the United Nations, New York, 24 September 1996, 3–7; see also L. Axworthy, 'Kosovo and the Human Security Agenda', Notes for an Address by the Honourable Lloyd Axworthy, Minister of Foreign Affairs, to the Woodrow Wilson School of Public and International Relations, Princeton University, Princeton, New Jersey, 7 April 1999.

[63] Report of the International Commission on Intervention and State Sovereignty, *The Responsibility to Protect* (Ottawa: International Development Research Centre, 2001), 15.

[64] Government of Canada, Department of Foreign Affairs and International Trade, *Human Security: Safety for People in a Changing World* (Ottawa: Department of Foreign Affairs and International Trade, 1999), 5–6; and *The Responsibility to Protect*, 17.

Tony Blair's claim that '[w]e are witnessing the beginnings of a new doctrine of international community'.[65] In this world, democracy is on the march; security is conceived in terms of the respect for liberty, the rule of law, and human rights; and prosperity is ensured by the expansion of free trade and market economies. These changes are both far-reaching and fundamental, for he argues, in language that would seem to confirm Fukuyama's claims, that '[w]e cannot refuse to participate in global markets if we want to prosper. We cannot ignore new political ideas in other countries if we want to innovate. We cannot turn our backs on conflicts and the violation of human rights within other countries if we want still to be secure'.[66] The world is moving, perhaps irreversibly, towards a condition of mutual dependence. States can no longer afford 'go it alone', as isolation is sure to result in poverty and insecurity: '[w]e are all internationalists now, whether we like it or not.'[67] There is, it seems, no real alternative in sight.

The voice of Fukuyama and the principles of the new international legitimacy are even more pronounced in the corresponding American idea of the good society, an idea that finds its heritage in the grand Wilsonian aspiration of making the world safe for democracy. For example, while speaking about the Balkans, Talbott describes European political life in darker times as resembling a 'musty, sprawling laboratory in the basement of a gothic castle, where mad scientists were experimenting with competing yet similar political monstrosities—two in particular: fascism and communism'.[68] But out of these catastrophic experiments emerged a concert of European democracies which subscribes to a common creed that rests on the principles of tolerance, justice, and respect for human dignity. These are the values that the United States must defend against modern-day barbarism. And it is in defence of those values that Talbott proposes the American answer to the Balkan question and other problems of a similar sort:

A state should let its people choose their leaders through elections, it should derive strength and cohesion from the diversity of its population, and it should protect the rights of minorities, especially those of the ultimate minority—the individual citizen. In short, to be successful and strong, to survive and prosper, a state should be a liberal democracy.[69]

This view of democracy presupposes the belief that a society which respects the rights of minorities and the rule of law domestically will respect the rights of the weak and refrain from the illegitimate use of force internationally.

---

[65] T. Blair, 'Doctrine of the International Community', Speech by the Prime Minister to the Economic Club of Chicago, Hilton Hotel, Chicago, USA, Thursday, 22 April 1999, Foreign and Commonwealth Office, London, 3.   [66] Ibid. 3.
[67] Ibid. 3.   [68] Talbott, 'The Balkan Question and the European Answer', 3.
[69] Ibid. 1.

George W. Bush similarly embraced the principles of the new legitimacy when he proclaimed, in the aftermath of the al-Qaeda directed attacks on New York and Washington on 11 September 2001, that '[t]he 20th century ended with a single surviving model of human progress, based on non-negotiable demands of human dignity, the rule of law, limits on the power of the state, respect for women and private property and free speech and equal justice and religious tolerance.'[70] It would seem, then, that the American notion of the good society, as well as the doctrine of international community, blurs the moral distinction between domestic and international society: we are truly a universal family of peoples joined in the pursuit of a common purpose in a world in which there is but one single truth. All else must be error.

The idea of international community is grounded in the belief that in cases of egregious human suffering, the members of this international community are entitled, individually and collectively, to intervene on behalf of humanity and against barbarism. And in that respect we have returned to where we began this investigation of trusteeship—the thought of Edmund Burke. It is worth repeating that Burke attached a special obligation to the possession of political power: all political power that is set over men should be exercised for the benefit of the persons who are subject to it.[71] Thus, Burke justified the East India Company's political dominion and commercial monopoly only so long as they conferred benefits on the native inhabitants of India; and in the absence of such a benefit he approved of parliamentary interference in the Company's affairs, even so far as to extinguish those privileges. The underlying moral claim of Burke's argument has been used historically to interfere in the affairs of people in order to put down endemic warfare, chronic disorder, despotic government, slavery, mutilation, cannibalism, and religious and social customs that were repugnant to civilized life. Interference in the affairs of others has been justified in contemporary international society, at least in the case of Kosovo, in response to modern day barbarism—failure to respect the principles of the new international legitimacy. The precedent established by Kosovo, if it can be said to constitute a precedent, suggests a rather tenuous future for states that commit grievous offences against their populations. A society that is paralysed by disorder or falls into a state of unconscionable tyranny must be instructed in becoming a good society, a society whose public arrangements correspond with the values of

---

[70] G. W. Bush, 'Remarks by the President at 2002 Graduation Exercise at the United States Military Academy, West Point, New York', The White House, Office of the Press Secretary, 1 June 2002.

[71] E. Burke, 'Speech on Mr. Fox's East India Bill, December 1, 1783', *The Works of the Right Honourable Edmund Burke*, vol. 2 (Boston: Little, Brown, and Company, 1899), 439.

the new legitimacy. This project entails nothing less than reconstructing public life, radically if necessary, so that it is consistent with the highest standards of international recognized human rights, adheres to democratic principles of governance, and results in the creation of a viable market-based economy.[72] And until such a society has been adequately educated, to use Frost's term, it must be placed under the tutelage of an authority capable of cultivating the habits of a legitimate member of international society.

The IICK takes on the project of international community in putting forth 'conditional independence', a condition that is distinct from 'full independence', as the best way of resolving questions about Kosovo's future. Conditional independence is justified by the conviction that 'the case for self-determination arises from the systematic abuse of the human rights of Kosovo Albanians over a long period and the consequent withdrawal of the consent of Kosovar Albanians to Serbian rule'.[73] However, the Commission is most anxious to distinguish the measure of self-government permitted by UNMIK and the degree of self-government that justifies conditional independence. The achievement of meaningful self-government must see the progressive transfer of powers reserved to UNMIK, powers it describes as being more appropriate to a colonial dependency than a self-governing people, to a government conducted by the Kosovars themselves.[74] But in this proposal there is little basis on which differentiate conditional independence from the type of trusteeship that informed Lord Lugard's approach to political development in nineteenth century British Africa. The people of Kosovo are to be prepared for eventual independence by granting to them 'conditional' powers of self-government, the exercise of which will be 'explicitly supervised' by the international community. It is difficult to see how this arrangement differs substantially from Lugard's view that political development in British Africa should allow the greatest possible measure of liberty and self-development, 'subject to the laws and policy of the [British colonial] administration'.[75] Indeed, it seems as if the Commission reduces the juridical concept of sovereignty to the sociological concept of autonomy in order to call trusteeship another name: conditional independence.

Sovereignty presupposes, not supreme power, but supreme authority to enter into agreements that may very well limit the things for which the possessor of

---

[72] In the context of Kosovo, see 'Report of the Secretary-General', S/1999/1250, para. 20, 36, 103.

[73] Independent International Commission on Kosovo, *The Follow-up of the Kosovo Report: Why Conditional Independence?* (Stockholm: IICK/Olof Palme Center, 2001), 22.

[74] Ibid. 25.

[75] F. D. Lugard, *The Dual Mandate in Tropical Africa*, 4th edn. (London: William Blackwood & Sons, 1929), 94.

that authority can rightly aspire. Authority implies the right to act; autonomy implies the liberty to act. Thus, a sovereign state possesses the authority, because it is sovereign, to undertake voluntary obligations, such as those which condition membership in the EU, WTO, and NATO, which may (or may not) restrict its autonomy. But absent in the Commission's notion of conditional independence is the supreme authority that, unlike the autonomy to act as one wishes, is a necessary requirement of sovereign statehood. The sovereignty that is the goal of conditional independence is in fact not properly called sovereignty at all; for it entails an arrangement that is 'not voluntarily chosen' and which is contained 'within limits prescribed by the international community'.[76] That arrangement is called trusteeship.

A Universal Society of States?

The resurrection of trusteeship represented by the international administration in Kosovo raises several cogent questions that have attracted considerable scholarly attention. How shall future trusteeships be funded, staffed, and supported? Who should lead them? Is the United Nations competent to undertake these missions? Or, as the Brahimi Report asks, is international administration something in which the United Nations should be involved at all?[77] What role should the Security Council play? Is Security Council authorization always necessary? Must trusteeship always be approached as a multilateral enterprise? Or should it be left to 'coalitions of the willing' or perhaps to a single state, most probably a great power? How far should local populations be entrusted with conducting the affairs of government? What balance should be struck between the claims of justice and those of reconciliation in territories ravaged by civil war? And when do efforts to protect civilians in distress slide into what the IICK derides as 'imperial condenscion'?[78]

Curiously, though, some of the most consequential and far-reaching implications of a resurrected practice of trusteeship have been left largely unexamined. One of the most obvious of these implications must be the very real possibility that a world made safe for trusteeship may also make for a more violent world—a world in which interstate war is more commonplace as other failed and unjust states are placed into international receivership. Still more important is the implication that a resurrected practice of trusteeship might be corrosive of the post-colonial project of a universal society of states grounded in the universal legal equality of its members. Indeed, renewed

---

[76] *The Follow-up of the Kosovo Report*, 28–31.   [77] Brahimi Report, 13.
[78] *The Follow-up of the Kosovo Report*, 20.

enthusiasm for trusteeship suggests that the time has come to abandon this project for a world order that is tolerant of some form of political hierarchy. What, then, are the consequences of abandoning the strictly egalitarian world order that emerged out of decolonization, a world order that equates political dependence with an infringement of fundamental human rights and freedoms? The answer to this most crucial of questions comes into view after exploring the procedural ethics of trusteeship.

Through much of this book it has been argued that the idea of trusteeship joins ruler and subject in a relation of inequality. However, the procedural ethics of trusteeship, that is, the way in which trusteeship obliges one to act, are better expressed in terms of two kinds of equality: natural and proportionate. The idea of natural equality presupposes a formal mode of conduct that tells us nothing about how particular persons should be treated in particular situations. Thus, where men are regarded as being equal in respect of human personality, they must be treated as men, and not as beasts, gods, or property. This conception of equality often provides the starting point for theorizing the states system and its attendant practices. For example, the Hobbesian account of natural equality, which views all men as being by nature equal in the faculties of body, mind, and, crucially, strength, supposes that each is governed by his own reason and is at absolute liberty to act according to that reason. Thus, every man possesses a right to every thing, a right that is subject only to the limits of power a man can enlist in support of his cause; and it is this right to everything that succours an inclination in all men towards competition, diffidence, and glory—what are for Hobbes the principal causes of war. And in a state where the fear of war is ever present, where strength and cunning have the greatest purchase on security, life is, in the those oft-repeated words, 'solitary, poor, nasty, brutish, and short'.[79]

This notion of natural equality has been cultivated by international theorists in order to describe the states system as consisting in a 'precontractual state of nature' that discloses no more than a non-progressivist 'theory of survival'.[80] However, it is a challenge of some magnitude to locate the obligations of trusteeship in a world that is distinguished by the will to power. It makes little sense to speak of obligation, much less of law or justice, in a world understood as a Hobbesian state of nature. The obligations of trusteeship are wholly at odds with an ethics of power premised on the principle, expressed plainly in the Melian dialogue, that 'the strong do what they have the power

---

[79] T. Hobbes, *Leviathan*, ed. M. Oakeshott (Oxford: Basil Blackwell, 1949), 80–5.

[80] M. Wight, 'Why Is There No International Theory', in H. Butterfield and M. Wight (eds.), *Diplomatic Investigations: Essays in the Theory of International Politics* (Cambridge, MA: Harvard University Press, 1968), 30–3.

to do and the weak accept what they have to accept'.[81] Trusteeship is not justified by the possession of preponderant power, but it is keenly interested in questions of power. It is concerned with the disparities that preponderant power creates and the obligations that attach to that power, the most important of which demands that preponderant power be exercised for the benefit of the disadvantaged.

This relation between power and obligation invoked by trusteeship suggests that the Lockian account of natural equality, and the consequences that derive from it, casts more light on the procedural ethics of trusteeship. For Locke, man enjoys by nature a state of perfect freedom, a state that is neither confirmed nor altered by any power on earth, apart from that power which is his own. Thus, each man is entitled to live his own life, according to his own reason, subject only to the law of nature. And because all men are endowed with the same faculties, the ability to know and to understand the law of nature, all men are rightly regarded as perfect equals. There are no ranks within the human family: man is by nature independent of, as opposed to dependent on, the will, authority, and jurisdiction of his fellows. This condition is such that, in Locke's words, 'all the Power and Jurisdiction is reciprocal, no one having more than another'.[82] And, as is consistent with formal notions of equality, all men are equal because they are men, not because they are equal in strength, knowledge, wisdom, courage, position, experience, or beauty. This fundamental and irreducible condition of equality leads Locke to elaborate a rather more extensive theory of preservation than is articulated by Hobbes. Locke, persuaded by Hooker's claim that equality amongst men imposes an obligation of mutual love, argues that every man is bound to preserve himself and, in a departure from Hobbes, to act so far as he is capable to 'preserve the rest of Mankind'.[83] It is this obligation of mutual love, an obligation that arises from the natural equality from men, which sanctions the legitimacy of trusteeship.

The movement to suppress slavery and the slave trade, a great crusade underwritten by the obligation of mutual love, more than any single event brings into sharp relief the relation of obligation and power that champions of trusteeship had in mind. Abolitionists like William Wilberforce argued that keeping men in a state of perpetual bondage was not wrong because slaves were too often under-fed and over-worked, or because they laboured under the stern discipline inflicted by the slave-driver's whip. Nor was it

[81] Thucydides, *History of the Peloponnesian War*, trans. R. Warner (London: Penguin Books, 1972), 400–8.
[82] J. Locke, 'The Second Treatise of Government', *Two Treatises of Government* ed. P. Laslett (Cambridge: Cambridge University Press, 1988), 269–70.   [83] Ibid. 270–1.

wrong because slave labour generated less wealth than free labour, as Adam Smith argued to great effect. Rather, for Wilberforce, slavery was wrong because it ran counter to all that is sacred about being human: it was contrary to the natural rights of all human beings just as it was categorically repugnant to the 'moral character of the human species'.[84] So great was the crime of slavery that no consideration of circumstance or expediency could justify its continuation. And for opponents of slavery the duty imposed on the powerful to eradicate such a thoroughly criminal enterprise was no less plain. The duty of mutual love, the duty to work for the preservation of mankind, presupposed the belief that '[p]ower always implies responsibility; and the possessor of it cannot innocently be neutral, when by his exertion moral good may be promoted, or evil lessened or removed'.[85] It did not matter that the black man was more often than not despised and treated with contempt. Europeans, even some who wished to see a speedy end to the practice of slavery, typically indulged feelings of cultural and racial superiority in order to castigate the black man as being selfish, indolent, and licentious. Still, Wilberforce maintained, the black man ought to be treated as 'those whom the Almighty had made capable of enjoying our own civil blessings in this world'.[86] It is in this claim that we encounter the argument of natural equality, an argument that recognises the irreducible sanctity of human personality and therefore demands that the black man be treated as a man rather than as an article of property.

But for the committed abolitionist it was not enough to put down the slave trade and to emancipate the black man from the bonds of servitude. Emancipation had to be accompanied by redemption. The victims of slavery had to be instructed in the grace of the Christian God and the perfect morality of the Gospel. They had to be introduced to the advantages of science, industry, and commerce. And they had to be instilled with the virtues of temperance, truthfulness, and fair play. It is in this project of emancipation, so that the peoples of Africa may share in the benefits of civilization, that we encounter a different sort of equality, a type of equality that is premised on the belief that all men are not equal in all things. In other words, the moral and material condition of Africa's native population constituted a substantive difference that justified derogation from the principle of natural equality. The idea of proportionate equality represents a way of coming to terms with the practical

---

[84] W. Wilberforce, *An Appeal to the Religion, Justice, and Humanity of the Inhabitants of the British Empire, in Behalf of the Negro Slaves in the West Indies* (London: J. Hatchard and Son, 1823), 7–15; and A. Smith, *The Wealth of Nations*, vol. 1, eds. R. H. Campbell and A. S. Skinner (Indianapolis, IN: Liberty Fund, 1981), 98–9.

[85] Wilberforce, *Negro Slaves in the West Indies*, 77.

[86] Ibid. 68; and H. A. C. Cairns, *Prelude to Imperialism: British Reactions to Central African Society 1840–1890* (London: Routledge & Kegan Paul, 1965), chs 2–3.

difficulties that arise when men substitute life in society for life in the state of nature—or, in the context of trusteeship, it is a way of making sense of the great differences that emerge when a people of 'advanced' civilization come into contact with a people of 'primitive' civilization. Proportionate equality demands that the enjoyment of rights, duties, or privileges must be subject to some test of merit, so that particular persons who disclose particular qualities may, for example, assert a claim of preference in respect of political power. It is this test of merit that secures Lugard's argument that 'the extent to which native races are capable of controlling their own affairs must vary in proportion to their degree of development and progress in social organization'.[87] Thus, proportionate equality is justified insofar as participation in political life is subject to a test of merit, a test that colonial administrators understood as the standard of civilization.

If the procedural ethics of trusteeship are intelligible in terms of both natural equality and proportionate equality, as has been argued thus far, then it seems as if the idea of trusteeship itself is hopelessly flawed. How can it be that each man is naturally equal in such a way that he cannot claim authority or jurisdiction over any other and, at the same time, some of these men rule over the rest on account of some special qualification? The usual way of getting at this question is to take refuge in the concept of consent. Locke reminds us that men remain in a state of perfect freedom and perfect equality, so that no one may act as lord of another, until 'by their own Consents they make themselves Members of some Politick Society'.[88] However, trusteeship disallows relations based on mutual consent. A public charge cannot render consent because he does not understand the conditions of his happiness; or because he is ignorant of his situation; or because he lacks the moral and intellectual faculties required for self-direction. A ward must be coerced towards some good because he cannot secure that good for himself. Trusteeship sanctions this mode of conduct, and thereby reconciles the demands of natural equality and proportionate equality, by taking refuge in the idea of non-age. It implies a temporary condition not unlike that which joins father and child in a relation of authority and obedience; and the duty which attaches to that authority enjoins a father to instruct a child in a state of minority until maturity takes its place. Thus, the procedural ethics of trusteeship may be stated as follows: respect the natural equality of men who, on account of that equality, disclose an irreducible unity amongst them; recognize authority and jurisdiction in proportion to a test of merit interpreted in terms of an universal scale of values that express their common humanity;

---

[87] Lugard, *The Dual Mandate in British Tropical Africa*, 194.
[88] Locke, 'The Second Treatise of Government', 278.

and, in concord with the duty of mutual love that follows from the natural equality of men, exercise power in such a way that it remedies the imperfect moral and material state in which a portion of the human family subsists.

The moral reasoning upon which this mode of conduct rested collapsed very suddenly under the onslaught of the anti-colonial movement. Post-colonial international society embraced an Aristotelian notion of statehood that was fundamentally at odds with the conditional world of empire. The state or *polis* is for Aristotle the natural end of all other human associations because it alone is self-sufficient.[89] Of course, self-sufficiency does not refer to an empirical condition. To be self-sufficient is to be independent; or, in the vocabulary of contemporary world affairs, to be self-sufficient it is to be answerable to no higher authority, a status that we commonly know as sovereign. Such a condition of self-sufficiency, it is assumed, holds out the possibility that men might live the good life; for it is within the framework of a state that an ongoing dialogue about what is desirable, what is good, what is right, and what is just takes place. This necessary connection between the state and the good life suggests that the state is by its nature an arrangement of justice; and outside of this arrangement of justice the good life is either an impossible ideal or an inchoate fiction.[90] It is this justification of statehood that rendered independence a categorical right and dependence of any kind a categorical wrong. Independence endowed dependent peoples with the authority to choose their own ends of life and to determine the best way in which to achieve them. And it is recognition of this idea, the conception that human beings aspire to organize their individual and collective lives according to their own will, that justifies the universal society of states that emerged out of decolonization. Thus, the society of states that emerged out of decolonization is, in Jackson's words, 'horizontal rather than hierarchical, inclusive rather than exclusive, and is based expressly on the pluralist ethics of equal state sovereignty, self-determination, and non-intervention'.[91]

At this point it is not difficult to understand the irreducible tension between trusteeship and universal equality: the resurrection of the former necessarily entails the death of the latter. An international society constituted by sovereign states, each of which is formally equal to all others in respect of authority and jurisdiction, cannot at the same time be proportionately equal in respect of that same authority and jurisdiction. Indeed, the constitution of contemporary international society affords no possibility of reconciling these

---

[89] Aristotle, *The Politics*, trans. T. A. Sinclair (London: Penguin Books, 1992), 59.
[90] Ibid. 60–1.   [91] Jackson, *The Global Covenant*. 14.

two kinds of equality in the way that they are reconciled in a relation of trusteeship. With the onset of decolonization, it was no longer possible to take refuge in the concept of non-age. Decolonization homogenized the political organization of humankind in such a way that our world is, politically speaking, devoid of children. Apart from a small handful of territories, most of which are marginal in size and importance, our world is one composed solely of political adults—that is, sovereign states. Post-colonial international society is, if we are to accept Jackson's view, an inclusive arrangement in which there are no barbarians, savages, infidels, or pagans standing outside what is now a universal political order: everyone is an insider.[92] Thus, it makes no sense whatsoever to speak of trusteeship as a legitimate relation within international society. To do so, that is, to treat a sovereign state as if it has no will of its own, is to deny, and not merely infringe upon, the personality that makes it what it is. The moral objection underlying this line of argument is that it proposes to treat an equal unequally. It is to deny that a state is a state, and thereby deny rights that go with being a state, just as it is to deny that a man is a man, and thereby deny rights that express what it means to be human. To withhold recognition of rights that one claims for oneself, and hence extinguish the freedom of a state or person for the sake of their own good and happiness, is to act without regard for their status as independent rather than dependent beings. And to behave towards independent beings in this way is to treat them paternally—a mode of conduct that Immanuel Kant denounced as the 'greatest conceivable *despotism* [emphasis in original]'.[93]

The demise of the post-colonial practice of universal equality that must necessarily accompany the resurrection of trusteeship does not mean that future manifestations of trusteeship will form a perfect identity with those of the past. It is hardly conceivable that future arrangements of trusteeship would be justified in places like Sierra Leone or the Congo because their populations are, as J. C. Smuts once described the peoples of Africa, happy and amiable but child-like in psychology and outlook. And James Mill's justification of British rule in India, on account of a devious Hindu priest-craft and oppressive system of law and government that left a vast population destitute and impoverished, is equally unintelligible in our world.[94] It is no more conceivable that the resurrection of trusteeship will be accompanied by the resurrection of great empires.

[92] Ibid. 13.

[93] I. Kant, 'On the Common Saying: "This May Be True in Theory, But It Does Not Apply in Practice"', *Kant: Political Writing*, ed. H. Reiss and trans. H. B. Nisbet (Cambridge: Cambridge University Press, 1991), 74.

[94] J. C. Smuts, *Africa and Some World Problems* (Oxford: Clarendon Press, 1930), 75; and J. Mill, W. Thomas (abrg.) *The History of British India*, (Chicago: University of Chicago Press, 1975), 60–72, 108–11, 138, 190–2, 226.

At present there is no alternative in sight to a world dominated by the sovereign state, despite the challenges posed by globalization, the changing nature of war, the proliferation of weapons of mass destruction, growing inequalities in wealth and power, and all else that is deficient about sovereign statehood. What the resurrection of trusteeship does mean, if objections to it are overcome, is a return to a hierarchical world order. Trusteeship will in the future place some territories, and the people residing in them, outside the moral and political order expressed by the idea of international society. These people will be subject to law, but not law of their own making. They will live their joint lives, but not according to their own reason and their own purpose. And they will be treated as human beings, because they are human beings and not something else, but not as members of a society of states based on reciprocal recognition and consent. Ultimate authority and jurisdiction will reside elsewhere, perhaps in a supervising power or, as is the case with Kosovo, in the United Nations. Indeed, trusteeship of the future will, as it did in the past, deprive some people of their independence, make them dependent on the will of someone else, and guide them in this state of minority until they are ready to take their place as equals in the society of states.

Answering the Call of Humanity

If trusteeship is to be justified in protest against injustice, and if it is to answer the call of humanity, then we must also be forthright in recognizing its consequences. The ICISS concludes its report on intervention to protect civilians by saying: 'the very term "international community" will become a travesty unless the community of states act decisively when large groups of human beings are being massacred or subjected to ethnic cleansing'.[95] The human family, like human security, is indivisible. And derived from the indivisible nature of the human family is a 'responsibility to protect' that is vested in an equally indivisible international community. Indeed, the Commission argues—and Wilberforce would have certainly agreed—that 'all human beings are equally entitled to be protected from acts that shock the conscience of us all'.[96] This responsibility extends, not only to preventing and reacting to human catastrophes that shock the conscience of humankind, but, crucially, to rebuilding states that have collapsed into disorder and tyranny. Indeed, the Commission suggests that the reconstruction of failed states should be guided by the objectives of the United Nations Trusteeship System that are enumerated in Article 76 of the Charter. In staking out this position, the Commission concedes that 'any resurrection of the "trusteeship" concept'

---

[95] *The Responsibility to Protect*, 75.   [96] Ibid. 75.

would likely meet with resistance, but it maintains nonetheless that some situations simply cannot be ignored.[97] But what would it mean if the world's
most powerful states made good use of the 'residual responsibility' to protect
civilians in distress that resides in the international community? And what
would the normative landscape of international society look like if we were to
answer the call of humanity with trusteeship?

It would be misleading, if not dishonest, to simply dismiss renewed interest
in trusteeship as a dubious project aimed at overthrowing a society of states
that is often criticized for clinging to discredited notions of nineteenth century
sovereignty rather than looking forward to the heady promise of a post-
modern twenty-first century. No less disingenuous is the view that regards
trusteeship as part of an ill-intentioned plot designed to shore-up informal
empires established by Western economic dominance, or to reclaim formal
empires lost in the rush to decolonization. Moreover, resurrecting trusteeship in
order to redress 'international wrongs' is not an idea whose currency trades only
in the rich and powerful West. While many voices in the non-western world
remain deeply suspicious of any encroachment that might threaten their independence, others, as debate within the United Nations makes clear, are increasingly willing to support the type of forcible intervention that might lead to
trusteeship being a more prominent part of international life. Indeed, Kofi Annan
argues that the developing norm in favour of humanitarian intervention—
which is difficult to separate from questions of trusteeship—should be wel-
comed as 'testimony to a humanity that cares more, not less, for the suffering in
its midst, and a humanity that will do more, and not less, to end it'.[98] In this
respect, Lyon is certainly right in suggesting that a United Nations trusteeship
would be preferable to the miserable conditions that an all too large proportion
of the world's population endures. UNMIK continues to be criticized for its
failure thus far to establish a viable multi-ethnic society in Kosovo[99], but it cannot be charged with failing to establish reasonably tolerable conditions of life,
at least from a material standpoint, for the vast majority of Kosovo's population. Infusions of foreign aid and investment, generating access to jobs and
public services, and rebuilding shattered homes and public works have by all
measures improved the quality of daily life in Kosovo. But to justify trusteeship
solely for the sake of material advantage is to neglect the anti-paternal claim
of post-colonial international society, if not to miss it entirely. Despite the
popularity of materialist accounts of history, it seems as if ideas, and the very

[97] Ibid. 43.

[98] Secretary-General of the United Nations, 'Secretary-General Presents His Annual Report
to the General Assembly', Press Release, 20 September 1999, SG/SM/7136-GA9596. See also
Wheeler, *Saving Strangers*, 307.

[99] See, for example, International Crisis Group, 'UNMIK's Kosovo Albatross: Tackling
Division in Mitrovica', *Balkans Report No. 131*, 3 June 2002.

powerful feelings that attach to them, move most human beings to action. And the idea of freedom must be included amongst the most important ideas for which human beings have been willing to risk and, indeed, lay down their lives.

But unlike the idea of freedom, paternalism is an ugly idea in world affairs because there is something ugly about it. Hence it is not enough to call trusteeship by another name in order to escape the opprobrium of this ugliness. It is not enough to merely assert a preference for human rights or some other value in order to embrace trusteeship while avoiding the stigma of empire. Nor it is enough to ground trusteeship in the universal claims of human rights in order to seek immunization from the reproach that often attaches to anti-paternal critiques. The value of human rights, and all else that human beings cherish, must be argued. And, as argument that expresses moral claims, it can never state something that is true, much less something that is self-evidently true. Moral argument is always contingent and open to challenge and revision; and it is, in the end, inconclusive, perhaps frustratingly so, no matter how obvious its conclusion may be to those who offer it.[100] The purpose of moral argument, if it can be said to have a purpose as such, is to persuade. It is way of saying that in our relations with our fellow creatures we should conduct ourselves in a particular way; that, before acting, we should consider some enduring interest or the consequences of our actions; or that there is some boundary that must never be crossed, even for the sake of great advantage. And it is within the framework of a universal society of states, an association in which all its members are equal in respect of authority and jurisdiction, which such conversations can and do take place. An equal must be persuaded rather than coerced, even when disagreements arise. And when amongst equals we must be prepared to say: 'you are the best judge of your happiness although I disagree, sometimes vehemently and perhaps categorically, with your judgements'. Trusteeship stands wholly outside this mode of relations. Command and obedience, rather than persuasion and consent, are its guiding principles. There is no response to disagreement because there can be no response. Trusteeship rules out dialogue about what is thought to be good, right, and just. A trustee acts on behalf of someone who is thought to be incapable of navigating the choices, dilemmas, and responsibilities of ordinary life, just as a parent acts on behalf of a child that is not yet ready to take on responsibilities of adulthood. Thus, trusteeship answers the call of humanity by treating states, and the peoples residing within them, as if they have no will of their own; for it denies the personality that makes a sovereign state what it is: free, equal to all others of its kind, and entitled to strive for the good life that is distinctly its own.

---

[100] A. MacIntyre, *Three Rival Versions of Moral Enquiry: Encyclopaedia, Genealogy, and Tradition* (Notre Dame, IN: Notre Dame University Press, 1990), 173–4.

7

Trusteeship, International Society, and the Limit of Obligation

It might be said that this book has been thus far devoted to interrogating characteristics that are internal to the idea of trusteeship, and it has been suggested that the character of the idea of trusteeship is intelligible in certain beliefs about virtue, inequality, and tutelage. But to leave it at that would be to bring our investigation to a premature close. Therefore this chapter offers some thoughts about the idea of trusteeship and its place in the history of international society. The first section puts forward the claim that trusteeship is an historic idea that is distinctive of a particular time and place, and, specifically, that it is intelligible in relation to other ideas that are especially characteristic of the Enlightenment. Thus, trusteeship discloses moral excellence, and indeed obtains powerful justification, when it contributes to the unity, progress, and perfection of the human family. The second section argues that these ideas call forth an understanding of international life that conceives international society and human society as forming a perfect identity, and which is underwritten by the duty that we should act so as to secure the good of our fellows. The third section considers the limits of this duty, and concludes that in seeking the good of our fellows we must stop short of treating people paternally. This conclusion casts a pall of doubt on the legitimacy of trusteeship in contemporary international society, even when it is aimed at protecting fundamental human rights, because it proposes to treat an equal unequally. Indeed, trusteeship is morally objectionable because it offends the irreducible sanctity of human personality by repudiating the essence of what it means to be human—a thinking and choosing agent.

Unity, Progress, and Perfection of Humankind

The idea of trusteeship is, according to Giambiattista Vico's understanding of history, a novelty that cannot be wholly disconnected from the past, and yet it is at the same time an idea that is distinctly of the present—the here and now. Indeed, Vico believed that the reappearance over time of characteristics that distinguished one age from another enabled human beings to argue analogically between different periods of history. He did not, however, suppose that history repeated itself in the strictly cyclical fashion that attached to the Graeco-Roman conception of historical movement. Rather, he understood each period of history as disclosing a peculiar character that distinguished it from what had gone before, so much so that 'the Christian barbarism of the Middle Ages is differentiated from the pagan barbarism of the Homeric age by everything that makes it distinctively an expression of the Christian mind'.[1] If Vico's view is to be taken seriously, then the distinguishing characteristics of a particular period of history are at once old and new. Thus, the idea of trusteeship is as much a product of its time as the Greek polis or the medieval Christian Church. It is a response to a particular problem, in a particular place, involving particular people. And, indeed, the idea of trusteeship is intelligible in other ideas, that is, general ideas that are definitive of the context of life in a particular age, which say something about the nature of the human family, its relation to history, and the possibilities of its future.

The first of these ideas is concerned with the presumed equality of all human beings and the concomitant unity of the human family. In Christian teachings, the equality of humankind is implied, among other places, in Paul's letter to the Romans: 'I am under obligation both to Greeks and to barbarians.'[2] From the rightness of this obligation followed the belief that Greek and barbarian should be treated as brothers in common fellowship. Thus, Warren Hastings stood accused of high crimes and misdemeanours for waging an unjust war against the Rohilla nation, in contravention of the respect that should obtain between brothers, and for reducing that nation to a condition of servitude. Conversely, Thomas Fowell Buxton embraced the Pauline message of brotherhood, and thereby rejected the proposition that Africans were not men in the ordinary sense of the word, by working for their spiritual as well as temporal salvation. The moral basis of brotherhood, the unity that arises out of fellowship, is intelligible in the law of nature as it is set out by Cicero: 'there will not be different laws at Rome and at Athens, or different laws now and in the future, but one eternal unchangeable law will be valid for all nations and for all times, and there will be one master and one ruler, that is, God, over us all, for He is the author of this law, its promulgator, and its enforcing judge'.[3] Substantially, then, humankind consists in a universal community, an all inclusive human family premised upon the fundamental equality of all human beings, that is the direct consequence of what unites

---

[1] R. G. Collingwood, *The Idea of History* (New York: Oxford University Press, 1956), 67–8.

[2] The Letter of Paul to the Romans, *The Old and New Testaments of the Holy Bible*, revised standard version (Philadelphia: Lutheran Church in America, 1971), 1.14.

[3] Quoted in A. P. D'Entreves, *Natural Law: An Introduction to Legal Philosophy* (London: Hutchinson University Library, 1970).

them: a law that is derived from their common nature. And the members of this community, in spite of the differences that might otherwise divide them, are equipped by nature to know and to understand the law that is common to them; for the eternal precepts of this law are inscribed in the hearts of every man and woman, and its content and meaning is discerned with the light of reason that their creator instilled in each of them.[4] It is this notion of fundamental human equality, what Christians call respect for human personality and secular traditions call human rights, that imposed a duty on the strong to assist the weak. Thus, it was possible to argue, as did J. H. Oldham, that all human beings possess a personality that is intrinsically worthy of respect and that 'they are equal in the right to the development of that personality, so far as may be compatible with the common good'.[5]

But in order to appreciate the strength of Oldham's claim, and the way in which it shapes the idea of trusteeship, it is worth considering the distinction that W. W. Tarn draws between the 'irreconcilable opposition between Stoicism and the theory of kingship, between the belief that unity and concord existed and you must try and get men to see it, and the belief that unity and concord did not exist and that it was the business of the rulers of the earth to try and bring them to pass'.[6] The Stoic tradition assumes that the unity of the universe exists by an act of God; and it is through education, rather than remedying the consequences of bad actions, that the unity of the human family is realized. Thus, once men are taught to see and to think right, all that is wrong in the world will in due course vanish. But the unity to which trusteeship aspires is less intelligible in the Stoic tradition than in the thought of Alexander the Great, who sought to be the harmonizer of the world, at least the one known to him, in a mission he believed to be ordained by God. It is important to recognize, Tarn argues, that Alexander sought unity in a world divided between good men and bad men, a division not unlike Aristotle's division of humanity between Greek and barbarian, but one which recognized good men as true Greeks and bad men as barbarians. Alexander understood it as the business of a king to promote fellowship among men, to reconcile all men to a unified brotherhood, even though God favoured the best men as peculiarly his own.[7] Advocates of trusteeship believed, as did Cicero, that 'if bad habits and false beliefs did not twist the

---

[4] T. Aquinas, 'Summa Theologica', *The Political Ideas of St. Thomas Aquinas*, ed. D. Bigongiari (London: Collier Macmillan Publishers, 1953), 12–14, 42–54; and D'Entreves, *Natural Law*, 26.

[5] J. H. Oldham, *Christianity and the Race Problem* (New York: George H. Doran Company, 1924), 82–92.

[6] W. W. Tarn, 'Alexander the Great and the Unity of Mankind', *Proceedings of the British Academy, 1933* (London: Oxford University Press, 1934), 137.   [7] Ibid. 136–7, 147.

weaker minds and turn them in whatever direction they are inclined, no one would be so like his own self as all men would be like all others'.[8] However, in the tradition of Alexander, they saw as the duty of the corporate agent, colonial administrator, mandatory power, and international trustee to promote deliberately the unity of humankind by sweeping away all that prevented people from seeing it. They were not satisfied merely to educate, to do no more than impart knowledge so that all human beings might see clearly for themselves, so long as slavery and other abuses impeded the universal fellowship of all human beings. Thus, Alfred Zimmern argued that '[t]he process by which the Western peoples have risen to a sense of their duty towards their weaker and more ignorant fellow citizens is indeed one of the chief stages in that progress of the common life of mankind with which we are concerned'.[9]

The claim that all human beings are fundamentally equal, and are therefore entitled to the development of their personality, immediately comes up against the reality that human beings are undeniably unequal in so many aspects of their common lives. Some people are stronger than their fellows, others more intelligent, and a few more virtuous than the ordinary person. The idea of trusteeship is distorted beyond recognition when it is removed from a discourse of inequality, a discourse that makes it possible to speak of people being advanced and backward or strong and weak. However, Zimmern alludes to a second idea in which trusteeship is intelligible, the idea of progress, which overcomes the dilemma posed by the manifest inequality of the human condition. The origins of the idea of progress may be traced to the thought of Jean Bodin who, according to J. B. Bury, announced a rather optimistic vision of man's career on earth. In the periodic ebbs and flows of history, Bodin detected a regularity of motion that ruled out a past golden age that, since the splendour of Rome, had degenerated into a condition of superstition and prejudice. History was to be interpreted as a gradual ascent in which the politics, art, literature, law, and custom of past ages could be usefully compared to the present. Thus, Bodin understood history in terms of a general progression, disclosing a definite direction, which revealed a past of some demonstrable value and a present of still greater value. Bury argues that Bodin anticipated the growth of an idea of progress, which established man's emancipation from tradition and supremacy over nature, by issuing a decisive rejection of the theory of degeneration, in so far as he regarded the achievements of his own age to be equal or superior to those of antiquity.[10]

[8] Quoted in D'Entreves, *Natural Law*, 26.
[9] A. E. Zimmern, 'Progress in Government', in F. S. Marvin (ed.), *Progress and History* (Freeport, NY: Books for Libraries Press, 1969), 161.
[10] J. B. Bury, *The Idea of Progress: An Inquiry Into Its Origin and Growth* (New York: Dover Publications, 1932), 37–44.

It is in this approach to history that Bodin, perhaps unwittingly, overcame without the help of theology a seemingly impossible contradiction between nature and convention. In other words, the idea of progress was one way of reconciling the moral equality that Christian thought and secular traditions of human rights attached to all human beings with the conventional inequality that is such a ubiquitous feature of the human condition.

The principal claim of the idea of progress, that the present is somehow better than the past which preceded it, encouraged a manner of thinking that conceived the seeming backwardness of the non-European world as a problem of development. However, the idea of trusteeship encompasses not one but several contending theories of progress that are intelligible in terms of assimilation, separation, and evolution. Assimilationist theories of progress assume, as Lord Hailey put it, that the social and political institutions of the non-European world are destined to be similar to those of Europe.[11] Theories of this sort rely heavily upon some notion of corruption, the eradication of which could be achieved quite rapidly, but only through the direct application of right principle. The utilitarian version of this theory understands the impediments to progress as the same in all places so that, for example, the irrational organization of society and the dogma of religion obstructed the attainment of good government in England and India alike. Eradicating ignorance and superstition amounted to little more than a technical affair; it was, as Jeremy Bentham makes clear, a matter of being made to see that 'the same arrangement that would serve for the jurisprudence of any one country, would serve with little variation for that of any other'.[12] This approach to progress differs only slightly in form and in logic from a rival Christian theory of progress that is intelligible, not in terms of salvation through grace, but in terms of a historical project that could realize improvement on earth. Christian thinking also conceived backwardness as a problem of corruption, whereby savage custom obscured the self-evident truth of God's law, but it substituted divine law for the principle of utility so that God was Bentham's first and supreme legislator. And it was man's task on earth to help the ignorant and blind along the road of enlightenment in the belief that '[t]rue civilization and Christianity are inseparable; the former has never been found but as a fruit of the latter'.[13] Thus, Christian as well as utilitarian theories of

---

[11] Lord Hailey, *An African Survey: A Study of Problems Arising in Africa South of the Sahara*, rev. edn. (London: Oxford University Press, 1957), 150.

[12] J. Bentham, *A Fragment on Government* (Cambridge: Cambridge University Press, 1994), 26; and J. W. Burrow, *Evolution and Society: A Study of Victorian Social Theory* (Cambridge: Cambridge University Press, 1970), 41.

[13] Quoted in T. F. Buxton, *The African Slave Trade and Its Remedy* (London: Frank Cass & Co., 1967), 507. On the possibility of a Christian theory of progress, see C. Berry, 'On the

progress presuppose a rationally ordered universe that discloses an irreducible harmony of interests and values; and it was the duty of the missionary and the legislator to sweep away the impediments that prevented others from seeing its perfection.

In the writings of Arthur de Gobineau we encounter a theory of progress which, unlike assimilationist theories that aspired to a universal standard of sameness, presupposes the separation of political, economic, and social life on the basis of race. On this view, progress and degeneration are understood as being innately connected with evidence of racial genius. The achievement of progress depended on the separation of the races, in order that each should perform the function for which nature intended; for it was the adulteration of blood, as opposed to fanaticism, misrule, irreligion, or the corruption of morals, that resulted in degeneration. From this argument, Gobineau quite naturally concluded that some races were intrinsically suited to rule, while others lacked the inner impulse to take the first step towards civilization.[14] Colonial arrangements that ensured the primacy of European civilization were often predicated on a racial distribution of power that bears a striking resemblance to this mode of thinking. The white race formed a ruling caste that governed; the Indian race acted as a racial link between black and white; and the black race formed a class of labourers and thus occupied positions of servitude. It is in this spirit that Charles Dilke proclaimed: 'nature seems to intend the English for a race of officers, to direct and guide the cheap labour of the Eastern peoples.'[15]

But no matter how self-evidently wrong such thinking appears to us now, it would be a mistake to simply dismiss it as a crude attempt to disguise naked domination and exploitation. The idea of race that shaped the character of trusteeship during the nineteenth century furnished answers to questions great and small that were in their time no less authoritative than those furnished by religion or science. It is in this context that J. C. Smuts parried charges of malice by arguing that the essential differences of the white and black races dictated that the African should be preserved in his natural state, for the hope of Africa had to be built on distinctly African foundations. Moreover, he argued that the intermingling of the races would lead to all

Meaning of Progress and Providence in the Fourth Century', *Heythrop Journal*, 18/3 (1977), 257–70.

[14] A. de Gobineau, *The Inequality of Human Races*, trans. A. Collins (New York: Howard Fertig, 1967), 4, 25–8, 33, 50; and H. Arendt, *The Origins of Totalitarianism* (New York: Harcourt Brace & Company, 1985), 171.

[15] C. Dilke, *Greater Britain: A Record of Travel in English-Speaking Countries During 1866 and 1867* (New York: Harper, 1869), 192; and H. A. C. Cairns, *Prelude to Imperialism: British Reactions to Central African Society 1840–1890* (London: Routledge & Kegan Paul, 1965), 207.

manner of social evil that would in the end enfeeble both races: racial antipathy, public disorder, moral deterioration, and, as Gobineau feared, the 'debasement of the higher race and culture'.[16] This approach to progress assumed that the possibility of advancement remained open so long as racial divisions remained intact. Respect for the genius of race would see the world to a future that was better than the present, and better still than the past that preceded it. Thus, Lothrop Stoddard, an influential demographer in his day, concluded that '[w]hat we to-day need above all else is a changed attitude of mind—a recognition of the supreme importance of heredity, not merely in scientific treatises but in the practical ordering of the world's affairs.'[17]

The most influential theory of progress, at least so far as the idea of trusteeship is concerned, disclosed a gradualist disposition that classified tribes, nations, and civilizations in terms of stages of development. It is in this idiom of progress that the notion of peoples being differently placed on the ladder of civilization makes most sense. Gradualist theories of progress began to take hold in the mid-nineteenth century, when the Indian Mutiny of 1857 shattered the Anglicist hope championed by T. B. Macaulay of creating a class of Indians that were English in all respects but the colour of their skin.[18] And once the concept of evolution entered the social field, these theories were endowed with a powerful quasi-scientific basis in an attempt to replicate the heady achievements of natural science. Herbert Spencer is perhaps the most important nineteenth century thinker to compare societies and organisms in the belief that the laws of the social world were analogous to those of the natural world. Thus, the most primitive societies exhibit little evidence of mutual dependence; more advanced societies composed of 'savages' disclose a rudimentary degree of social structure and governmental organization; and the most advanced societies display levels of specialization and aggregation that are indicative of nations. Hence, for Spencer, 'society is a growth and not a manufacture'.[19]

Evolutionary concepts of development, competition, and gradation are at the very centre of the gradualist theories of progress. For example,

---

[16] Smuts, *Africa and Some World Problems* (Oxford: Clarendon Press, 1930), 30, 93.

[17] L. Stoddard, *The Rising Tide of Color Against White World-Supremacy* (New York: Charles Scribner's Sons, 1921), 305–6.

[18] T. B. Macaulay, 'T. B. Macaulay's Minute on Education', in C. H. Philips (ed.), *The Correspondence of Lord William Cavendish Bentinck, Governor-General of India, 1828–1835* (Oxford: Oxford University Press, 1977), 1412.

[19] H. Spencer, 'The Social Organism', *The Man Versus the State: With Six Essays on Government, Society, and Freedom* (Indianapolis, IN: Liberty Fund, 1981), 388, 392–405. On Spencer's thought generally, see E. Barker, *Political Thought in England, 1848–1914* (London: Oxford University Press, 1954). For a survey of how the idea of evolution shaped attitudes toward empire, see W. L. Langer, *The Diplomacy of Imperialism, 1890–1902*, 2nd edn. (New York: Alfred A. Knopf, 1965), 86–94.

Lord Lugard ascribed value to the Islamic religion, a force responsible for destroying the most heinous native superstitions and customs, but he expressed grave doubt that it could carry the people of Africa beyond a stage of barbarism. The idea of trusteeship in both the League of Nations covenant and the United Nations charter implies a competitive world in which underdeveloped nations require the guidance of developed nations. And on the eve of decolonization, Lord Hailey saw fit to describe the colonial peoples of the British Empire as a 'procession of peoples in which great distances separate the van from the rear guard'.[20] The great achievement of social theories of evolution is that they reconciled diverse social facts with established ways of thinking; and, when combined with the idea of progress, they revealed something about the past as well as something about the possibilities of the future.[21]

But the word 'progress' is merely a name given to the direction of history; the end of progress, the point towards which history is moving, is better described by the word 'perfection'. Indeed, the idea of trusteeship is not fully intelligible outside of a conception of perfection that emerged in the seventeenth century. Before then, John Passmore submits, thinking about perfection fell generally into two categories: either human beings could perfect themselves or they could become perfect through God's grace. Trusteeship is intelligible in a third possibility: 'men could be perfected not by God, not by the exercise of their own free will, not even by some combination of the two, but by the deliberate intervention of their fellow-men.'[22] Intimations of this mode of thinking are evident in the sixteenth century writings of Francisco de Vitoria, who included mental incapacity on the part of the Indians among the just titles by which a Christian prince may lay claim to dominions in the New World. Spanish dominion in the Americas would be justified, he argued, if the Indians were incapable of administering a government in accord with European concepts of civil and human legitimacy; and, then, only if it benefited the Indians rather than amassed profit for the Spaniards.[23] Vitoria's theological account of duty eventually gave way to a modern account whereby duty joined man with man as opposed to man with God. Thus, duty demanded that we act for the sake of our fellow man for no other reason than he is a man. Passmore argues that the idea of perfection secured in this notion of duty supposes that individual human beings should be perfected only as the entire human family is perfected as a whole. It asks that the ideal to which

[20] Lugard, F. D., *The Dual Mandate of Africa*, 4th edn. (London: William Blackwood & Sons, 1929), 75–8; and Lord Hailey, *The Future of Colonial Peoples* (Oxford: Oxford University Press, 1943), 62.   [21] Burrow, *Evolution and Society*, 267.

[22] J. Passmore, *The Perfectibility of Man*, 3rd edn. (Indianapolis, IN: Liberty Fund, 2000), 226.

[23] F. de Vitoria, 'On the American Indians', *Political Writings* eds. A. Pagden and J. Lawrance (Cambridge: Cambridge University Press, 1991), 290–1.

human beings aspire be attainable on earth and in their present life; and it recognizes, as did James Lorimer, that the 'right of undeveloped races, like the right of undeveloped individuals, is a right not to recognition as what they are not, but to guardianship—that is, to guidance—in becoming that of which they are capable, in realising their special ideals'.[24] The idea of perfection, then, at least the one that is our concern, specifies an ideal that some human beings might approach through the intervention of their fellows. And with this objective in mind, Passmore argues, the moralists of the seventeenth and eighteenth centuries 'set out to remake the world in the image of universal benevolence, to perfect it in secular charity'.[25] The idea of trusteeship is undoubtedly one way of answering the call.

Of course, the pursuit of perfection by intervening in the lives of others, caring for them so that they too might approach some ideal condition of good, runs a great risk of destroying much or all that is of value to them. Passmore warns that attempts at achieving the collective perfection of humanity aspire to total order and harmony, that is, 'a kind of unity which is destructive of that diversity which is the glory of the world and the secret of all man's achievements'.[26] The idea of trusteeship is no doubt an historical response to the diversity of life on this planet, but rarely has it recognized diversity as disclosing ways of life that, while alien and perhaps detestable, are valuable to some people and therefore require no further justification. Rather, the story of trusteeship in international history is unavoidably tied up in what Gerrit Gong refers to as a confrontation of civilizations and cultures,[27] whereby members of civilized (European) international society endeavoured to substitute true religion, true science, true knowledge, true law, and true custom for the putatively defective institutions, practices, and traditions of African and Asian societies. Thus, the idea of trusteeship in international history assumes that Europeans were the best judges of African and Asian welfare.

But for all the deprecation of non-European ways of life, it would be a mistake, and a hasty one at that, to dismiss the claims of trusteeship as merely manifestations of selfishness, greed, or malice. Lord Hailey was right when he suggested that 'the value of a doctrine such as that of trusteeship must be judged by the inspiration it brings to noble minds, rather than by the excuses it affords to the baser instincts of mankind.'[28] But even if the history of trusteeship is distinguished by proofs of kindness, heroism, and devotion to

---

[24] J. Lorimer, *The Institutes of the Law of Nations: A Treatise of the Jural Relations of Separate Political Communities*, vol. 1 (Edinburgh: William Blackwood and Sons, 1883), 101–58.

[25] Passmore, *The Perfectibility of Man*, 230–1, 239.   [26] Ibid. 511.

[27] G. Gong, *The Standard of 'Civilization' in International Society* (Oxford: Clarendon Press, 1984), 5–7.   [28] Hailey, *The Future of Colonial Peoples*, 15.

the cause of disadvantaged peoples, its most enduring legacy is the consistency with which those peoples denounced the enlightened despotism of empire and demanded the right to be masters of their own affairs. Indeed, this sentiment, the still very powerful claim that destroyed the legitimacy of trusteeship, is expressed best in an unnamed African's protest to Margery Perham: 'We do not wish for any special treatment. We do not wish to be protected; we want to be allowed to make our own mistakes, and to work out our own salvation, as you did.'[29]

A Society of States and a Family of Peoples

The idea of trusteeship expressed in terms of these ideas—unity, progress, and perfection—calls forth an understanding of international life that is rather different from accounts that form the basis of most international society theorising. Martin Wight's conception of international society, which provides as good a starting point as any other, depends on a distinction borrowed from Grotius in an attempt to bridge the universalism of human society and the particularism of a society of states.[30] The external boundary of this international society was delimited by an eternal natural law that presupposed a universal moral life of humankind. Even the barbarians of the Americas, as Las Casas endeavoured to demonstrate, were owed the respect of Christian love obliged by God's command: love your neighbour as yourself. All men, Christian and infidel alike, as creatures created in God's image, must be treated as brothers: 'This we owe to all men. Nobody is excepted.'[31] But within this human society—a society in which nothing more than human fellowship entailed obligation—the Christian princes of Europe instituted positive obligations, based on historical and cultural unity rather than the legal unity of the Christian republic, which marked the internal boundary of a particular society of states. That limit, according to Wight, is indicated in the Grotian claim: 'between contracting parties there is a kind of league closer than that between men in general.'[32] The particular bonds of contract saw the degrees of precedence that structured the hierarchical relations of *respublica Christiana* give way to an egalitarian principle of organization.

[29] Quoted in M. Perham, 'Some Problems of Indirect Rule', *Colonial Sequence, 1930 to 1949* (London: Methuen & Co., 1967), 103.

[30] M. Wight, *Systems of States*, ed. H. Bull (Leicester: Leicester University Press, 1977), 125–8.

[31] B. de Las Casas, in *Defence of the Indians*, trans. S. Poole (DeKalb, IL: Northern Illinois University Press, 1974), 38–9.

[32] H. Grotius, in *De Jure Belli ac Pacis*, trans. L. R. Loomis (Roslyn, NY: Walter J. Black, 1949), 147.

Distinctions would be made on the basis of power, but no corresponding rank obtained in respect of authority or jurisdiction. Communication transpired through resident embassies and periodic summits and congresses. And the defence of common interests, those related mainly to questions of peace and war, were interpreted in view of collective security and the balance of power. Indeed, it is within this 'inner circle' that international society 'comes of age' as an association of states, each of which exercised authority and jurisdiction over a particular population and territory, that conducted their relations according to principles of law common to them.[33]

Although many of these ideas are discernible in Hedley Bull's account of international society, the notion of human society that informs such an important part of Wight's thinking is but a faint outline in his classic work, *The Anarchical Society*. The so-called solidarist ideas that are insensitive to the constraints of time and place, while not entirely absent, are pushed to the margins of inquiry in the belief that a community of humankind, as Bull once tersely asserted, is not yet a 'going concern'.[34] But the authority of shared rules and institutions, which are necessary conditions of life in society, are not derived from God or from nature, just as the moral order represented by international society is neither revealed nor discovered. Artifice and convention are the watchwords of the association that Bull has in mind. Questions of origin and limit are answered in terms of history; and speculation about the nature and extent of obligation as well as the content and meaning of justice, once the exclusive domain of theology, is an appropriate activity for the layman. In short, then, international society, and all that pertains to it, belongs to the world of human conduct. It is an arrangement that can extend no further than Wight's inner circle because, as Bull makes clear, the rules and institutions of international society derive from the consent of the states that created them.[35]

This contractual understanding of international society is even more pronounced in Robert Jackson's notion of a universal ethical standard called the global covenant. Crucially, though, this claim of universality is justified, not by the actual or potential unity of the human family, but by the manifest difference of international life and the value of preserving that difference. The global covenant is concerned with procedural means rather than substantive ends. It is 'by and large' a procedural association in which states are joined in respect of the authority of a practice—the most important of which include sovereign equality, territorial integrity, and non-interference—rather than in pursuit of common substantive ends. And the arrangements of this association,

---

[33] Wight, *Systems of States*, Ch. 5.
[34] H. Bull, *The Anarchical Society: A Study of Order in World Politics* (New York: Columbia University Press, 1977), 23.   [35] Ibid. 34.

the rules and institutions that make mutual coexistence possible, are distilled from the historical world of practice and enjoy positive recognition in international law on a voluntary, reciprocal, and consensual basis.[36] Hence, Jackson trims the obligation of Christian love, and its contemporary secular equivalents, to the barest of negative meanings. Loving your neighbour as yourself can mean no more than respecting his freedom to act within what amounts to a private space bounded by the jurisdiction of a sovereign state. In this sort of international society, if taken to its logical conclusion, the voice of human society falls silent.

This contractual basis of international society is of particular importance because without it trusteeship collapses into practical irrelevance. In other words, an international society grounded in a relation of contract also required arrangements in order to conduct relations with persons who could not enter into a contractual relation. Thus, if Wight is correct in saying that international society comes of age in the seventeenth century, we might also say that the idea of contract as the source of authority, right, and duty in international life comes of age in the eighteenth century. It was in this period that authority ordained by God, the essential premise of the theory of the divine right of kings, gave place to authority conferred by the people. And the claim that kings were accountable to no authority but God came to be regarded as a tendentious argument aligned against the interests of the people. The relation of contract that displaced the theory of divine right supposed that will and consent should form the basis of human association, as well as the conventions of justice that are fundamental to it.[37] This theory of popular legitimacy began to take hold internationally, as Wight argues, when the American Revolutionaries proclaimed to the world in 1776 that men institute governments to secure their unalienable rights that derive 'their just powers from the consent of the governed'.[38] Thirteen years later, in 1789, the National Assembly of France signalled the death knell of the competing theory of dynastic legitimacy when it declared: 'No body nor individual may exercise any authority which does not proceed directly from the nation.'[39] The idea that will and consent should legitimize the arrangements of domestic life

---

[36] R. Jackson, *The Global Covenant: Human Conduct in a World of States* (Oxford: Oxford University Press, 2000), 22–5, 416–19.

[37] J. N. Figgis, *The Divine Right of Kings*, 2nd edn. (Cambridge: Cambridge University Press, 1922), 5–6; and E. Barker, 'Introduction', *Social Contract: Essays by Locke, Hume, and Rousseau* (Oxford: Oxford University Press, 1971), vii–ix.

[38] 'The Declaration of Independence, July 4, 1776', in H. S. Commager (ed.), *Documents of American History*, 4th edn. (New York: Appleton-Century-Crofts, 1948), 100; and Wight, *Systems of States*, 160.

[39] 'Declaration of the Rights of Man and Citizen (1789)', in M. Rosen and J. Wolff (eds.), *Political Thought* (Oxford: Oxford University Press, 1999), 394.

proved to be no less influential when it came to legitimizing the arrangements of international life. But the clarity of relations based on contract made for a rather sharp distinction between insiders and outsiders. A society of states, the arrangements of which were grounded in contract and legitimated by consent, necessarily excluded persons (natural or legal) who lacked a functioning will, or who could not render consent. Thus, we might think of trusteeship as a way of ordering relations between the society of states and what lay beyond it without appealing, at least explicitly so, to a law of nature of the sort that underpins Grotian thinking. It is in this respect that relations of contract and trusteeship imply one another; they are, so to speak, opposing sides of the proverbial coin of international life.

But the idiom of contract that pervades so much of international society thinking is on the one hand misleading and on the other incomplete. It is misleading because it tends to promote the view that theorizing international life begins and ends with states. International society is thus an association in which only sovereign states are eligible for membership. They are the principal actors, as well as the principal bearers of rights and duties, within this association. And institutions that are distinctive of international society, diplomacy, great powers, war, international law, and the balance of power are predominantly, if not exclusively, the domain of the states that created them. Indeed, the importance of states is such that Bull regards them as '[t]he starting point of international relations' and Jackson treats them as the 'building blocks' of international society.[40] Thus, we might reasonably conclude that the questions most deserving of scholarly attention, even those that pertain to issues that allegedly defy the hegemony of the state, such as human rights, globalization, environmental degradation, terrorism, and transnational crime, must not deviate too far from this omnipresent feature of international life.

But a world theorized in terms of states, especially one that is principally procedural in organization, is incomplete in so far as it can provide no more than a partial account of the obligations of international life. The procedural world that Jackson portrays is essentially an autonomous realm that exists independently of other forms of human association. However, a society of states, procedural or otherwise, cannot be constituted solely by a theory of contract, and the binding nature of that contract cannot be derived ultimately from an expression of consent. The difficulty with treating contract as the basis of international society is illuminated by H. L. A. Hart's claim that an exchange of promises, which gives rise to obligations, depends on pre-existing rules that authoritatively establish that promises must be kept prior to entering into such an agreement. It follows, then, he continues, that 'such rules

---

[40] Bull, *The Anarchical Society*, 8; and Jackson, *The Global Covenant*, 116.

presupposed in the very notion of a self-imposed obligation obviously cannot derive *their* obligatory status from a self-imposed obligation to obey them'.[41] In other words, a theory of contract cannot of itself provide an account of the obligatory nature of the global covenant. That account must be sought somewhere else.

Identifying the idea that underpins the obligatory nature of the global covenant requires an examination of what it means to be joined in a relation of society and, conversely, in a relation of trusteeship. R. G. Collingwood argues that '[a] society or partnership is constituted by the social will of the partners, an act of free will whereby the person who thereby becomes a partner decides to take upon himself a share in a joint enterprise.'[42] Society is constituted internationally by sovereign states, each of which is endowed with a common personality, and the rights and duties that attach to that personality are confirmed, not by an assertion of power, but in a freely given act of recognition. And because society is created and sustained by free will, its members must be equal in respect of authority in order to form and to recognize such a partnership. Thus, on Collingwood's terms, an association that is rightly named 'society' must have a will, that is, a joint will, by which it rules itself according to its own design and purpose.[43]

In contrast, the idea of trusteeship, and the mode of relations it entails, is fundamentally opposed to life in society. A trustee must act on behalf of a ward because he cannot act for himself. Ignorance or immaturity may obscure the nature of the good, so that true happiness is realizable only under someone else's tuition. Hence, trusteeship is intelligible in terms of an association that Collingwood calls a non-social community—a type of human association that lacks a joint will of its own. It is an association that is dependent on the guidance of an alien will and, as such, it is not self-ruling according to its own lights and purposes. Indeed, a non-social community is ruled by force understood, not as the application of physical force, but as a type of mental superiority that in an earlier age was expressed as the standard of civilization. And it is this asymmetrical and non-consensual character of life in a non-social community that leads Collingwood to conclude: '[t]he members of a non-social community are faithful, not of their own free will but in virtue of some force brought to bear upon them, to a communal order or way of life originated and maintained in them by something that is not their will but, for example, the will of a society upon which they are dependent.'[44]

---

[41] H. L. A. Hart, *The Concept of Law* (Oxford: Clarendon Press, 1961), 219–20.
[42] R. G. Collingwood, *The New Leviathan* (Oxford: Clarendon Press, 1942), 133, 139.
[43] Ibid. 140–1.   [44] Ibid. 142–3, 150.

But the ideas of society and non-social community cannot provide an adequate account of the obligatory status of self-imposed rules so long as they are treated as being independent of one another. They invoke distinctive modes of association that are intelligible in terms of irreconcilable postulates that make it impossible to assimilate one to the other. Indeed, it makes no sense whatsoever to speak of a relation of trusteeship between members of a society of states. To do so would mean that an entity that lacks a will is capable of participating in an association that is constituted by the will of its members; or, alternatively, it would mean that an entity that is a member of such an association might be treated as if it possessed no will. What is needed, then, if the category 'international society' is to be meaningful at all, is a mode of association that is inclusive of both society and non-social community. Collingwood's notion of family, 'a mixed community consisting of a social nucleus of parents and a non-social community of children', goes some way towards accommodating these mutually irreconcilable ideas within the framework of a single mode of association.[45] The social part of a family is signified by an exchange of promises that results in a contract of marriage; and, like all social relations, the institution of marriage depends on the will of its constituent partners if it is to exist at all. The non-social part of a family is signified by children that, on account of their physical and mental immaturity, require the guidance and care of their parents. These children are of course expected to grow up, so that they will eventually possess a fully functioning will of their own that will enable them to make contracts and to participate in social life. At that point they no longer require the tutelage of their parents: with adulthood comes independence and equality. But emergence from a child-like state of immaturity does not alter the bonds of family. The language of contract, which is definitive of social life, is wholly irrelevant in making sense of family life, as neither will nor consent has any bearing on familial membership. Membership in a family does not follow from an expression of intent to become a partner in a joint enterprise called 'family'. We are members of a family for no other reason than we are born into it.[46] Thus, the ideas of will and consent are equally irrelevant when it comes to understanding the nature of obligations that arise from the fact of kinship.

The idea of family is not offered here as an arbitrarily chosen analogy with which to make a rather fine point regarding how we think about an abstractly theorized international society. Colonies, and the peoples residing in them, were in history and in law likened to children that in time, and with the education that all responsible parents should provide, would grow up to be adult nations. But until they reached a state of maturity, that is, until they could be

---

[45] Ibid. 166.   [46] Ibid. 160.

counted upon to conduct themselves in accordance with the values of (European) civilization, they were to be treated with the care and discipline that joins parent and child. Even the most strident critics of imperialism, such as John Hobson, indulged in the tutelary language of family in order to effect its reform: '[t]he analogy furnished by the education of a child is prima facie a sound one, and is not invalidated by the dangerous abuses to which it is exposed in practice.'[47] And the perils of immaturity led Herbert Morrison, the Home Secretary in Churchill's wartime coalition, to caution against any retreat from empire: '[i]t would be ignorant, dangerous nonsense to talk about grants of full self-government to many of the dependent territories for some time to come. In those instances it would be like giving a child of ten a latch-key, a bank account, and a shot-gun.'[48] It seems that, in view of the historical as well as philosophical account of family in international society, the obligations of trusteeship and those of the global covenant find their ultimate sanction in the same source, even though they demand conflicting action. Whereas trusteeship asks that we come to the assistance of people that, like children, cannot help themselves, the global covenant asks that we respect the freedom of people that, like adults, are entitled to act for themselves. That we should assist or, alternatively, respect our fellows speaks to obligations that are owed to all human beings, because they are members of a unitary human family that transcends all determinations of rank and status. Thus, taken together, the obligatory status of trusteeship and the global covenant—the fundamental condition of their rightness—is grounded in the duty that we should all seek the good of our fellow man.

The Limit of Obligation

The principal moral claim of family, that we should seek the good of our fellow man, brings the idea of human society back to the forefront of international life. However, in doing so, I do not want merely to re-state Martin Wight's dualistic conception of international society as an inner circle of sovereign states embedded within an all-embracing outer circle of humanity. In our world it makes little sense to speak of insiders and outsiders. There are no geographical boundaries that separate members from non-members, and there are no rival systems of law that distinguish the universal from the particular. Everyone is an insider. Thus, it no longer makes sense to ask questions

[47] J. A. Hobson, *Imperialism* (London: George Allen & Unwin, 1938), 229.
[48] Quoted in W. R. Louis, *Imperialism at Bay, 1941–1945: The United States and the Decolonization of the British Empire* (Oxford: Clarendon Press, 1977), 14.

about what stands beyond the society of states. But I do not mean to suggest as well that we are unable to make meaningful distinctions as we attempt to come to grips with the problems of world affairs. It is hardly possible to get at those problems, much less to communicate their significance in a way that is comprehensible to others, without employing some manner of political, economic, or cultural distinction. Nor do I wish to suggest that it is impossible to make distinctions in order to offer substantive judgements about the rightness of human conduct internationally. Indeed, one of the most historically significant ways of conveying such judgements, the discourse civilization, was clothed in a newly found respectability in wake of the terrorist attacks on New York and Washington in September 2001. But when George W. Bush proclaimed that '[t]he civilized world is rallying to America's side',[49] he cannot be understood to mean a world outside of which exists a rival barbarous world. There are no barbarians clamouring outside the gates of civilization. Adjudging something as barbarous in our world, for example, flying aeroplanes into buildings in order to kill thousands of innocent civilians, depends on an inside judgement made in relation to norms of conduct that are internal to a singular world composed of persons who are at once men and citizens. The distinction that has been foreclosed, however, is that between independent (parent) states and dependent (child) communities. Our world is composed of a family of peoples that are all adults: the children have all grown up yet, as family members, they still live in the neighbourhood. In other words, our world is one in which human society and the society of states, that is, the universal and the particular, form a perfect identity.

This conception of international life proposes a much broader understanding of duty than what might be reasonably derived from a procedural association aimed at the achievement of mutual coexistence. But how far should we act to ensure that every man receives his due? Must we do anything in our power to answer the call of humanity? And are there limits of which we should take notice in seeking the good of our fellow man? With the idea of human society squarely in view, it is possible to argue on a more secure platform that interference in the lives of others may be justified in order to ensure that every man receives his due. For example, it breathes life into Nicholas Wheeler's argument that the claim of human society, the solidarist argument as he calls it, enjoins the world's most powerful states to put a stop to 'loud emergencies' such as genocide, mass murder, and ethnic cleansing.[50] But in

---

[49] G. W. Bush, 'Address to a Joint Session of Congress and to the American People', Washington, D.C., The White House, The Office of the Press Secretary, 20 September 2001.

[50] N. Wheeler, *Saving Strangers: Humanitarian Intervention in International Society* (Oxford: Oxford University Press, 2000), 285–310.

accepting a broad interpretation of duty, we are left to ask if our obligation to act is in respect of trusteeship subject to limitation. Discerning the extent of this duty is all the more cogent when we consider that the society of states, the universal association that emerged out of decolonization, seems to be sagging under the weight of its principal moral claim. A frighteningly large proportion of the world's population lives in states that cannot be described as repositories of the good life; and the person who experiences the misfortune of being a citizen of the wrong state is likely to be condemned to a life of fear, deprivation, and chronic insecurity. Indeed, Oxfam reports that in Africa alone three-hundred million people subsist on less than US$1 per day; life expectancy is falling from its current level of 48 years; HIV/AIDS afflicts twenty-eight million people; more than one-third of all children suffer from malnutrition; and war is a part of daily life for more than one-hundred million people.[51] States that are home to this sort of diversity cannot be regarded as arrangements that are crucial to the moral and material well-being of their citizens. And it is this sobering reality that provides a compelling counterpoint to the value that Jackson ascribes to the global covenant, a counterpoint that excites demands for an alternative ethics of human conduct.

The search for an alternative ethics usually starts with asking questions about the relation of state sovereignty and individual sovereignty. For example, Kofi Annan asserts the primacy of the latter by arguing: '[s]tates are now widely understood to be instruments at the service of their peoples, and not vice versa.'[52] But relegating state sovereignty to the realm of the instrumental, that is to say, to a realm in which it discloses no moral value in its own right, dispenses with the understanding of states as moral communities far too easily. To characterize states as little more than arrangements of convenience, temporary arrangements meant to address some passing interest, is to deny much of the history of the world in which we live. The universal society of states that emerged out of decolonization embraced an Aristotelian notion of statehood that is fundamentally at odds with the idea of states as strictly instrumental arrangements. There is, on this view, a necessary connection between the good life and life in a state. Independent statehood holds out the possibility that men might live well by their own lights, because it is within the framework of the state that they participate in an ongoing dialogue about what is good, what is right, and what is just. The substance of this dialogue, as well as the framework within which it takes place, leads Aristotle to conclude that the state is an arrangement of justice; and outside of this arrangement of

---

[51] A. Van Woudenberg, 'Africa at the Crossroads: Time to Deliver', *Oxfam Briefing Paper 19* (Oxford: Oxfam GB, 2002), 1.

[52] K. Annan, 'Two Concepts of Sovereignty', *The Economist*, 18 September 1999.

justice, the good life is either an impossible ideal or an inchoate fiction. For the man who is separated from the life of the state, who has no need to be a member of a state, or who is incapable of participating in its life, is not a man properly so-called but is rather a 'god' or 'beast'.[53] But acceptance of this understanding of statehood, which treats the state as having a natural priority over any particular individual, does not entail a concomitant abandonment of the value of individual sovereignty; it is, rather, to argue from a position of human dignity and from an explicit acknowledgement thereof. Indeed, it is to recognize that the realization of human potential, the development of the faculties and the virtues that separate human beings from the subhuman and the superhuman, cannot be fulfilled fully outside of the life of a state.

The relation between human dignity and independent statehood proposes a very clear limit of which we must take notice in seeking the good of our fellow man. State sovereignty and individual sovereignty imply one another in such a way that one cannot be made subservient to the other if justice is to be done. In other words, if human beings are to be recognized as being fully human, and, indeed, if they are to live well as human beings and not as something else, they must live in a state of their own. Thus, we must act so far as we are able to assist our neighbours, to help them in achieving their goals, and to protect them when they are in danger, but we must stop short of treating them paternally. The value that attaches to human personality asks that we treat all persons as thinking and choosing agents that are entitled to direct their own affairs, for no other reason than they are human beings. We must treat them as subjects of law that they know by their own faculties rather than as objects of law that is imposed by an alien authority. And it requires absolute respect of at least a minimal sphere of freedom in which they are certain to realize great achievements and, likewise, to commit great mistakes as they pursue their own ends by their own lights and according to their own purposes.

Crucially, then, the sanctity of human personality expresses a condition of independence that cannot be separated from, subordinated to, or placed above the independence of the political community. The development of human personality, and, by extension, the fulfilment of what Annan means by individual sovereignty, demands that all persons be members of an independent political community in which they are entitled to be equal members. This argument should not be misconstrued to mean that the sovereign state is destined to dominate the political landscape of international life; nor should it be interpreted to mean that future generations are precluded from organizing themselves politically in ways that are vastly different from our own.

---

[53] Aristotle, *The Politics*, trans. T. A. Sinclair (London: Penguin Books, 1992), 59–60.

Human potential might be realized just as well in a single world community or in hundreds of small communities that come into contact infrequently or not at all. What it does mean is that to be fully human one must be a citizen and to be a citizen one must be recognized as fully human.

The idea of trusteeship stands fundamentally opposed to the demands of human dignity as we have come to understand it in contemporary international society. Trusteeship assumes that some people do not understand their situation; they may be ignorant of 'true' knowledge, 'true' law, 'true' science, 'true' politics, and 'true' economy in some way so that 'true' happiness escapes their grasp; and, on account of this ignorance, they must be ruled for their own good until they are able to comprehend and understand the 'true' nature of things. People that are treated as children, because they do not understand their situation, are necessarily excluded from the moral order expressed by the idea of the state; and communities that are treated as children, because they are immature, depraved, or destitute, are similarly excluded from the moral order expressed by the idea of international society. They will be subject to law, but not law of their own making. They will live their lives, but not according to their own reason and purpose. And they will be treated as members of the human family, because they are human beings and not something else, but not as autonomous individuals that are possessed of a fully developed personality, which establishes their authority to think and to choose for themselves. That is why a paternal relation between equals is always wrong. Indeed, to treat a thinking and choosing person as if he is not so is to deny, and not merely to infringe upon, the essence of what it means to be human. And it is the iniquity of denying the absolute sanctity of human personality that shattered the legitimacy of empire and, along with it, trusteeship in international society. Giving every man his due means that we must respect his right to seek his own salvation and to make mistakes in doing so.

The fundamental importance that attaches to human dignity in our world suggests that the space between anarchy and society that trusteeship once occupied has been and remains closed. For reopening that space would entail nothing less than depriving people of their independence, making them dependent on the will of someone else, and guiding them in this state of minority until they are ready once again to take their place as equals in the society of states. It is in this respect that the idea of trusteeship cannot escape its imperial past, no matter how enlightened or well-intentioned it might be, because it belongs to a mode of conduct that is imperial by its nature. It belongs to a mode of conduct that is fundamentally irreconcilable with the idea that we should respect the dignity of all human beings, not because it is conducive to peace, order, security, efficiency, wealth, happiness, utility, enlightenment, or some other interest, but because they are human.

Bibliography

ALEXANDROWICZ, C. H. (1967). *An Introduction to the History of the Law of Nations in the East Indies*. Oxford: Clarendon Press.

ANGELL, N. (1933). 'The International Anarchy', in *The Intelligent Man's Way to Prevent War* (ed. L. Woolf). London: Victor Gollancz.

—— (1953). 'The Commonwealth Idea: Past and Future', *United Empire*, 44/4, 149–52.

ANGOULVANT, G. L. (1969). 'General Instructions, 26 November 1908', in *France and West Africa: An Anthology of Historical Documents* (ed. John Hargreaves). London: Macmillan.

ANNAN, K. (1999). 'Two Concepts of Sovereignty', *The Economist*, 18 September.

AQUINAS, T. (1953). 'Summa Theologica', in *The Political Ideas of St. Thomas Aquinas* (ed. D. Bigongiari). London: Collier Macmillan Publishers.

ARENDT, H. (1985). *The Origins of Totalitarianism* (New York: Harcourt Brace & Company).

ARISTOTLE (1992). *Politics* (trans. T. A. Sinclair) London: Penguin Books.

ART, R., and K. WALTZ (1983). 'Technology, Strategy, and the Uses of Force', in *The Use of Force: International Politics and Foreign Policy* (eds. R. Art and K. Waltz). New York: University Press of America.

ASHDOWN, P. (2002). 'Inaugural Speech by Paddy Ashdown, the New High Representative for Bosnia and Herzegovina', Office of the High Representative Press Office, 27 May. (www.ohr.int)

—— (2002). 'What I Learned in Bosnia', *New York Times*, 28 October. (www.nytimes.com)

AXWORTHY, L. (1996). Notes for an Address by the Honourable Lloyd Axworthy, Minister of Foreign Affairs, to the 51st General Assembly of the United Nations, New York, 24 September. (www.dfait-maeci.gc.ca)

—— (1999). 'Kosovo and the Human Security Agenda', Notes for an Address by the Honourable Lloyd Axworthy, Minister of Foreign Affairs, to the Woodrow Wilson School of Public and International Relations, Princeton University, Princeton, New Jersey, 7 April 1999. (www.dfait-maeci.gc.ca)

BARKER, E. (1954). *Political Thought in England, 1848–1914*. London: Oxford University Press.

—— (1971). *Social Contract: Essays by Locke, Hume, and Rousseau*. Oxford: Oxford University Press.

BEARCE, G. D. (1961). *British Attitudes Towards India, 1784–1858*. Oxford: Oxford University Press.

BEER, G. L. (1923). *African Questions at the Paris Peace Conference* (ed. L. H. Gray). New York: Macmillan.

BENTINCK, W. C. (1977). *The Correspondence of Lord William Cavendish Bentinck, Governor-General of India, 1828–1835* (ed. C. H. Philips). Oxford: Oxford University Press.

BENTHAM, J. (1994). *A Fragment on Government*. Cambridge: Cambridge University Press.

BERRY, C. (1977). 'On the Meaning of Progress and Providence in the Fourth Century', *Heythrop Journal*, 18/3, 257–70.

BLAIR, T. (1999). 'Doctrine of the International Community', Speech by the Prime Minister to the Economic Club of Chicago, Hilton Hotel, Chicago, USA, Thursday, 22 April, Foreign and Commonwealth Office, London. (www.fco.gov.uk)

BODELSEN, C. A. (1924). *Studies in Mid-Victorian Imperialism*. London: Gydendalske Boghandel.

BRAILSFORD, H. N. (1928). *Olives of an Endless Age: Being a Study of This Distracted World and Its Need of Unity*. New York: Harper & Brothers Publishers.

—— (1971). *The War of Steel and Gold: A Study of Armed Peace*. New York: Garland Publishing.

BRIGHT, J. (1914). 'Principles of Foreign Policy, Birmingham, October 29, 1858' in *Selected Speeches on British Foreign Policy, 1738–1914* (ed. E. R. Jones). London: Oxford University Press.

British Documents on Foreign Affairs: Reports and Papers From the Foreign Office Confidential Print (1989). Part II, ser. H., vol. 4. Frederick, MD: University Press of America.

BROWNLIE, I. (1992). *Basic Documents on Human Rights*, 3rd edn. Oxford: Clarendon Press.

BUELL, R. L. (1928). *The Native Problem in Africa*, vol. 1. New York: Macmillan Company.

BULL, H. (1966). 'International Theory: The Case for the Classical Approach', *World Politics*, 18, 361–77.

—— (1977). *The Anarchical Society: A Study of Order in World Politics*. New York: Columbia University Press.

—— (1984). 'The Revolt Against the West', *The Expansion of International Society* (eds. H. Bull and A. Watson). Oxford: Clarendon Press.

BULL, H., and A. WATSON (eds.), (1984). *The Expansion of International Society*. Oxford: Clarendon Press.

BURKE, E. (1899). 'Ninth Report of the Select Committee of the House of Commons on the Affairs of India, June 25, 1783', *The Works of the Right Honourable Edmund Burke*, vol. 8. Boston: Little, Brown, and Company.

—— (1899). 'Speech on Mr. Fox's East India Bill, December 1, 1783', *The Works of the Right Honourable Edmund Burke*, vol. 2. Boston: Little, Brown, and Company.

—— (1899). 'Speeches in the Impeachment of Warren Hastings, Esquire, Late Governor-General of Bengal, February 15, 1788', *The Works of the Right Honourable Edmund Burke*, vol. 9. Boston: Little, Brown, and Company.

—— (1899). 'Articles of Charge Against Warren Hastings, Esq., Late Governor-General of Bengal', *The Works of the Right Honorable Edmund Burke*, vol. 8. Boston: Little, Brown, and Company.

—— (1981). 'Speech on North's East India Resolutions, 5 April 1773', *The Writings and Speeches of Edmund Burke*, vol. 2 (ed. Langford). Oxford: Oxford University Press.

BURROW, J. W. (1970). *Evolution and Society: A Study of Victorian Social Theory.* Cambridge: Cambridge University Press.

BURY, J. B. (1932). *The Idea of Progress: An Inquiry Into Its Origin and Growth.* New York: Dover Publications.

BUSH, G. W. (2001). 'Address to a Joint Session of Congress and to the American People', Washington, DC, The White House, Office of the Press Secretary, 20 September 2001. (www.whitehouse.gov)

—— (2002). Remarks by the President at 2002 Graduation Exercise at the United States Military Academy, West Point, New York, The White House, Office of the Press Secretary, 1 June 2002. (www.whitehouse.gov)

—— (2002). 'President Calls for New Palestinian Leadership', The White House, Office of the Press Secretary, 24 June 2002. (www.whitehouse.gov)

—— (2002). 'Securing Freedom's Triumph', *New York Times*, 11 September 2002. (www.nytimes.com)

BUTTERFIELD, H. (1965). *The Whig Interpretation of History.* New York: W. W. Norton & Company.

—— and M. WIGHT (eds.) (1968). *Diplomatic Investigations: Essays in the Theory of International Politics.* Cambridge, MA: Harvard University Press.

BUXTON, T. F. (1967). *The African Slave Trade and Its Remedy.* London: Frank Cass & Co.

CAIRNS, H. A. C. (1965). *Prelude to Imperialism: British Reactions to Central African Society 1840–1890.* London: Routledge & Kegan Paul.

CAPLAN, R. (2002). 'A New Trusteeship?: The International Administration of War-torn Territories', *Adelphi Paper, No. 341.* London: IISS.

CARR, E. H. (1970). *The Twenty Years' Crisis.* London: Macmillan.

CASEMENT, R. (1904). 'Mr. Casement to the Marquess of Landsdowne—(Received December 12), December 11, 1903', *Parliamentary Papers*, Cmd. 1933 lxii.

CHAMBERLAIN, J. (1953). 'Speech at the Imperial Institute, 11 November 1895', in *The Concept of Empire: Burke to Attlee, 1774–1947* (ed. G. Bennett). London: Adam and Charles Black.

CHANDLER, D. (2000). *Bosnia: Faking Democracy After Dayton*, 2nd edn. London: Pluto Press.

—— (2002). 'Bosnia's New Colonial Governor', *The Guardian*, 9 July. (www.guardian.co.uk)

CHAR, S. V. D. (ed.) (1983). *Readings in the Constitutional History of India 1757–1947.* Delhi: Oxford University Press.

'Charter of the United Nations', (1993). in *United Nations, Divided World* (eds. A. Roberts and B. Kingsbury). Oxford: Clarendon Press.

CHESTERMAN, S. (2002). 'East Timor in Transition: Self-determination, State-building and the United Nations', *International Peacekeeping*, 9/1, 45–76.

CHOPRA, J. (2000). 'Introductory Note to UNTAET Regulation 13', *International Legal Materials*, 39, 936–44.

CHOPRA, J. (2000). 'The UN's Kingdom in East Timor', *Survival*, 42/3, 27–40.

CHURCHILL, W. (1950). *The Hinge of Fate*. Boston: Houghton Mifflin Company.

—— (1950). *The Grand Alliance*. Boston: Houghton Mifflin Company.

COBDEN, R. (1953). 'England, Ireland, America, 1835', in *The Concept of Empire: Burke to Attlee, 1774–1947* (ed. G. Bennett). London: Adam and Charles Black.

—— (1953). 'Speech at Manchester, 10 January 1849', in *The Concept of Empire: Burke to Attlee, 1774–1947* (ed. G. Bennett). London: Adam and Charles Black.

COHEN, A. (1959). *British Policy in Changing Africa*. Evanston, IL: Northwestern University Press.

COLLINGWOOD, R. G. (1942). *The New Leviathan*. Oxford: Clarendon Press.

—— (1956). *The Idea of History*. New York: Oxford University Press.

COMMAGER, H. S. (ed.) (1948). *Documents of American History*. New York: Appleton-Century-Crofts.

Correspondence Respecting the Affairs of the Congo (1912–1913). (February 1913). *Parliamentary Papers*, Cmd. 6606 lix.

Correspondence Respecting the Taxation of Natives, and Other Questions, in the Congo State (1908). (June 1908). *Parliamentary Papers*, Cmd. 4135 lxxi.

Correspondence Respecting the Report of the Commission of Inquiry into the Administration of the Independent State of the Congo (1906). (June 1906). *Parliamentary Papers*, Cmd. 3002 lxxix.

COUPLAND, R. (1923). *Wilberforce*. Oxford: Clarendon Press.

—— (1933). *The British Anti-Slavery Movement*. London: Thornton Butterworth.

CROMER, Earl of, (1913). 'The Government of Subject Races', *Political and Literary Essays, 1908–1913*. London: Macmillan.

'Declaration of the Rights of Man and Citizen (1789)', (1999). in *Political Thought* (eds. M. Rosen and J. Wolff) Oxford: Oxford University Press.

D'ENTREVES, A. P. (1970). *Natural Law: An Introduction to Legal Philosophy*. London: Hutchinson University Library.

DICKINSON, G. L. (1916). *The European Anarchy*. London: George Allen & Unwin.

—— (1917). *The Choice Before Us*. New York: Dodd, Mead and Company.

—— (1972). *Causes of International War*. New York: Garland Publishing.

DILKE, C. (1869). *Greater Britain: A Record of Travel in English-Speaking Countries During 1866 and 1867*. New York: Harper.

Documents of the United Nations Conference on International Organization, 10 vols. (1945). London: United Nations Information Organizations.

DONELAN, M. (1984). 'Spain and the Indies', in *The Expansion of International Society* (eds. H. Bull and A. Watson). Oxford: Clarendon Press.

DWORKIN, G. (1971). 'Paternalism', in *Morality and the Law* (ed. R. Wasserstom). Belmont, CA: Wadsworth Publishing Company.

EASTON, S. (1961). *The Twilight of European Colonialism: A Political Analysis*. London: Methuen & Co.

EGERTON, G. (1978). *Great Britain and the Creation of the League of Nations: Strategy, Politics, and International Organization, 1914–1919*. Chapel Hill, NC: University of North Carolina Press.

EMBREE, A. T. (1962). *Charles Grant and British Rule in India*. London: George Allen & Unwin.

Ferguson, A. (1995). *An Essay on the History of Civil Society* (ed. F. Oz-Salzberger). Cambridge: Cambridge University Press.

FIELDHOUSE, D. (1965). *The Colonial Empires: A Comparative Survey from the Eighteenth Century*. London: Weidenfeld and Nicolson.

FIGGIS, J. N. (1922). *The Divine Right of Kings*, 2nd edn. Cambridge: Cambridge University Press.

'Final Warsaw Declaration: Toward a Community of Democracies', (2000). Warsaw, Poland, 27 June. (www.state.gov)

Fox, G., and B. ROTH (2001). 'Democracy and International Law', *Review of International Studies*, 27/3, 327–52.

FRANKLAND, N. (ed.) (1958). *Documents on International Affairs, 1955*. Oxford: Oxford University Press.

FRIEDMAN, T. (2001). 'A Way Out of the Middle East Impasse', *The New York Times*, 24 August. (www.nytimes.com)

FROST, M. (1991). 'What Ought to be Done about the Condition of States?', in *The Condition of States: A Study in Normative Political Theory* (ed. C. Navari). Milton Keynes: Open University Press.

—— (1996). *Ethics in International Relations: A Constitutive Theory*. Cambridge: Cambridge University Press.

FUKUYAMA, F. (1993). *The End of History and the Last Man*. New York: Avon Books.

GANN, L. H., and P. DUIGNAN (1967). *Burden of Empire: An Appraisal of Western Colonialism in Africa South of the Sahara*. New York: Praeger.

—— (1979). *The Rulers of Belgian Africa, 1884–1914*. Princeton, NJ: Princeton University Press.

General Act of the Conference of Berlin (1886). *Parliamentary Papers*, LXVII, mf. 92.353.

General Act of the Brussels Conference (1889–1890). With Annexed Declaration, *Parliamentary Papers*, 1890 LI, mf. 96.405.

General Framework Agreement for Peace in Bosnia and Herzegovina (1996). Annex 10, *U.S. Department of State Dispatch*, supplement 1. (www.state.gov)

GEORGES, E. H. M. (1918). 'Report on the Natives of South-West Africa and Their Treatment by Germany', *Parliamentary Papers*, Cmd. 9146, xvii.

DE GOBINEAU, A. (1967). *The Inequality of Human Races* (trans. A. Collins). New York: Howard Fertig.

GONG, G. (1984). *The Standard of 'Civilization' in International Society*. Oxford: Clarendon Press.

Government of Canada, Department of Foreign Affairs and International Trade (1999). *Human Security: Safety for People in a Changing World*. Ottawa: Department of Foreign Affairs and International Trade.

Government of India (1949). *The Constituent Assembly Debates: Official Report, 14-11-1949 to 26-11-1949*, vol. 11. New Delhi: Lok Sabha Secretariat, undated.

Government of Great Britain (2000). Fourth Report from the Foreign Affairs Committee, Session 1999–2000. HC 28-1, 7 June 2000. (www.fco.gov.uk)

Government of the United States of America (1943). *The Paris Peace Conference,* vol. 3. Washington, DC: Government Printing Office.

—— (1955). *Foreign Relations of the United States: The Conferences at Malta and Yalta, 1945.* Washington, DC: Government Printing Office.

—— (1961). *Foreign Relations of the United States: The Conferences at Cairo and Tehran, 1943.* Washington, DC: Government Printing Office.

—— (2002). 'The National Security Strategy of the United States of America', September. (www.whitehouse.gov)

GRANT, C. (1812–1813). 'Observations on the State of Society Among the Asiatic Subjects of Great Britain'. *Parliamentary Papers,* (282) x.31, mf. 14.63–64.

GRANT, R. (1990). *Oakeshott.* London: The Claridge Press.

GRENVILLE, J. A. S., and BERNARD WASSERSTEIN (eds.) (2001). *The Major International Treaties of the Twentieth Century,* vol. 1. London: Routledge.

GRIFFITHS, P. (1965). *The British Impact on India.* London: Archon Books.

GROTIUS, H. (1949). *De Jure Belli ac Pacis* (trans. L. R. Loomis). Roslyn, NY: Walter J. Black.

HAILEY, LORD (1943). *The Future of Colonial Peoples.* Oxford: Oxford University Press.

—— (1957). *An African Survey: A Study of Problems Arising in Africa South of the Sahara* (rev. edn.). London: Oxford University Press.

HALL, H. D. (1948). *Mandates, Dependencies, and Trusteeship.* London: Stevens & Sons.

—— (1967). 'The British Commonwealth and the Founding of the League Mandate System', in *Studies in International History* (eds. K. Bourne and D. C. Watt). London: Longman.

HARGREAVES, J. D. (1963). *Prelude to the Partition of West Africa.* London: Macmillan.

HARLOW, V. (1964). *The Founding of the Second British Empire, 1763–1793,* 2 vols. London: Longman.

HART, H. L. A. (1961). *The Concept of Law.* Oxford: Clarendon Press.

HOBBES, T. (1949). *Leviathan* (ed. M. Oakeshott). Oxford: Basil Blackwell.

HOBSON, J. A. (1938). *Imperialism.* London: George Allen & Unwin.

—— (1971). *Towards International Government.* New York: Garland Publishing.

HOCHSCHILD, A. (1998). *King Leopold's Ghost: A Story of Greed, Terror, and Heroism in Colonial Africa.* London: Macmillan.

HOFFMANN, S. (2001). 'On the War', *The New York Review of Books,* 48/17. (www.nybooks.com)

HOLBORN, L. W. (ed.) (1943). *War and Peace Aims of the United Nations: September 1, 1939–December 31, 1942.* Boston: World Peace Foundation.

—— (1948). *War and Peace Aims of the United Nations: From Casablanca to Tokio Bay: January 1, 1943–September 1, 1945.* Boston: World Peace Foundation.

HOLSTI, K. J. (1996). *The State, War, and the State of War.* Cambridge: Cambridge University Press.

HULL, C. (1948). *The Memoirs of Cordell Hull,* 2 vols. New York: Macmillan.

Independent International Commission on Kosovo, (2000). *Kosovo Report: Conflict, International Response, Lessons Learned.* Oxford: Oxford University Press.

—— (2001). *The Follow-up of the Kosovo Report: Why Conditional Independence?* Stockholm: IICK/Olof Palme Center.

'Indians in Kenya, July 1923', (1923). *Parliamentary Papers*, Cmd. 1922 xviii.

INDYK, M. (2002). 'A U.S.-Led Trusteeship for Palestine', *Washington Post*, 29 June. (www.washingtonpost.com)

International Court of Justice (1995). Case Concerning East Timor (Portugal *v.* Australia), 30 June. (www.icj.org)

International Crisis Group (2002). 'UNMIK's Kosovo Albatross: Tackling Division in Mitrovica', *Balkans Report No. 131*, 3 June.

JACKSON, R. (1990). 'Martin Wight, International Theory and the Good Life', *Millennium*, 19/2, 26–67.

—— (1990). *Quasi-States: Sovereignty, International Relations and the Third World*. Cambridge: Cambridge University Press.

—— (1996). 'Is There a Classical Theory?', in *International Theory: Positivism and Beyond* (eds. S. Smith, K. Booth, and M. Zalewski). Cambridge: Cambridge University Press.

—— (2000). *The Global Covenant: Human Conduct in a World of States*. Oxford: Oxford University Press.

JAMES, A. (1999). 'The Practice of Sovereign Statehood in Contemporary International Society', in *Sovereignty at the Millennium* (ed. R. Jackson). Oxford: Blackwell Publishers.

JONES, A. C. (1959). 'The Labour Party and Colonial Policy 1945–51', in *New Fabian Colonial Essays* (ed. A. C. Jones). London: Hogarth Press.

JONES, W. (1958). 'The Orientalist Viewpoint', in *Sources of Indian Tradition* (ed. W. T. de Bary). New York: Columbia University Press.

—— (1999). 'On the Origin and Families of Nations', in *Slavery, Abolition and Emancipation: Writings in the British Romantic Period*, vol. 8 (ed. P. J. Kitson). London: Pickering & Chatto.

KANT, I. (1952). 'The Science of Right', *Great Books of the Western World* (ed. R. M. Hutchins and trans. W. Hastie). Chicago: Encyclopaedia Britannica.

—— (1970). 'An Answer to the Question: "What Is Enlightenment?" ', *Kant's Political Writings* (ed. H. Reiss and trans. H. B. Nisbet). Cambridge: Cambridge University Press.

—— (1991). 'On the Common Saying: "This May Be True in Theory, But It Does Not Apply in Practice" ', *Kant: Political Writing* (ed. H. Reiss and trans. H. B. Nisbet). Cambridge: Cambridge University Press.

KAPLAN, R. (2000). *The Coming Anarchy: Shattering the Dreams of the Post Cold War*. New York: Random House.

KEDOURIE, E. (1971). *Nationalism*. London: Hutchinson University Library.

KEITH, A. B. (1919). *The Belgian Congo and the Berlin Act*. Oxford: Clarendon Press.

KELSEN, H. (1951). *The Law of the United Nations: A Critical Analysis of Its Fundamental Problems*. London: Stevens & Sons.

KERR, P. H. (1916). 'Political Relations Between Advanced and Backward Peoples', in *An Introduction to the Study of International Relations*. London: Macmillan.

KEYLOR, W. R. (1998). 'Versailles and International Diplomacy', in *The Treaty of Versailles: A Reassessment After Seventy-Five Years* (eds. M. F. Boemeke, G. D. Feldman, and E. Glaser). Cambridge: Cambridge University Press.

KEYNES, J. M. (1920). *The Economic Consequences of the Peace*. New York: Harper Torchbooks.

KIPLING, R. (1988). *Kim*. New York: Bantam Books.

KNOCK, T. J. (1998). 'Wilsonian Concepts and International Realities at the End of the War', in *The Treaty of Versailles: A Reassessment After Seventy-Five Years* (eds. M. F. Boemeke, G. D. Feldman, and E. Glaser). Cambridge: Cambridge University Press.

KONDOCH, B. (2001). 'The United Nations Administration of East Timor', *Journal of Conflict and Security Law*, 6/2, 245–65.

LANGER, W. L. (1965). *The Diplomacy of Imperialism, 1890–1902*, 2nd edn. New York: Alfred A. Knopf.

LANSING, R. (1921). *The Peace Negotiations: A Personal Narrative*. New York: Houghton Mifflin Company.

DE LAS CASAS, B. (1974). *In Defence of the Indians* (trans. S. Poole). DeKalb, IL: Northern Illinois University Press.

LECKY, W. (1970). 'The Empire: Its Value and Its Growth', *Historical and Political Essays*. Freeport, NY: Books for Libraries Press.

LENIN, V. I. (1968). 'Imperialism, the Highest Stage of Capitalism', in *Lenin on Politics and Revolution* (ed. J. E. Connor). Indianapolis, IN: Pegasus.

LEWIN, E. (1915). *The Germans in Africa: Their Aims on the Dark Continent and How They Acquired Their African Colonies*. New York: Frederick A. Stokes Company.

LIPPMANN, W. (1944). *U.S. War Aims*. Boston: Little, Brown and Company.

LIVINGSTONE, D. (1999). 'Cambridge Lecture No. 1 (1858)', in *Imperialism and Orientalism: A Documentary Sourcebook* (eds. B. Harlow and M. Carter). Oxford: Blackwell.

—— (2001). 'Missionary Correspondence (1841–42)', in *Politics and Empire in Victorian Britain* (ed. A. Burton). Basingstoke: Palgrave.

LLOYD GEORGE, D. (1936). *War Memoirs of David Lloyd George*, 5 vols. London: Ivor Nicholson & Watson.

—— (1938). *The Truth About Peace Treaties*, 2 vols. London: Victor Gollancz.

LOCKE, J. (1988). 'Second Treatise of Government', *Two Treatises of Government* (ed. P. Laslett). Cambridge: Cambridge University Press.

LORIMER, J. (1883). *The Institutes of the Law of Nations: A Treatise of the Jural Relations of Separate Political Communities*, 2 vols. Edinburgh: William Blackwood and Sons.

LOUIS, W. R. (1967). *Great Britain and Germany's Lost Colonies, 1914–1919*. Oxford: Clarendon Press.

—— (1977). *Imperialism at Bay, 1941–1945: The United States and the Decolonization of the British Empire*. Oxford: Clarendon Press.

LOUIS, W. R., and J. STENGERS (1968). *E. D. Morel's History of the Congo Reform Movement*. Oxford: Clarendon Press.

LUGARD, F. D. (1929). *The Dual Mandate of Africa*, 4th edn. London: William Blackwood & Sons.

LYON, P. (1993). 'The Rise and Fall and Possible Revival of International Trusteeship', *The Journal of Commonwealth and Comparative Politics*, 31/1, 96–110.

MACAULAY, T. B. (1879). *The Works of Lord Macaulay* (ed. Lady Trevelyan). London: Longman's, Green, and Co.

—— (1977). 'T. B. Macaulay's Minute on Education', *The Correspondence of Lord William Cavendish Bentinck, Governor-General of India, 1828–1835* (ed. C. H. Philips). Oxford: Oxford University Press.

MACINTYRE, A. (1990). *Three Rival Versions of Moral Enquiry: Encyclopaedia, Genealogy, and Tradition*. Notre Dame, IN: Notre Dame University Press.

MACMILLAN, W. M. (1953). 'African Growing Pains', *United Empire*, 44/3, 97–104.

MALCOLM, J. (1856). *The Life and Correspondence of Major-General Sir John Malcolm*, vol. 2 (ed. J. W. Kaye) London: Smith, Elder, and Co.

MALLABY, S. (2002). 'The Lesson of MacArthur', *Washington Post*, 23 October. (www.washingtonpost.com)

MARSHALL, P. J. (ed.) (1968). *Problems of Empire, 1757–1813*. London: George Allen and Unwin.

MARTIN, I. (2001). *Self-determination in East Timor: The United Nations, the Ballot, and International Intervention*. London: Lynne Rienner.

MARX, K., and F. ENGELS (1978). 'Manifesto of the Communist Party', *The Marx-Engels Reader* (ed. R. Tucker) 2nd edn. New York: W. W. Norton.

MATHESON, M. J. (2001). 'United Nations Governance of Postconflict Societies', *American Journal of International Law*, 95/1, 76–85.

MEEK, R. (1976). *Social Science and the Ignoble Savage*. Cambridge: Cambridge University Press.

Memorandum (1908). Respecting the Taxation of Natives, and Other Questions, in the Congo State, November 1908, *Parliamentary Papers*, Cmd. 4178.

MILL, J. (1975). *The History of British India*, abrg. W. Thomas. Chicago: University of Chicago Press.

MILL, J. S. (1973). 'A Few Words on Non-Intervention', *Essays on Politics and Culture* (ed. G. Himmelfarb). Gloucester, MA: Peter Smith.

—— (1973). 'Civilization', *Essays on Politics and Culture* (ed. G. Himmelfarb). Gloucester, MA: Peter Smith.

—— (1978). *On Liberty* (ed. E. Rapaport). Indianapolis, IN: Hackett Publishing Company.

—— (1991). *Considerations on Representative Government*. Amherst, MA: Prometheus Books.

MILLER, D. H. (1928). *The Drafting of the Covenant*, 2 vols. New York: G.P. Putnam's Sons.

MILTON, J. (1961). *Paradise Lost and Other Poems*. New York: Mentor Books.

MONTESQUIEU (1977). *The Spirit of the Laws* (ed. D. W. Carrithers). Berkeley, CA: University of California Press.

MOREL, E. D. (1906). *Red Rubber*. London: T. Fisher Unwin.

Morel, E. D. (1920). *The Black Man's Burden*. London: The National Labour Press.
—— (1972). *Truth and the War*. New York: Garland Publishing.
Morgan, D. J. (1980). *Guidance Towards Self-Government in British Colonies, 1941–1971*, vol. 5. London: Macmillan.
Nafziger, E. W., F. Stewart, and R. Vayrynen (eds.) (2000). *War, Hunger, and Displacement: The Origins of Humanitarian Emergencies*. Oxford: Oxford University Press.
Nehru, J. (1946). *The Discovery of India*. New York: The John Day Company.
Newbury, C. W. (ed.) (1965). *British Policy Toward West Africa: Select Documents 1786–1874*. Oxford: Clarendon Press.
Nkrumah, K. (1962). *Towards Colonial Freedom: Africa and the Struggle Against World Imperialism*. London: Heinemann.
Notter, H. A. (ed.) (1949). *Postwar Foreign Policy Preparation, 1939–1945*. Washington, DC: US Government Printing Office.
Nussbaum, M. (2005). *Women and Human Development: The Capabilities Approach*. Cambridge: Cambridge University Press.
Nyerere, J. (1973). *Freedom and Development: A Selection from Writings and Speeches, 1968–1973*. Oxford: Oxford University Press.
Oakeshott, M. (1991). 'The Voice of Poetry in the Conversation of Mankind', *Rationalism and Politics and Other Essays* (new and expanded edn.). Indianapolis, IN: Liberty Fund Press.
—— (1991). 'Political Education', *Rationalism and Politics and Other Essays* (new and expanded edn.). Indianapolis, IN: Liberty Fund Press.
—— (1993). *Morality and Politics in Modern Europe* (ed. S. R. Letwin). New Haven, CT: Yale University Press.
—— (1996). *On Human Conduct*. Oxford: Clarendon Press.
O'Hanlon, M. (2002). 'The Price of Stability', *The New York Times*, 22 October 2000. (www.nytimes.com)
The Old and New Testaments of the Holy Bible (1971). (revised standard version). Philadelphia, PA: Lutheran Church in America.
Oldham, J. H. (1924). *Christianity and the Race Problem*. New York: George H. Doran Company.
Organization of American States (1991). 'Representative Democracy', Resolution Adopted at the Fifth Plenary Session of the Organization of American States, 5 June 1991, AG/RES. 1080 (XXI-O/91).
—— (2001). 'Inter-American Democratic Charter' Adopted at the Twenty-Eighth Special Session of the OAS General Assembly, 11 September 2001, AG/doc. 8 (XXVIII-E/01).
Parekh, B. (1982). *Contemporary Political Thinkers*. Oxford: Martin Robertson & Company.
Passmore, J. (2000). *The Perfectibility of Man*, 3rd edn. Indianapolis, IN: Liberty Fund Press.
Perham, M. (1961). *The Colonial Reckoning*. London: Collins.
—— (1967). *Colonial Sequence, 1930 to 1949*. London: Methuen & Co.
Plamenatz, J. (1960). *On Alien Rule and Self-Government*. London: Longman.

PLATO, (1993). *Republic* (trans. R. Waterfield). Oxford: Oxford University Press.

PORTER, A. N., and A. J. STOCKWELL (eds.) (1987). *British Imperial Policy and Decolonization, 1938–64*, 2 vols. London: Macmillan.

PORTER, B. (1968). *Critics of Empire: British Radical Attitudes to Colonialism in Africa 1895–1914*. London: Macmillan.

Protocols and the General Act of the West African Conference (1885). *Parliamentary Papers*, LV mf. 91.435–37.

'Queen Victoria's Proclamation, 1 November 1858' (1962), in *The Evolution of India and Pakistan, 1858 to 1947* (ed. C. H. Philips). London: Oxford University Press.

Report of the Commission on Global Governance (1995). *Our Global Neighbourhood*. Oxford: Oxford University Press.

Report of the International Commission on Intervention and State Sovereignty (2001). *The Responsibility to Protect*. Ottawa: International Development Research Centre.

RICE, C. (2000). 'Promoting the National Interest', *Foreign Affairs*, 79/1, 45–62.

ROBINSON, K. (1965). *The Dilemmas of Trusteeship: Aspects of British Colonial Policy Between the Wars*. London: Oxford University Press.

ROBINSON, R., and J. GALLAGHER (1965). *Africa and the Victorians: The Official Mind of Imperialism*. London: Macmillan.

ROSSELLI, J. (1974). *Lord William Bentinck: The Making of a Liberal Imperialist 1774–1839*. London: Chatto & Windus.

ROUSSEAU, J. J. (1971). 'The Social Contract', *Social Contract: Essays by Locke, Hume, and Rousseau*. Oxford University Press.

——(1987). *The Basic Political Writings* (ed. and trans. D. Cress). Indianapolis, IN: Hackett Publishing Company.

ROY, R. (1958). 'Letter on Education', in *Sources of Indian Tradition* (ed. W. T. de Bary). New York: Columbia University Press.

SCHWARZENBERGER, G. (1951). *Power Politics: A Study of International Society*. New York: Frederick A. Praeger.

Secretary-General of the United Nations (1999). 'Secretary-General Presents His Annual Report to the General Assembly', Press Release, 20 September 1999, SG/SM/7136-GA9596.

SMITH, A. (1981). *The Wealth of Nations*, 2 vols. (eds. R. H. Campbell and A. S. Skinner). Indianapolis, IN: Liberty Fund.

SMUTS, J. C. (1928). 'The League of Nations: A Practical Suggestion', *The Drafting of the Covenant*, vol. 2 (ed. D. H. Miller). New York: G.P. Putnam's Sons.

——(1930). *Africa and Some World Problems*. Oxford: Clarendon Press.

——(1966). *Selections from the Smuts Papers*, vol. 4 (eds. W. K. Hancock and J. Van Der Poel). Cambridge: Cambridge University Press.

SPENCER, H. (1981). 'The Social Organism', *The Man Versus the State: With Six Essays on Government, Society, and Freedom*. Indianapolis, IN: Liberty Fund.

STODDARD, L. (1921). *The Rising Tide of Color Against White World-Supremacy*. New York: Charles Scribner's Sons.

STOKES, E. (1959). *The English Utilitarians and India*. Oxford: Clarendon Press.

TALBOTT, S. (1999). 'The Balkan Question and the European Answer', Address at the Aspen Institute, Aspen, Colorado, 24 August 1999. (www.state.gov)

TARN, W. W. (1934). 'Alexander the Great and the Unity of Mankind', *Proceedings of the British Academy, 1933*. London: Oxford University Press.

TAYLOR, A. J. P. (1957). *The Trouble Makers: Dissent Over Foreign Policy, 1792–1939*. London: Hamish Hamilton.

THORNTON, A. P. (1959). *The Imperial Idea and Its Enemies: A Study in British Power*. London: Macmillan.

—— (1965). *Doctrines of Imperialism*. New York: John Wiley & Sons.

THUCYDIDES (1972). *History of the Peloponnesian War* (trans. R. Warner). London: Penguin Books.

TOUSSAINT, C. E. (1956). *The Trusteeship System of the United Nations*. London: Stevens & Sons.

TOYNBEE, A. (1953). *The World and the West*. New York: Oxford University Press.

TROTSKY, L. (1984). 'To Peoples and Governments of Allied Countries', in *The Papers of Woodrow Wilson*, vol. 45 (ed. A. S. Link). Princeton, NJ: Princeton University Press.

United Nations, *Yearbook of the United Nations, 1950*. New York: United Nations Department of Public Information.

—— (1953). *Yearbook of the United Nations, 1952*. New York: United Nations Department of Public Information.

—— (1968). *Yearbook of the United Nations, 1966*. New York: United Nations Department of Public Information.

—— (1972). *Yearbook of the United Nations, 1970*. New York: United Nations Department of Public Information.

United Nations Development Programme (1994). *Human Development Report, 1994*. New York: Oxford University Press.

United Nations General Assembly (1960). 926th Plenary Meeting, 28 November 1960, United Nations General Assembly Official Records, A/PV 926.

—— (1960). 927th Plenary Meeting, 29 November 1960, United Nations General Assembly Official Records, A/PV 927.

—— (1960). 928th Plenary Meeting, 30 November 1960, United Nations General Assembly Official Records, A/PV 928.

—— (1960). 929th Plenary Meeting, 30 November 1960, United Nations General Assembly Official Records, A/PV 929.

—— (1960). 'Transmission of Information Under Article 73e of the Charter', United Nations General Assembly Resolution 1542 (XV), A/RES/1542.

—— (1975). Resolution 3485 (XXX), A/RES/3485.

—— (1999). 'Question of East Timor, Progress Report of the Secretary-General', General Assembly, 13 December 1999, A/54/654.

United Nations General Assembly/Security Council, 'Report of the Panel on United Nations Peace Operations (Brahimi Report)', A/55/305-S/2000/809.

UNMIK (1999). 'Regulation No. 1999/1, On the Authority of the Interim Administration in Kosovo, 25 July' 1999, UNMIK/REG/1999/1.

United Nations Security Council (1963). Resolution 183, S/RES/183.

—— (1975). Resolution 384, S/RES/384 (1975).

—— (1976). Resolution 389, S/RES/389 (1976).

—— (1999). Resolution 1244, S/RES/1244 (1999).

—— (1999). Resolution 1272, S/RES/1272 (1999).

—— (1999). 'Report of the Secretary-General on the Interim Administration Mission in Kosovo, 12 July 1999', S/1999/779.

—— (1999). 'Report of the Secretary-General on the United Nations Interim Administration Mission in Kosovo, 23 December 1999', S/1999/1250.

UNTAET (1999). 'Regulation No. 1999/1, On the Authority of the Transitional Administration in East Timor, 27 November 1999', UNTAET/REG/1999/1.

VAN WOUDENBERG, A. (2002). 'Africa at the Crossroads: Time to Deliver', *Oxfam Briefing Paper 19*. Oxford: Oxfam GB.

DE VITORIA, F. (1991). *Political Writings* (eds. A Pagden and J. Lawrance). Cambridge: Cambridge University Press.

WALWORTH, A. (1986). *Wilson and His Peacemakers: American Diplomacy at the Paris Peace Conference, 1919*. New York: W. W. Norton & Company.

WATT, D. C. (ed.) (1971). *Documents on International Affairs, 1962*. Oxford: Oxford University Press.

WHEELER, N. (2000). *Saving Strangers: Humanitarian Intervention in International Society*. Oxford: Oxford University Press.

WHITEHEAD, J. (1903). 'Rev. J. Whitehead to Governor-General of the Congo State, July 28', *Parliamentary Papers*, Cmd. 1933 lxii (1904).

—— (1903). 'Rev. J. Whitehead to Governor-General of the Congo State, September 7', *Parliamentary Papers*, Cmd. 1933 lxii (1904).

WIGHT, M. (1948). 'Christian Commentary', BBC Home Service Broadcast, Friday 29, October 1948.

—— (1952). *British Colonial Constitutions, 1947*. Oxford: Clarendon Press.

—— (1968). 'Why Is There No International Theory?', in *Diplomatic Investigations: Essays in the Theory of International Politics* (eds. H. Butterfield and M. Wight). Cambridge, MA: Harvard University Press.

—— (1977). *Systems of States* (ed. H. Bull). Leicester: Leicester University Press.

WILBERFORCE, W. (1823). *An Appeal to the Religion, Justice, and Humanity of the Inhabitants of the British Empire, in Behalf of the Negro Slaves in the West Indies*. London: J. Hatchard and Son.

WILDE, R. (2001). 'From Danzig to East Timor and Beyond: The Role of International Territorial Administration', *The American Journal of International Law*, 95/3, 583–606.

WILSON, W. (1966–1992). *The Papers of Woodrow Wilson*, 69 vols. (ed. A. S. Link). Princeton, NJ: Princeton University Press.

WOOLF, L. (1920). *Empire and Commerce in Africa: A Study in Economic Imperialism*. London: George Allen and Unwin.

WRIGHT, Q. (1930). *Mandates Under the League of Nations*. Chicago: University of Chicago Press.

ZIMMERN, A. (1934). *The Third British Empire*. Oxford: Oxford University Press.

—— (1969). 'Progress in Government', in *Progress and History* (ed. F. S. Marvin). Freeport, NY: Books for Libraries Press.

Index